THE FAILURES OF OTHERS

Arguments from failure – arguments that an institution must expand its powers because another institution is failing in some way 'to do its job' – are commonplace. From structural reform litigation, where courts sometimes assume administrative or legislative functions, to the Uniting for Peace Resolution of the UN General Assembly, to the recent bill quashing British subpostmasters' convictions, such arguments are offered in justification for unorthodox exercises of public power. But in spite of their popularity, we lack a good understanding of these arguments in legal terms. This is partly because failure itself is a highly malleable concept and partly because arguments from failure blur into other more familiar legal doctrines about implied powers or emergencies. We can do better. We should recognize arguments from failure as a distinct concept of public law and understand that contemporary constitutional theory offers us tools to evaluate such arguments in different settings. This title is also available as open access on Cambridge Core.

MICHAELA HAILBRONNER holds the chair for German and International Public Law and Comparative Law at the University of Münster, Germany. She is Co-President of the International Society of Public Law (ICON-S) and has done research in Germany, South Africa, the US and the UK. Her 2014 article on German constitutionalism won the inaugural Best Paper Award of the International Journal of Constitutional Law.

What should we do when those who wield power fail? In a subtle and nuanced analysis, Michaela Hailbronner tackles this question with insight and originality. Drawing on case studies from comparative constitutional law, the European Union, and international law, Hailbronner makes a powerful case that we need to take institutional failure seriously – not just as a cause for lament or an automatic licence to deviate from established legal norms, but as a stimulus for a more measured, proportionate, and context-specific approach. In a time of widespread democratic dysfunction and political failure, all public lawyers will benefit from engaging with Hailbronner's illuminating and compelling arguments.

– Aileen Kavanagh, Professor of Constitutional Governance, Law, Trinity College Dublin

The theory and practice of constitutionalism are filled with arguments, but not all have been adequately captured. This brilliant and imaginative work underscores how legal efforts are often a response to our broken institutional reality. *The Failures of Others* not only clarifies our doctrinal landscape – it offers us a new way to inform and shape our constitutional future.

– Madhav Khosla, B. R. Ambedkar Professor of Indian Constitutional Law and Professor of Political Science, Columbia University

Institutions fail in ways that spell bad news for a project of democratic constitutionalism – but can also provide invaluable lessons for scholars and practitioners looking to promote future institutional success. In the here and now, the failure of one institution is also a powerful reason for other institutions to step up and in to uphold constitutional norms -and Hailbronner constructs a sophisticated account of what this kind of failure-sensitive approach to judicial review might look like at a domestic and transnational level. The book should be compulsory reading for all those interested in the future of constitutionalism nationally and transnationally.

– Rosalind Dixon, Professor of Law and Director of the Gilbert + Tobin Centre of Public Law, University of New South Wales, Sydney

Michaela Hailbronner has written an exceptional and well-argued book, in which she studies the problem of institutional failure. She does so in a very attractive way, particularly for those of us interested in comparative political process theory, concerned about the (tragic) phenomenon of 'authoritarian erosion', and still hopeful about structural reform litigation.

– Roberto Gargarella, Professor of Law at the Torcuato di Tella University and the University of Buenos Aires

CAMBRIDGE STUDIES IN CONSTITUTIONAL LAW

The aim of this series is to produce leading monographs in constitutional law. All areas of constitutional law and public law fall within the ambit of the series, including human rights and civil liberties law, administrative law, as well as constitutional theory and the history of constitutional law. A wide variety of scholarly approaches is encouraged, with the governing criterion being simply that the work is of interest to an international audience. Thus, works concerned with only one jurisdiction will be included in the series as appropriate, while, at the same time, the series will include works which are explicitly comparative or theoretical - or both. The series editors likewise welcome proposals that work at the intersection of constitutional and international law, or that seek to bridge the gaps between civil law systems, the US, and the common law jurisdictions of the Commonwealth.

Series Editors

David Dyzenhaus

Professor of Law and Philosophy, University of Toronto, Canada

Thomas Poole

Professor of Law, London School of Economics and Political Science

Books in the Series

The Failures of Others: Justifying Institutional Expansion in Comparative Public and International Law Michaela Hailbronner

Constitutionalizing the Private Sphere: A Comparative Inquiry Christina R. Bambrick

Beyond Expropriation Without Compensation: Law, Land Reform and Redistributive Justice in South Africa Edited by Olaf Zenker, Cherryl Walker and Zsa-Zsa Boggenpoel

Trust, Courts and Social Rights: A Trust-Based Framework for Social Rights Enforcement David Vitale

The Collaborative Constitution Aileen Kavanagh

Non-Statutory Executive Powers and Judicial Review Jason Grant Allen

The Law as a Conversation among Equals Roberto Gargarella

Micronations and the Search for Sovereignty Harry Hobbs and George Williams

Fundamental Rights and the Legal Obligations of Business David Bilchitz

Courting Constitutionalism: The Politics of Public Law and Judicial Review in Pakistan Moeen Cheema

Ruling by Cheating: Governance in Illiberal Democracy András Sajó

Local Meanings of Proportionality Afroditi Marketou

Property Rights and Social Justice: Progressive Property in Action Rachael Walsh

Carl Schmitt's Early Legal-Theoretical Writings: Statute and Judgment and the Value of the State and the Significance of the Individual Lars Vinx and Samuel Garrett Zeitlin

Remedies for Human Rights Violations: A Two-Track Approach to Supranational and National Law Kent Roach

Europe's Second Constitution: Crisis, Courts and Community Markus W. Gehring

A.V. Dicey and the Common Law Constitutional Tradition: A Legal Turn of Mind Mark D. Walters

Administrative Competence: Reimagining Administrative Law Elizabeth Fisher and Sidney A. Shapiro

Legal Sabotage: Ernst Fraenkel in Hitler's Germany Douglas Morris

Proportionality in Action: Comparative and Empirical Perspectives on the Judicial Practice Edited by Mordechai Kremnitzer, Tayla Steiner and Andrej Lang

Constitutional Dialogue: Democracy, Rights, Institutions Edited by Geoffrey Sigalet, Grégoire Webber and Rosalind Dixon

The Veiled Sceptre: Reserve Powers of Heads of State in Westminster Systems Anne Twomey

Vigilance and Restraint in the Common Law of Judicial Review Dean Knight

The Alchemists: Questioning Our Faith in Courts as Democracy-Builders Tom Gerald Daly

Australia's Constitution after Whitlam Brendan Lim

Building the Constitution: The Practice of Constitutional Interpretation in Post-Apartheid South Africa James Fowkes

Dimensions of Dignity: The Theory and Practice of Modern Constitutional Law Jacob Weinrib

Reason of State: Law, Prerogative, Empire Thomas Poole

Bills of Rights in the Common Law Robert Leckey

The Guardian of the Constitution: Hans Kelsen and Carl Schmitt on the Limits of Constitutional Law Translated by Lars Vinx, with an introduction and notes by Lars Vinx

Parliamentary Bills of Rights: The Experiences of New Zealand and the United Kingdom Janet L. Hiebert and James B. Kelly

Lawyering for the Rule of Law: Government Lawyers and the Rise of Judicial Power in Israel Yoav Dotan

Balancing Constitutional Rights: The Origins and Meanings of Postwar Legal Discourse Jacco Bomhoff

Judges on Trial: The Independence and Accountability of the English Judiciary Shimon Shetreet and Sophie Turenne

Proportionality and Constitutional Culture Moshe Cohen-Eliya and Iddo Porat

The Politics of Principle: The First South African Constitutional Court, 1995–2005 Theunis Roux

The New Commonwealth Model of Constitutionalism: Theory and Practice Stephen Gardbaum

Searching for the State in British Legal Thought: Competing Conceptions of the Public Sphere Janet McLean

Judging Social Rights Jeff King

Proportionality: Constitutional Rights and their Limitations Aharon Barak

Parliamentary Sovereignty: Contemporary Debates Jeffrey Goldsworthy

THE FAILURES OF OTHERS

Justifying Institutional Expansion in Comparative Public and International Law

MICHAELA HAILBRONNER

University of Münster

CAMBRIDGE
UNIVERSITY PRESS

CAMBRIDGE UNIVERSITY PRESS

Shaftesbury Road, Cambridge CB2 8EA, United Kingdom

One Liberty Plaza, 20th Floor, New York, NY 10006, USA

477 Williamstown Road, Port Melbourne, VIC 3207, Australia

314–321, 3rd Floor, Plot 3, Splendor Forum, Jasola District Centre, New Delhi – 110025, India

103 Penang Road, #05-06/07, Visioncrest Commercial, Singapore 238467

Cambridge University Press is part of Cambridge University Press & Assessment,
a department of the University of Cambridge.

We share the University's mission to contribute to society through the pursuit of
education, learning and research at the highest international levels of excellence.

www.cambridge.org
Information on this title: www.cambridge.org/9781009646666

DOI: 10.1017/9781009646659

First published 2026

Cover image: Angelus Novus. Museum: Israel Museum, Jerusalem. Author: Paul Klee / Album / Alamy
Stock Photo

A catalogue record for this publication is available from the British Library

Library of Congress Cataloging-in-Publication Data
Names: Hailbronner, Michaela author
Title: Arguments from failure : institutional expansion in comparative public and international law /
Michaela Hailbronner, University of Münster.
Description: Cambridge, United Kingdom ; New York, NY : Cambridge University Press, 2025. | Series:
Cambridge studies in constitutional law | Includes bibliographical references and index.
Identifiers: LCCN 2025014310 (print) | LCCN 2025014311 (ebook) | ISBN 9781009646666 hardback |
ISBN 9781009646635 paperback | ISBN 9781009646659 epub
Subjects: LCSH: Public law | International law
Classification: LCC K3150 .H35 2025 (print) | LCC K3150 (ebook) | DDC 342–dc23/eng/20250331
LC record available at https://lccn.loc.gov/2025014310
LC ebook record available at https://lccn.loc.gov/2025014311

ISBN 978-1-009-64666-6 Hardback

For my family
(some failures are one's own)

CONTENTS

ACKNOWLEDGEMENTS

I did not mean to write another book right after the first one. When I left in 2014 for South Africa with my soon-to-be husband James, I cheerfully abandoned the plan to write a Habilitation to become a German law professor. However, things turned out otherwise, and when we returned to Germany in 2016, it was clear to me I had to write a book, and I better make a move on it since I had already spent two years in South Africa writing other things and having a child. But even though I started out in Münster with a privileged position as research assistant to Niels Petersen, who was very supportive and kindly left me alone to work on things, writing this book was not straightforward. This is partly because writing a book when one is just starting a family will always be less than ideal. For me, it meant writing this book during my son's first years. It also meant writing it during a time in which I had two miscarriages and two ectopic pregnancies. As statistics attest, this happens to many women. It didn't help with the writing that all miscarriages happened right at the start of my semester breaks when I had carefully reserved weeks on end to finally sit down to think and write, in February 2017, in August 2017, in August 2019 and in February 2020.

All of this contributed to lingering doubts whether an academic career was the right one to pursue at all. There is much to dislike about academia: most importantly for me, it was about how much networks and connections matter. I often resented not being invited to some or other thing where I felt I would have been better qualified than others. After a while, however, I realized that I myself was also increasingly invited to events or projects, where other people clearly knew a lot more. This struck me as fairly ironic. Nevertheless, the fact that these things seem to balance each other out somehow doesn't mean that we couldn't do better as academics.

Funding from the University of Münster made it possible for this book to be published open access, making the digital version freely available for anyone to read under a Creative Commons licence.

That in my case everything worked out in the end, or so it seems right now, is due to a mix of luck and to those people who supported me at varying stages over the last few years.

I owe a big thanks first of all to my parents for their support over the years. I am also very grateful to my colleagues at the law faculty of Giessen, where I had my first tenure-track appointment. They always treated me as someone who belonged. Since a kindly anonymous reviewer of the DFG had previously suggested that I had no place in German academia as an outsider who mostly wrote in English in international journals, their trust and community could not have been more important. And I have been very lucky that in Münster, too, there are colleagues and now friends who have my back and whom I enjoy learning from, most importantly Nora Markard, Niels Petersen and Oliver Lepsius. At Humboldt University, Philipp Dann and Christoph Möllers agreed to shepherd this book, which made for a rather unconventional Habilitation, through the process, with Susanne Baer chairing the faculty commission. All of them could have chosen to be difficult about things, but were very supportive instead.

Not least, I am grateful to all of those who have taken the time to read and comment on draft chapters and discuss aspects of this book in different workshops and have given me the opportunity to present it in their conferences and fora over the past years. This includes Micaela Alterio, Gráinne de Búrca, Aparna Chandra, Timothy Endicott, Guy Fiti Sinclair, Roberto Gargarella, Raphael Grenier-Benoit, Tom Ginsburg, Mark Graber, Aileen Kavanagh, Tarunabh Khaitan, Jeff King, David Kosar, Roberto Niembro, Colm O'Cinneide, Tom Poole, Silvia Suteu and Sergio Verdugo. But the biggest professional debt for these past few years I owe to Gráinne de Búrca, Rosalind Dixon and Joseph Weiler, who have taught and encouraged me, included me in their networks and opened doors for me. I learned a lot when working as book review editor for the International Journal of Constitutional Law and later at the International Society of Public Law. And Rosalind Dixon has been an extremely generous mentor and good friend for some years now.

I dedicate this book to my family. My father has always been an important influence on me, and while our political views diverge, I cannot help writing partly still to convince him, too. (No therapy is that good.) Edward, now ten years old and bursting with ideas of his own, has had to put up with an often distracted and sometimes rather impatient mother over the past few years, which is one of my biggest regrets. He also sat patiently through countless conferences where I have been presenting this book. And it was really my husband James who originally came up with the observation that courts often act expansively when there is a sense that other institutions have failed and then let me write about it. James was also always there, doing an equal share of what needed to be done and sometimes more. He remains the most kind, generous, funny and inspiring person I know.

Introduction

I.1 Failure in Public Law

Policy failures, state failures, dysfunction, systemic deficiencies and structural problems seem to be everywhere. No longer are these labels reserved mostly for 'developing states', justifying intervention by well-meaning international bureaucracies in one form or another. Increasingly, they are applied to more established democracies, too. In the United States, 'dysfunction' and 'failures' in the context of the political and health crises of the past years have become a staple of both media and academic commentary.[1] Britain, too, has repeatedly been called a failed or failing state, and not just by tabloids.[2] And even in Germany, supposedly home to a well-functioning rational Weberian bureaucracy, talk of 'Staatsversagen' (state failure) has become commonplace, especially in the context of the Covid pandemic.[3] Populist movements in particular thrive on the rhetoric of disaster and failure, sowing discontent against institutions and elites to push demands for radical change.[4] But of course, governmental failure is a necessary part of our attempts to make things work. It occurs in all

1 For many, see Y. Abutaleb et al., 'The U.S. Was Beset by Denial and Dysfunction as the Coronavirus Raged', *The Washington Post*, 4 April 2020, https://tinyurl.com/2v6d49yw see also, e.g., S. Levinson and J. M. Balkin, *Democracy and Dysfunction* (University of Chicago Press, 2019).

2 For some recent accounts, see S. Freedman, *Failed State: Why Nothing Works and How We Fix It* (Pan Macmillan, 2024); J. Calvert and G. Arbuthnott, *Failures of State: The Inside Story of Britain's Battle with Coronavirus* (Mudlark/HarperCollins, 2021); see also K. Viner, 'The Guardian View on Broken Britain: It Won't Be Fixed with the Status Quo', *The Guardian*, 9 June 2023, https://tinyurl.com/4zj9kr6c.

3 J. Hermann, 'Staatsversagen im Corona-Winter: Deutschlands Regierung wird von der vierten Welle überrollt', *Neue Züricher Zeitung*, 2 December 2021, https://tinyurl.com/ed7tvbna; or S. Gennies, 'Steingefechte um Grenzwerte – Wenn Corona weiterherrscht, ist es Staatsversagen', *Tagesspiegel*, 3 March 2021, https://tinyurl.com/yjbuxab6.

4 This represents a broader hallmark of populist movements; see B. Moffitt, 'How to Perform Crisis: A Model for Understanding the Key Role of Crisis in Contemporary Populism' (2015) 50:2 *Government and Opposition* 189; see also more broadly, e.g.,

political systems, domestic and international, Northern and Southern. And talk of failure is part of our ordinary arsenal of opposition rhetoric in a democracy.

In the last ten years, the themes of institutional failure and dysfunction have increasingly become a field of research of their own among political economists and scientists.[5] The theme has its roots in parallel earlier debates in economics around the concept of market failure. Market failure represented a challenge to the liberal economic theories of Adam Smith and others, which stressed the ability of the market to self-regulate and provide for a socially efficient distribution of wealth.[6] If such economic self-regulation did not work and market failure arose, theorists suggested that state institutions must fill the gap.[7] Since states were of course not infallible either, there soon emerged the parallel concept, and research field, of governmental or institutional failure.

Lawyers are, as usual, late to the party. This is not surprising given that 'failure' is not prima facie a legal concept, but a weapon for political combat and often part of populist rhetoric. And especially in Europe, lawyers all too often allow themselves to assume that they are dealing with a basically functional system and to proceed to address legal issues from there.

This is a mistake. Institutional failure – which I will use as a shorthand for a range of other terms, such as policy or state failure, dysfunction and structural or systemic deficits[8] – features frequently in public law, including international and European Union law. Law and lawyers have to grapple with the phenomenon in different forms and circumstances, but frequently we encounter what I call in this book *arguments from failure*. The standard template of these arguments is that the failure of one (state) institution

J. Müller, *What Is Populism?* (University of Pennsylvania Press, 2016); E. Laclau, *On Populist Reason* (Verso, 2005).

5 P. Zittoun, 'Analysing Policy Failure as an Argumentative Strategy in the Policymaking Process: A Pragmatist Perspective' (2015) 30:3 *Public Policy and Administration* 243; see also for the broader debate A. Prakash and M. Potoski, 'Dysfunctional Institutions? Toward a New Agenda in Governance Studies' (2016) 10:2 *Regulation & Governance* 115; and for a recent literature survey P. Derwort, N. Jager and J. Newig, 'Towards Productive Functions? A Systematic Review of Institutional Failure, Its Causes and Consequences' (2019) 52:2 *Policy Sciences* 281.

6 A. Smith, *The Wealth of Nations* (1776).

7 J. M. Buchanan, 'Market Failure and Political Failure' (1988) 8:1 *Cato Journal* 1; on the origins of market failure, see A. Marciano and S. G. Medema, 'Market Failure in Context: Introduction' (2015) 47 *History of Political Economy* 1 and other contributions in the same issue.

8 I address some of the differences between those terms in later chapters.

provides a justification for other institutions to act 'to get a job done', even though they ordinarily do not have the competence to tackle the issue in question. In other words, institutional failure serves as an argument for expanding institutional competences and for legal innovation.

Consider the following examples:

In November 1950, the General Assembly of the United Nations argued in its famous Uniting for Peace Resolution:

> If the Security Council, because of lack of unanimity of the permanent members, fails to exercise its primary responsibility for the maintenance of international peace and security in any case where there appears to be a threat to the peace, breach of the peace, or act of aggression, the General Assembly shall consider the matter immediately with a view to making appropriate recommendations to Members for collective measures, including in the case of a breach of the peace or act of aggression the use of armed force when necessary, to maintain or restore international peace and security.[9]

In German law, courts have allowed individual patients to obtain reimbursement for certain treatments or medications outside of publicly prescribed schedules in exceptional situations. This is permitted when they have encountered *a systemic deficiency or systemic failure* on part of the bodies responsible for drawing up these schedules, for example where new treatments had not been assessed for the purposes of adding them to what is covered. System failure (*Systemversagen*) is thus a doctrinal concept in German social law that provides a reason for courts to step in where they would ordinarily defer to other institutions.[10]

In March 2017, in one of its most detailed and expansive judgments to date, the South African Constitutional Court placed the South African Social Services Agency (SASSA) under court supervision. SASSA had failed to arrange for the payment of social grants after the Court had set aside a previous contract with a private service provider (CPS) because of an illegal tender process.[11] After reiterating that 'SASSA has adopted an unhelpful and almost obstructionist stance', the Constitutional Court noted that 'the problem to be addressed was the demonstrated inability of SASSA to get its own affairs in order, in relation to the performance of

[9] United Nations General Assembly (UNGA) Res. 377 V (1950) UN Doc A/1775.

[10] H. Lang, '§ 27 Krankenbehandlung', in Ulrich Becker and Thorsten Kingreen (eds.), *SGB V, Gesetzliche Krankenversicherung*, 8th edn (C.H. Beck, 2022), para. 69, with further references; see also Chapter 6.

[11] *Black Sash Trust v. Minister of Social Development* 2017 (3) SA 335 (CC) (S. Afr.).

the contract, a competitive bidding process and becoming able to make payment of grants under its own steam'.[12] In response, the Court set out duties for the future provision of social services, ordered independent auditing and required the Minister of Social Affairs and SASSA to provide reports on their progress every three months.

In all of these instances, failure drove innovation and the expansion of the competences and activities of institutions not usually responsible for the issue at hand. This is most straightforward in the Uniting for Peace Resolution, in which the General Assembly claims for itself a right to act if the Security Council fails to do its job. In the German example, systemic failure ultimately leads to an expansion of individual rights, but more importantly, the decision to step in represents an expansion of the court's own role in these cases. And in South Africa, the Constitutional Court justifies the adoption of unusually strong supervision and remedies on the basis of the previous obstructionism of the responsible state actors.

Many other examples from a range of different contexts could be added here and will feature throughout this book. Many of the ones I discuss are taken from a judicial context, involving courts acting in an expansive way, but not all of them are. Not only courts step in when other institutions are seen to be failing. As we will see, in some cases arguments from failure are explicit; in others, they are for various reasons hidden or entwined with other arguments. In many cases, they are bound up with discourses of modernization and efficiency. Sometimes this has a (neo-)liberal thrust, as in the jurisprudence of the European Court of Justice, or indeed neo-colonial undertones, as in the 1990s discourses on state failure and structural adjustment programmes. At other times, they are deployed in the service of progressive social transformation, to alleviate poverty, end governmental impunity and realize key human rights. In such contexts, failure usually serves as an argument for why courts need to act to realize constitutional values and rights where democratic systems or individual institutions are considered dysfunctional.

The different discourses around these themes tend to stay in their own siloes. We are not used to connecting the arguments we encounter in these different spheres. They seem to be apples and oranges. This, I believe, is another mistake. Despite the sharp ideological differences between the different discourses and contexts, the arguments presented operate with a similar argumentative structure: Failure implies the need

12 Ibid.

for distrust and for diverging from established paths, while at the same time holding out the promise of a better future. The arguments also share a common emphasis on output, whatever that may be, and come with a high risk of abuse. Looking at examples from different contexts and engaging with the different literatures dealing with them can help us better understand the risks and challenges that come with arguments from failure and, ultimately, develop ways to evaluate such arguments.

This is the project of this book, which sets itself three main objectives accordingly.

First, I seek to identify arguments from failure in a range of different settings. I analyze how they are framed and consider how they intersect with broader discourses of modernization, neoliberalism or more progressive themes of transformative constitutionalism and combatting poverty. Arguments from failure have a lot to tell us about power relationships and institutional self-perception. They also provide a window into the loss of trust in public institutions in our time. This becomes particularly clear if we draw on the connection to the (socio-)legal literature dealing with the relationship of law and disasters, connecting back to earlier scholarship on emergencies following September 11 and the ensuing 'war on terror'. Among the key insights of that literature is that neither disasters nor emergencies should be understood as merely objective events to which states then subsequently try to respond. Rather, they are always shaped by existing legal and governmental structures, which shape them in turn.[13] Disasters, Bandopadhyay argues in his recent book, are key to the formation of modern Western states, whose claim to authority is based on securing 'normalcy'. This echoes deeper legal theoretical insights of law as a plan[14] and as a tool for stabilizing normative expectations.[15] Where states fail to manage disasters, we typically observe a loss of trust, and we encounter discourses of state failure or policy failure, as Stephen Griffin notes for the United States.[16] A similar story can be told about the European Union.[17]

13 S. Bandopadhyay, *All Is Well: Catastrophe and the Making of the Normal State* (Oxford University Press, 2022); also K. Loevy, *Emergencies in Public Law: The Legal Politics of Containment* (Cambridge University Press, 2016).

14 S. J. Shapiro, 'Law, Plans, and Practical Reason' (2002) 8:4 *Legal Theory* 387.

15 N. Luhmann, *Rechtssoziologie* (Springer, 2008).

16 S. M. Griffin, *Broken Trust: Dysfunctional Government and Constitutional Reform* (University Press of Kansas, 2015).

17 M. Hailbronner, 'Beyond Legitimacy: Europe's Crisis of Constitutional Democracy', in M. Graber, S. Levinson and M. Tushnet (eds.), *Constitutional Democracy in Crisis?* (Oxford University Press, 2018), p. 277.

Second, I argue that arguments from failure constitute a distinct category of legal and constitutional argument that we should take seriously and analyze on its own terms, for both analytical and normative reasons. We need to distinguish such arguments from other related and more familiar concepts of public law, such as emergency arguments and broader teleological approaches to interpretation, including doctrines of implied powers. As we will see, there is a tendency to invoke emergency arguments in cases of institutional failure and accordingly to justify institutional overreach in response to the magnitude of the problem. I argue that this is a temptation we should resist. Not only do emergency arguments open up a very dangerous slippery scale – in which the greater the problem, the more it seems legally permissible to set aside existing rules – but they are also ultimately different from arguments from failure, which are concerned with institutional relationships and responsiveness.

Third, I draw up a set of standard questions and considerations for evaluating arguments from failure in a host of different settings – international, federal and domestic – as well as in different institutional contexts. That there are such shared considerations and something of a shared framework is not self-evident, given the different discourses and settings in which we encounter arguments from failure. Nevertheless, there is a common set of factors that are central to evaluating all such arguments. In a nutshell, I argue that arguments from failure are only ever defensible within a context of a legal order in which legal arguments about institutional cooperation and mutual support as well as checks have a place. This typically presupposes a constitutional framework, and it is why such arguments become more problematic when we encounter them in the international realm. We also typically need to identify a violation of law and consider the broader institutional and legal context in which arguments from failure are employed – whether there exists a 'gap' in the law, in other words. Depending on the intervening institution, it also matters whether there are other more democratic mechanisms available to address the problem, thus requiring what I will call a no-more-democratic-means test.

Finally, we will need to assess the functionality, necessity and costs associated with the transgression of an institution's ordinary role. This amounts to a kind of proportionality test. In this context, we need to consider the likelihood of success, which is not a given in many cases and which I can only address very partially in this book. *What kind* of intervention is likely to be successful *when* is often an extremely difficult question to answer from a comparative perspective. A wide range of background factors will impact on the chances of success, even if we confine ourselves to a judicial context. As we will see in Chapter 4, there is, for example, a considerable discussion in the US literature about how successful structural reform litigation is and to what degree it might make things worse rather than better. Examples for both sides of this argument are not hard to come by. Things are no different elsewhere. Some judicial interventions have done relatively little to change matters. Others have brought about positive changes, albeit often slowly and incrementally, as in the case of the Colombian Court's famous decision on displaced persons, which is mostly considered a success in the literature.[18] The basic premise of this book is therefore that attempts to 'fill the gap', including in the context of structural reform litigation, work at least sometimes, and we should not therefore rule out such actions a priori on the basis that they will not succeed. When and under what conditions success is more likely than not is a question I touch on occasionally, but to which I do not provide a comprehensive answer. Evaluating success is a highly complex task. It involves both factual questions that lawyers have a hard time answering, as well as difficult normative questions about what counts and how much, in particular whether indirect and long-term consequences should be taken into account.[19] I nevertheless offer some preliminary thoughts in the second part of this book as to how we might think about functionality and costs so as to better address situations where we encounter these questions.

To evaluate proportionality and in particular necessity, we will also need to consider the problem at issue in more detail: how long it has existed, how many people are affected by it and how serious it is. In the context of structural reform litigation – a practice standardly justified with reference to the failure of other institutions – the problem in question will typically be a rights violation. We thus need to consider the number of cases and affected people, the seriousness and duration of the violations and what the government's relationship or reaction to them has been. These factors are necessarily vague – and some may think that they are too vague to be helpful at all. Yet, I believe the

18 M. J. Cepeda Espinosa, 'The Constitutional Protection of IDPs in Colombia', in R. A. Rivadeneira (ed.), *Judicial Protection of Internally Displaced Persons: The Colombian Experience* (The Brookings Institution – University of Bern Project on Internal Displacement, 2009); on the likely reasons of success, also D. Landau, 'The Reality of Social Rights Enforcement' (2012) 53:1 *Harvard International Law Journal* 319.

19 See, e.g., the arguments and the discussion in O. L. M. Ferraz, *Health as a Human Right: The Politics and Judicialisation of Health in Brazil* (Cambridge University Press, 2020).

flexibility they afford is a necessary response to the complexities of real life in which we come across arguments from failure in very different contexts. These complexities and background conditions matter to how we assess the legitimacy of these arguments. At least in a comparative law context, therefore, I don't think that we can be much more determinate than the framework I propose here, which I spell out in more detail in the following chapters using some case studies from different jurisdictions.

However, in some cases, we should not even get to questions of proportionality, because arguments from failure are inappropriate outside a constitutional context due to the considerations above, that is because existing institutional frameworks are comprehensive or because there are more democratic means available to address the problem. Only where this is not the case, the questions of functionality, necessity and costs and thus proportionality arise and become central for assessing arguments from failure. This book, therefore, presents not just an argument for taking arguments from failure seriously and accepting them as legitimate arguments under certain conditions but also an argument for when and why to reject such arguments, namely in most cases.

I.2 Methodology

How can one study 'institutional failure' across multiple legal orders? Is there really a useful comparison to be drawn between the Uniting for Peace Resolution, the European Court of Justice's doctrine of systemic deficits and structural reform litigation in India? One standard approach to these questions might be to outline in Chapter 1 a normative concept of institutional failure and then demonstrate how different legal orders respond to failure thus defined, using that concept to measure their success. Such an inquiry raises the question of how we would go about defining institutional failure in the first place. Where would we look to come up with such a concept? To comparative law? To political theory?

In this book, I deliberately take a different approach. I don't narrow my inquiry upfront to one particular understanding of institutional failure defined at the outset. Instead, I focus on a type of public law argument: the argument from failure. This involves distinguishing such arguments from other doctrines and concepts, but it does not involve a definition of failure beyond the conceptual framework sketched out here and in Part I. Rather, my approach is best described as iterative, cycling back and forth between description and analysis of arguments from failure in different contexts and normative considerations. Thus, the theoretical arguments I put forward in Part I of this book include many examples and are built on the more specific cases and discourses I discuss in Parts II and III, where I subsequently refine some of my arguments and show how they might apply in specific settings.

I choose this somewhat unconventional approach for two reasons. First, I think it is at least as important to show and explain how 'arguments from failure' play a role in a range of different contexts as it is to evaluate them – and perhaps more so. This inquiry should not be limited upfront by focusing on cases that fit a certain definition of institutional failure. And though I cannot offer a comprehensive account here, and I will still be leaving out many instances where we encounter arguments from failure in many parts of the world, I have attempted to provide a big picture in this book. I include examples from a relatively wide range of different legal systems, international, regional and domestic, including states belonging to Global North and South jurisdictions – albeit focusing mainly on the 'usual suspects' where we already have plenty of English language scholarship to draw on. Analyzing arguments from failure in such different contexts, I am interested in both the commonalities and differences we find in the way these arguments are deployed and in their ideological underpinnings. I do not make any causal claims in an empirical sense in this book, but I do try to shed light on what appear to be some common threads and trends.

Second, from a comparative law perspective, I am not convinced that we can usefully operate with one comprehensive concept of institutional failure beyond the argumentative structure outlined in this book. Perhaps the most important point to emphasize upfront is what failure here is *not*, namely just any breach of law. For example, from a human rights lawyer's perspective, it may seem that every rights violation should be considered a failure. Many have suggested precisely this to me when I have presented my work at different conferences over the past years. However, if we call to mind the central purpose of arguments from failure – that is to justify an expansion of existing competences – we realize that this is not a useful definition of institutional failure. That rights will occasionally be violated is something we have built into most of our legal systems. We have institutions, namely courts (among others), to deal with such rights violations. More than that: With the proliferation of rights and rights talk, rights violations can happen and do happen anywhere and at any time, simply because no system or society is perfect. Speaking of failure in this context is therefore not a convincing use of that term. When institutions refer to failure to expand their competences in situations where ordinarily others would tackle the issue, the failure in question must therefore be special in some way. A rights violation as such is not enough to justify this.

And we can find ideas of what makes failure special in this sense in a range of public law constellations. For example, in international law some have argued that there is a legal concept of state failure.[20] Courts, too, sometimes use specific procedural or remedial tools to deal with certain kinds of rights violations, such as the pilot procedure in the European Court of Human Rights or the unconstitutional state of affairs doctrine in a range of Latin American countries.[21] Yet, attempts to define institutional failure wholesale in public law are scarce. The only genuine attempt to define it more broadly in legal terms to my knowledge is Simon and Sabel's famous paper on 'destabilization rights'.[22] They suggest that institutional failure exists whenever institutions no longer fulfil minimum standards of adequate performance, with reference to 'industry standards',[23] that is existing quantitative benchmarks of institutional performance in the United States. This sounds intuitively plausible, but there are a number of problems with their approach. It is already debatable if and to what degree failure or dysfunction can be objectively measured. In most cases in most of the world, there will not be readily available quantifiable benchmarks as to what constitutes adequate institutional performance. But their approach also runs into problems on a more principled level. Rights violations are not always and necessarily linked to institutional mandates, and so even massive violations of rights may therefore not appear as malperformance in the terms of their definition. For example, the police may lower criminality rates in a given area while at the same time violating rights on a massive scale. However, if we want to capture something like this – as courts do in practice – in terms of institutional failure, we will find that we often disagree about what counts as success.

In this situation, public lawyers may be tempted to turn to other disciplines for help. But political economists have so far mainly emphasized how concepts such as institutional or policy failure are not

[20] See in particular P. Starski, *The 'Unwilling or Unable' State as a Challenge to International Law*, Habilitation/Postdoctoral thesis, Bucerius Law School (2020).

[21] See Chapter 4 for details.

[22] C. F. Sabel and W. H. Simon, 'Destabilization Rights: How Public Law Litigation Succeeds' (2004) 117 *Harvard Law Review* 1016.

[23] Ibid., 1063.

straightforward. A literature survey demonstrates that no one definition of failure or dysfunction has emerged in that literature either. Thus, for example, Prakash and Potoski distinguish between four categories of dysfunction: (1) design failures, where institutions are designed in a way that does not enable them to pursue their function to channel private interests towards collective ends; (2) institutional mismatch and obsolescence, where new challenges to regulation have emerged, either in the form of external challenges or because those subject to regulation have devised new ways to avoid undesirable regulation or there is a new group of actors subject to regulation that the old rules do not fit; (3) adaptation failures, where institutions do not have sufficient flexibility to adapt to previously unforeseen problems; and finally (4) cases of institutional capture, where narrow interests subvert the common good orientation of particular institutions to their own benefit.[24] These categories are certainly helpful to better understand and distinguish between different types of dysfunction and devise a response to them. But operationalizing them for legal purposes is not always straightforward. Judges might decide to apply stricter scrutiny in cases of institutional failure thus defined, for example by treating capture or design flaws as forms of failure that warrant deviation from their standard of review.[25] However, it will often be difficult for judges to assess if and when these things are present. Moreover, using their categorization as a legal template would run into the same problem as Simon and Sabel's account: that some cases of failure are hard to capture in terms of dysfunction.

Something similar is true for Cass Sunstein's approach. He argues that we should understand dysfunction in terms of the state's ultimate goal of helping citizens to lead good lives.[26] Whatever our differences about what precisely a good life entails, Sunstein suggests we should be able to agree that five factors are important to that ability: namely subjective well-being, longevity, health, educational attainment and per capita income. Whether institutions fail or succeed then depends on what they contribute to the attainment of these goals. In the context of this book and its concern with the legal concept of failure, this approach is both too vague and insufficiently anchored in legal principles. Apart from the difficulties of measuring regulatory impact and for

[24] Prakash and Potoski, 'Dysfunctional Institutions'.

[25] T. W. Merrill, 'Capture Theory and the Courts: 1967–1983' (1997) 72:4 *Chicago-Kent Law Review* 1039–117 at 1039.

[26] C. R. Sunstein, 'Nonsectarian Welfare Statements' (2016) 10:2 *Regulation & Governance* 126.

that matter evaluating trade-offs between these indicators, lists of goods of this kind are always going to be endlessly contested.

Ultimately, scholarly discussions around the concept of policy failure and institutional failure in the political economy literature over the last few years show that it is not an objective one. While we may capture some aspects of policy failure in terms of quantifiable benchmarks, ultimately assessments of failure are rooted in particular discourses within particular communities, as well as, in some cases, among the broader public.[27] Philippe Zittoun in particular draws attention to this discursive function of failure as an argument used by stakeholders in the political process to serve multiple aims. This includes legitimizing an obligation to act – which is closest to my starting point here – but also its use as a prognostic argument intended to block reform proposals or challenge authority more broadly.[28] And as we will see in the course of this book, discourses about failure are frequently driven by powerful actors seeking to expand their power, but they are also used to challenge exclusionary politics and give voice to marginalized and vulnerable groups, articulating hopes for a better future.

Yet, the fact that arguments from failure will always be rooted in particular discourses is not to say that arguments from failure cannot be a legal concept. The trick, I believe, is to turn the question on its head. We should not ask for a legal concept or definition of institutional failure as such, but rather start by asking what it is that arguments from failure seek to justify and approach the question of whether we are dealing with a case of failure from there. In other words, failure and the response to it need to be tailored to each other.

And this, unlike the definitional question, is a question on which comparative constitutional theory can have something to say, or so I argue in this book. Arguments from failure confront a range of normative challenges that are sufficiently similar across different jurisdictions and contexts to engage with them from the perspective of comparative constitutional theory.

Though the nature and possibilities of comparative constitutional theory are still subject to debate, such an approach reflects one of the standard methodologies in comparative public law today. As Gary

[27] Zittoun, 'Analysing Policy Failure'; see also for the broader debate Prakash and Potoski, 'Dysfunctional Institutions' as well as Derwort, Jager and Newig, 'Towards Productive Functions?'.

[28] Zittoun, 'Analysing Policy Failure'.

Jacobsohn and Miguel Schor point out in the introduction to their edited volume on the subject, constitutional theorists have long worked with comparisons to other systems, going back to the writers of the Federalist Papers as well as key early authors such as Montesquieu, Bodin and Dicey. Each conceptualized their own (real or desired) constitutions by comparative references to others. Indeed, defining constitutional terms solely with reference to one particular constitutional text ignores to what degree such terms are a result of not only local but transnational and foreign struggles and debates.[29]

For more than a hundred years, constitutions have employed a host of identical terms – building blocks[30] – that constitutional framers have drawn upon when drafting their own texts. Though these universal components will take on a life of their own once they are integrated into a particular legal system,[31] and though some elements of a constitution may find no counterparts in other places, the universal/foreign origin of many components still provides a basis for comparison and for the approach Ran Hirschl labels 'concept formation through multiple description'.[32] Thus, if constitutional theorists *within one legal system* endeavour to theorize constitutional provisions with reference to their own particular system and other concepts within that system, *comparative* constitutional theorists construct concepts on the basis of a comparison of different legal systems, albeit without necessarily arriving at one definition or precise concept at the end. For example, constitutional theorists may shed light on the meaning of human dignity or the separation of powers in a particular legal system by reference to the history of those terms, including previous struggles that led to their introduction. They may also refer to other constitutional rights or concepts and broader considerations about the telos and origins of the constitution in question. In contrast, comparative constitutional theorists will consider and compare how different legal systems construct the meaning of such terms in constitutional scholarship and in judicial

[29] G. Jacobsohn and M. Schor (eds.), *Comparative Constitutional Theory* (Edward Elgar Publishing, 2018).

[30] G. Frankenberg, 'Constitutional Transfer: The IKEA Theory Revisited' (2010) 8:3 *International Journal of Constitutional Law* 563.

[31] Ibid.; for the classical argument (formulated in stronger terms than here), see P. Legrand, 'The Impossibility of "Legal Transplants"' (1997) 4 *Maastricht Journal of European & Comparative Law* 111.

[32] R. Hirschl, *Comparative Matters: The Renaissance of Comparative Constitutional Law* (Oxford University Press, 2014), p. 240–1.

practice. Of course, the bare fact that certain terms are understood in a particular way even in a majority of states provides no good argument for interpreting them in the same way within any one particular system. What is normatively relevant, however, is arguments about why they should be understood in a particular way. Such normative arguments may be grounded in constitutional and/or political theory, reasoning about what makes a just state and society, and they can be drawn from multiple scholarly traditions and regions. This is what I offer here: not a universal account of the legality of failure arguments, but a set of questions and considerations based on my analysis of practice and theory from multiple jurisdictions to help us think through such arguments in concrete cases.

I.3 Perspectives and Building Blocks

In exploring if and how arguments from failure might be justified (or not) in normative terms, my work resonates with Jeremy Waldron's call for more institutional analysis in public law in *Political Political Theory*.[33] It also echoes earlier work on interinstitutional comparison in law as championed by Neil Komesar,[34] building on political economists such as Douglass North.[35] However, unlike these earlier authors and unlike current work by political scientists on constitution drafting and institutional design, I focus here on the question whether exceptions to the default arrangement of competences may be legitimate from a public law perspective, rather than inquiring about the best institutional design or the optimal distribution of rights and obligations among private persons or vis-à-vis the state more broadly.

The questions I ask tend to be most explicitly addressed in contemporary debates about judicial review and the separation of powers. Such arguments often draw on political process arguments, sometimes based on previous work by John Hart Ely, for whom the question of trust and distrust vis-à-vis the political system was central to determining the

[33] J. Waldron, *Political Political Theory* (Harvard University Press, 2016).

[34] N. K. Komesar, *Imperfect Alternatives: Choosing Institutions in Law, Economics, and Public Policy* (University of Chicago Press, 1994); and id., *Law's Limits: Rule of Law and the Supply and Demand of Rights* (Cambridge University Press, 2001).

[35] D. North, *Institutions, Institutional Change and Economic Performance* (Cambridge University Press, 1990).

necessity (and scope) for judicial review.[36] The closest approach to my own in this regard is Rosalind Dixon's recent work on responsive review. Dixon argues that courts need above all to be responsive to the political environment in which they are operating. She sets out a nuanced template for judicial review that can range from super-strong review, where it is necessary to protect a democratic minimum core, to weak forms of review to address legislative blindspots and burdens of inertia as they arise even in well-functioning democratic systems.[37] My own work here builds on Dixon's approach as well as on David Landau's earlier work.[38] Landau has argued that political context and the existing institutional setup and functioning are key to evaluating the legitimacy of judicial intervention – an argument he has since expanded in other work.[39] He is not alone in building on the notion of malfunction as a justification for expansive judicial action, as we will see in Chapter 5.[40] Add to this strand of research another emerging line of comparative scholarship on structural remedies and the judiciary's ability to steer reform processes in public institutions, taken up inter alia by Po Jen Yap and[41] Kent Roach,[42] as well as by Alexandra Huneeus[43] in the international human rights context.

[36] J. H. Ely, *Democracy and Distrust: A Theory of Judicial Review* (Harvard University Press, 1980).

[37] R. Dixon, *Responsive Judicial Review: Democracy and Dysfunction in the Modern Age* (Oxford University Press, 2023).

[38] D. Landau, 'Political Institutions and Judicial Role in Comparative Constitutional Law' (2010) 51:2 *Harvard International Law Journal* 319.

[39] M. J. Cepeda Espinosa and D. Landau, 'A Broad Read of Ely: Political Process Theory for Fragile Democracies' (2021) 19:2 *International Journal of Constitutional Law* 548.

[40] See, e.g., S. Issacharoff and R. H. Pildes, 'Politics as Markets: Partisan Lockups of the Democratic Process' (1998) 50:3 *Stanford Law Review* 643; P. S. Karlan, 'Politics by Other Means' (1999) 85:8 *Virginia Law Review* 1697; N. Petersen, *Proportionality and Judicial Activism: Fundamental Rights Adjudication in Canada, Germany and South Africa* (Cambridge University Press, 2017); S. Issacharoff, *Fragile Democracies: Contested Power in the Era of Constitutional Courts* (Cambridge University Press, 2015); T. Daly, *The Alchemists: Questioning Our Faith in Courts as Democracy-Builders* (Cambridge University Press, 2017); S. Gardbaum, 'Comparative Political Process Theory' (2020) 18:4 *International Journal of Constitutional Law* 1429.

[41] P. J. Yap, *Constitutional Remedies in Asia* (Routledge, 2019); id., 'New Democracies and Novel Remedies' (2017) 1 *Public Law* 30; id., 'Remedial Discretion and Dilemmas in Asia' (2019) 69:1 *University of Toronto Law Journal* 84.

[42] K. Roach, *Remedies for Human Rights Violations: A Two-Track Approach to Supra-National and National Law (Cambridge Studies on Constitutional Law, Vol. 27)* (Cambridge University Press, 2021); id., 'Polycentricity and Queue Jumping in Public Law Remedies: A Two-Track Response' (2016) 66:1 *University of Toronto Law Journal* 3.

[43] A. Huneeus, 'Reforming the State from Afar: Structural Reform Litigation at the Human Rights Courts' (2015) 40 *Yale Journal of International Law* 1.

I see this book as a contribution to this work, but my aim here is both narrower and at the same time broader than the existing literature. My focus is narrower than existing theories of review insofar as I do not put forward a general theory of judicial review, of constitutionalism or the separation of powers. At the same time, I also pursue a broader project, because I am not only interested in courts and judicial review. Even though courts feature prominently throughout this book, I also seek to trace how arguments from failure are framed in different contexts and understand the larger normative stakes of such arguments in different fields of public law. The inclusion of examples from public international and European law has shaped my thinking and my theoretical approach, which understands arguments from failure as one among several efficiency- or output-focused arguments in public law. As such, it is not accidental that they are hard to capture and grapple with in legal terms. This is in fact a core property insofar as they are meant to destabilize existing rules in the interest of achieving certain results. To fully understand what this means and where this may lead without very careful constraints, the examples from international law and the jurisprudence of the European Court of Justice towards the end of this book are essential. They offer a perspective missing in the usual literature on structural reform litigation or remedies.

Finally, the normative framework I propose here fits into existing theories of a more collaborative approach to the separation of powers, as set out especially in Aileen Kavanagh's recent work.[44] It also aligns with theories of judicial review that emphasize the primacy of democratic mechanisms and the necessity of judicial responsiveness to them,[45] without, however, depending on any one particular theory of democracy or the separation of powers. This flexibility is intentional and necessary in light of the task of coming up with a comparative approach to arguments from failure. While consistent with a core understanding of constitutional democracy, I have attempted to be minimalist and pragmatic. I leave wide room for contextual adaptation to specific legal cultural backgrounds as well as a range of political positions within constitutional democracy. Thus, for example, in countries where constitutional review is rare and courts tend to exercise considerable deference, the framework I offer here might help judges determine where to intervene in the first place, rather than offering a path to structural reform

[44] A. Kavanagh, *The Collaborative Constitution* (Cambridge University Press, 2023).
[45] Dixon, *Responsive Judicial Review*.

litigation. Those who are generally sceptical of arguments for judicial intervention might therefore treat cases of institutional failure where trust in other institutions has been shattered as the rare exception to the presumption in favour of judicial restraint.

I.4 Outline

The book is divided into three main parts – a theoretical discussion; a discussion of failure arguments in a judicial context, with particular emphasis on structural reform litigation; and finally, a section on international and European law. I draw in Parts II and III on the theoretical arguments developed in Part I, but what I offer in these later parts is not a straightforward application of the earlier arguments. It is, rather, a mix of description, analysis and normative assessment in concrete circumstances, including in cases where I will argue there is ultimately no sufficient basis for arguments from failures.

In Part I, I engage with the normative questions raised by arguments from failure. I start in Chapter 1 by discussing what arguments from failure are and why we may need them, in light of other existing checks prevalent in many constitutional democracies. I argue that arguments from failure are one among several tools to respond flexibly to the challenges of governing. I distinguish them from their key competitors, implied powers arguments and emergency arguments. Neither of these, I argue, quite captures what is going on in arguments from failure. Nor is the normative framework they come with sufficient – and this suggests that arguments from failure are better treated as a distinct legal concept.

If Chapter 1 presents a prima facie case for why arguments from failure might be useful, this is not the same as saying that we should take them seriously as a *legal* argument. It may be that such arguments are just too political and abuse-prone and don't fit with standard ideas of constitutionalism as power grounded in law. In Chapter 2, I therefore engage in more detail with the normative stakes of arguments from failure, discussing different conceptions of the separation of powers as well as democracy and the rule of law to determine if and when arguments from failure can be justified in those terms. At the bottom line, I argue that we do have the theoretical resources to defend arguments from failure as a legal concept – in some narrowly circumscribed cases. A less scholarly way of expressing this would be to say that such arguments should be safe, legal and rare.

In Chapter 3, I further qualify the conditions for when arguments from failure might be defensible. I draw on the discussions and concepts that emerged when the UN Human Rights Commission first started to claim a mandate for dealing with concrete rights violations as well as the literature on structural reform litigation and on emergencies. All of these sources point to the need to consider the proportionality of interventions in response to failure, taking into account the functionality, necessity and costs of such interventions. I end the chapter by discussing a more recent example where an argument from failure might be usefully deployed, namely the statute deployed by the UK House of Commons to quash postmasters' wrongful convictions in response to the Horizon scandal.

Part II deals with the role of failure arguments in courts. Chapter 4 begins with the story of the development of structural reform litigation, discussing examples from the United States, India, South Africa and Colombia. Courts and scholars in these systems frequently invoke governmental failure to justify both novel judicial procedures and expansive remedies, but typically do so in the context of generally declining trust in the government. At the same time, structural reform litigation in these systems has developed in different ways and assumed different forms, from emphasizing compliance with past judgments as in South Africa to a much broader response to political malfunction and an outlet for judicial exasperation with politics in India and to some degree Colombia.

From there, I move in Chapter 5 to the normative questions. I pick up the discussion from Part I and examine its implications for evaluating structural reform litigation in the context of broader debates about the role of courts in addressing political malfunction, drawing on political process theory. I provide some more guidance here as to how judges and lawyers might approach the question of proportionality and flesh out how a range of factors, that is the quantity, duration and quality of rights violations, as well as the intent or lack thereof behind them, can help us to assess that question.

In Chapter 6, I turn away from the realm of structural reform litigation to consider courts that rely on arguments from failure as judicial trumps to override otherwise existing reasons for judicial deference. I show how arguments from failure can drive judicial innovation, but also discuss the difficulties in determining when to intervene, given that – unlike in typical cases of structural reform litigation – it is often not clear here that rights have been violated in the first place. To that end, I discuss a range of examples from Germany, South Africa and the Netherlands, including some of the emerging case law on climate change where arguments from failure are sometimes deployed to overcome the lack of explicit legal standards.

In the last part of the book, I deal finally with a set of examples from public international and European law where arguments from failure are occasionally deployed but often blur into other arguments. These include arguments about implied powers, including arguments about effective realization in European Union law and emergency arguments.

I begin in Chapter 7 by discussing one of the most explicit and famous examples of an argument from failure: the Uniting for Peace Resolution at the United Nations. From there, I dive into the murky waters of the discourse on state-failure in the 1990s, sketching out some of its most (in)famous manifestations from the law on the use of force and self-defense to the role of failure arguments in international development cooperation. Drawing on existing international law scholarship, I show how these examples speak to the central role of failure arguments as a justification for the expansion of the authority of international bodies. They highlight the need of taking power structures into account when assessing arguments from failure. But there are also broader questions about the appropriateness of invoking failure in an international context in the first place, given that we are typically operating here outside of a traditional constitutional context where principles such as the separation of powers are key concerns. Drawing on Part I, I reiterate that while arguments from failure may be legitimate outside of domestic contexts, they do suppose a quasi-constitutional context where expectations of mutual support and cooperation are normatively appropriate, something often lacking in the international realm.

Next, I turn to the European Union as a legal system where considerations of effectiveness, sometimes including arguments about failure, have long played a central role in driving European integration. I discuss in this context the recent concept of systemic deficiencies in European law as well the *Solange*-jurisprudence of the European Court of Justice, contextualizing these as part of the Court's broader functionalist approach. While some of my examples here involve arguments that are not strictly speaking arguments from failure, European law provides perhaps the best illustration of the risks and chances associated with a broad functionalist approach to legal interpretation.

In the final chapter of this book, Chapter 9, I summarize key findings and finally return to the bigger picture of rising distrust in state institutions, crises of governance and the simultaneous expansion of constitutional law and constitutional review. These developments not only increase our expectations in law and courts to fix existing problems, but they also drive arguments for legal flexibility, including based on arguments from failure, whenever it seems necessary to ensure certain outputs. Yet, the risks of thus enabling a slide into increasingly authoritarian patterns of governance are significant, as this book shows – and therefore suggest that great care and caution is needed in handling arguments for flexibility in public law.

I

Foundations

1

What Are Arguments from Failure and When Might We Need Them?

What happens when those holding political power fail? Political and constitutional theorists have thought about the answer to this question for centuries. Some thinkers have argued that failure justifies or even demands some response, be it in the form of a right to resistance or rebellion (like John Locke)[1] or indeed a right of other institutions to intercede and intervene. Thus, for example, the medieval philosopher William of Ockham argued that though the Pope should generally not intervene in the administration of non-religious affairs (temporal matters), exceptions existed in certain cases, for example when 'temporal matters were being handled by others to the danger of the community of Christians or to the subversion of faith, or in a similar case were being turned to evil, and there was no layman willing or able to prevent such dangers'.[2] In these circumstances, he argued, the Pope could intervene to remedy the situation – and thus, we encounter an early form of the argument for shifting powers in some specific cases of governmental failure.

For a current example, consider Art. 356 of the Indian Constitution, which reads as follows:

> If the President, on receipt of report from the Governor of the State or otherwise, is satisfied that a situation has arisen in which the government of the State cannot be carried on in accordance with the provisions of this Constitution, the President may by Proclamation assume to himself all or any of the functions of the Government of the State and all or any of the powers vested in or exercisable by the Governor or any body or authority in the State other than the Legislature of the State; . . .

It thus allows the Federal President in the case of a 'failure of constitutional machinery in a State' to take over the functions of the state government. This power does not just exist on paper but has been

[1] J. Locke, *Second Treatise on Government* (1689).
[2] W. of Ockham, Dialogus Part 3, Tract 1, Book 1, Opinion 5, a translation is available at http://publications.thebritishacademy.ac.uk/pubs/dialogus/t31d1new.html#zp16.

employed over a hundred times in post-independence India, frequently in a highly contested manner.[3]

Such explicit grants of power to intervene in cases of failure are, however, comparatively rare. Typically, arguments from failure have no explicit basis in law – and thus, treating them as a legal argument rather than merely a tool of political rhetoric will be controversial.

Nevertheless, we should take such arguments seriously as a matter of public law – or so I argue in this first part of the book. Arguments from failure should be recognized as concepts or doctrines of public law. Whether the expansion of power they seek to justify is in fact legal will, of course, depend on the existing legal frameworks in place and the specific case and context and is therefore not a question this book can conclusively answer. What I offer in the next few chapters is a way of thinking about the legality of such arguments through the prism of comparative constitutional theory.

1.1 'If men were angels…'

A long strand of liberal constitutional theory views the state as an answer to the failures of societal self-organization. Without a central power that holds a monopoly on force, contract theorists have argued, human beings will war against each other and live in a state of permanent fear.[4] Yet, rulers don't tend to be angels either, as the American framers were well aware,[5] and contemporary constitutions thus include a range of safeguards and tools to deal with this fact.[6]

I begin this chapter by sketching some of these accountability mechanisms while also giving a sense of their limitations when dealing with instances of failure. These limitations give rise to a range of legal arguments to expand institutional competences, which I discuss in the second part (Section 1.2) of this chapter. The overview I offer here is necessarily incomplete given the wide range of accountability mechanisms in different constitutional systems. Nevertheless, by giving us a sense of the

[3] R. Sagar, 'Chapter 13: Emergency Powers', in S. Choudhry, M. Khosla and P. B. Mehta (eds.), *The Oxford Handbook of the Indian Constitution* (Oxford University Press, 2016).

[4] The classic is of course T. Hobbes, *Leviathan*, J. C. A. Gaskin (ed.) (Oxford University Press, 2008).

[5] J. Madison, 'Federalist No. 51' in A. Hamilton, J. Madison and J. Jay, *The Federalist Papers*, C. Rossiter (ed.) (Dutton/Signet, 2012).

[6] See also for a contemporary argument P. Rosanvallon, *Counter-Democracy: Politics in an Age of Distrust* (Cambridge University Press, 2008).

bigger picture at the outset, it allows us to better understand the more specific contexts and cases I zoom in on later in this book.

1.1.1 Constitutional Mechanisms of Personal Control

The threat of removing rulers has long been the most important check on governmental power and the primary means to combat bad governance. Today, the obvious mechanism for removing bad rulers is an election. As Karl Popper argued – and Schumpeter subsequently affirmed[7] – democracy ensures that voters can remove the government without bloodshed, that is throw the rascals out.[8] Inefficient and incapable politicians will pay the cost at the ballot box and will simply be voted out of office, or so goes the theory.

Yet, we know that reality does not always neatly correspond to this idealized template. Elections provide some measure of governmental accountability, but they provide no comprehensive protection against politicians and administrators who fail to do their jobs conscientiously. Elections and election results are dependent on a host of factors, and existing failures are likely to be only one argument among many in the competition for votes. Different political regimes also come with different degrees of accountability. The possibility of holding politicians accountable depends on many things, including on how clearly responsibility can be attributed in the first place.[9] Coordination problems and capacity issues may lead to inefficiency and sometimes failure, which in turn may be hard to attribute to a particular government and harder still to remedy. And in some regimes, democratic processes themselves are largely dysfunctional, and thus elections provide only very limited means to change governmental policy and improve administrative capacity.[10]

Of course, elections are not the only means of controlling governments and removing incompetent or unwilling officials. In parliamentary systems, parliaments hold the power to force governments, and sometimes individual ministers, to resign. This is not true for presidential

[7] J. A. Schumpeter, *Capitalism, Socialism and Democracy*, 3rd edn (Harper & Row, 1950), p. 285.

[8] K. Popper, *The Open Society and Its Enemies. Volume I: The Spell of Plato* (Routledge, 2010), pp. 176 ff.

[9] T. Hellwig and D. Samuels, 'Electoral Accountability and the Variety of Democratic Regimes' (2008) 38:1 *British Journal of Political Science* 65.

[10] D. Landau, 'Political Institutions and Judicial Role in Comparative Constitutional Law' (2010) 51:2 *Harvard International Law Journal* 319, at 335 ff. and elsewhere.

systems, but here too, legislatures typically have some means to remove heads of government or state and sometimes other officials by impeaching them. Not all of these mechanisms are easy to operationalize in practice, however. It is rare for parliaments to force the resignation of governments as this requires the majority party to act against its own party members. Where parliaments take that step, it will typically be in situations where a political coalition has come apart – but we would expect a governmental failure of some magnitude before this would be the response to it.

Something similar is true for impeachment provisions. Whether they are suited to dealing with cases of dysfunction or failure will depend both on their concrete framing and interpretation by the relevant actors as well as political will. As Tom Ginsburg, Aziz Huq and David Landau argue, impeachment today often serves as a means not just to remove officials in cases of criminal offences but to address broader political crises where incumbents have lost support, which may involve dysfunction.[11] But while some constitutions explicitly include broader clauses, allowing for impeachment in light of persistent governmental dysfunctions, not all do. As a result, we sometimes find arguments for an expansive reading of impeachment provisions.[12] But impeachment often comes not just with high legal but also practical hurdles, given the influence and interests of political parties. The US example is a case in point[13] and by no means exceptional, if we consider, for example, the South African ANC's refusal to impeach then-President Zuma for corruption. Political parties often have little incentive to impeach their own leaders. Given that impeachment can be abused, the high hurdles that come with it are also not unreasonable, especially considering that (in presidential systems) it undermines the democratic choices of voters by removing directly elected officials and so should be a means of last resort. As a matter of addressing failure, impeachment may also not be the ideal tool because failure will often be less a matter of bad intent than a mix of

[11] T. Ginsburg, A. Huq, and D. Landau, 'The Comparative Constitutional Law of Presidential Impeachment' (2021) 88:1 *The University of Chicago Law Review* 81, specifically for South Korea at 96.

[12] D. E. Lewis, *The Politics of Presidential Appointments: Political Control and Bureaucratic Performance* (Princeton University Press, 2008); see also for a broad comparative perspective E. C. Page, *Policy Without Politicians: Bureaucratic Influence in Comparative Perspective* (Oxford University Press, 2012).

[13] E.g., K. E. Whittington, 'Impeachment in a System of Checks and Balances' (2022) 87:3 *Missouri Law Review* 835.

incapacity, neglect and coordination problems. Add to this that both no-confidence votes and impeachment of central figures are nuclear weapons in politics, triggering major changes.[14] As such, they will likely be deployed only to deal with problems of a certain magnitude rather than as a tool to address discrete cases of failure and dysfunction.

Within the administration, too, there are means for removing office-holders. Administrative oversight typically allows superiors and sometimes ministers to replace inefficient or corrupt officials with other more suitable candidates, though not all officials can be removed easily or without specific grounds for doing so. Typically, political appointees who 'serve at the pleasure of the President' may be dismissed more easily, whereas career civil servants enjoy stronger protections, both against being moved to different offices and even more so against dismissal. This would suggest that systems with a higher number of political appointees – such as the United States – overall do better than those operating largely with a career civil service, like Britain. Often, however, we think the reverse is true, and the more recent political science literature offers support for this intuition. Thus, for example, David Lewis shows how politicization in the United States enables and drives patronage appointments as well as leads to higher turnover in staff, both of which often hurt performance in the longer run.[15] And there are a range of factors that influence whether and how politicians might get involved in such oversight in the first place, including the broader political context, the nature of the problem, time pressures, etc.[16] Not all decisions on personnel are made by politicians, of course, but overall it is often difficult to dismiss career civil servants without a specific cause, which may be hard to establish. And moving them to other offices, if possible, may create new problems. More importantly still, an exchange of personnel will not always suffice if the problem at hand is structural and thus not tied to any particular officeholder. Broader legislative or administrative remedies will then be required.

[14] For an instructive US–German comparison on this, see M. Tokatlı, 'Impeachment as Last Resort to Safeguard Democracy? Removing the Head of Government in Different Institutional Settings' (2024) 65:2 *Politische Vierteljahresschrift* 395.

[15] D. E. Lewis, 'Revisiting the Administrative Presidency: Policy, Patronage, and Agency Competence' (2009) 39:1 *Presidential Studies Quarterly* 60; see also Lewis, *Presidential Appointments*, chapters 6–8.

[16] Page, *Policy Without Politicians*, chapter 1.

1.1.2 Issue-Specific Mechanisms of Control

Another way of grappling with institutional failure is not by exchanging personnel but by intervening directly in the issue in question. There are a range of constitutional and administrative mechanisms providing for such interventions. Sometimes, they merely involve the rights to publicly question officials about their and their departments' actions, as parliaments usually enjoy. Sometimes they provide the means to actually change existing policies, directly or indirectly.

The standard mechanisms for intervening directly on specific issues are judicial review and administrative oversight. Administrative oversight comes in different forms and may empower both politicians and administrative superiors to intervene at lower levels. Yet, there are many reasons why such mechanisms might not work: Bureaucrats may be overworked or may not care; bureaucracies may be too big to control effectively or be captured by certain lobby groups; close personal ties and personal loyalties may make intervention difficult; and tight budgets and coordination problems with other actors may get in the way of efficient oversight, even in reasonably well-functioning systems. And politicians, too, may not get involved for all these reasons and more. As Rosalind Dixon points out, even in well-functioning democratic systems there are routine malfunctions that may inhibit governmental responsiveness.[17] Current legislators have to consider a great deal of issues, often involving difficult and technical questions. Blind spots result from these pressures for time and attention within the ordinary legislative process, which may lead to some problems simply falling through the cracks. And previously declared priorities or the necessity for coalition building may prompt legislative inertia, with the result that some issues and rights violations may be ignored or sidelined, even in cases where they would arguably enjoy majority support.[18]

Judicial review, too, grants courts powers to intervene, subject to certain conditions. However, courts need support from the other institutions routinely tasked to implement their decisions – and such support

[17] R. Dixon, 'Creating Dialogue about Socioeconomic Rights: Strong-form versus Weak-form Judicial Review Revisited' (2007) 5:3 *International Journal of Constitutional Law* 391; in more recent work, Dixon connects these democratic blockages to the broader risk of democratic backsliding – as a part of general democracy-sensitive or 'responsive' approach to judicial review. See id., *Responsive Judicial Review: Democracy and Dysfunction in the Modern Age* (Oxford University Press, 2023).

[18] *Ibid.*

may or may not be forthcoming. (As we will see in the second part of this chapter, it is precisely when this assumption of support no longer holds that we see courts intervene more expansively, on the basis of governmental failure.) Judicial review is also limited by the fact that it typically happens ex post and in response to individual cases – and this in turn can make it a less than ideal tool to address broader structural and systemic problems, as we will see in Chapters 4 and 5.

Finally, there is a range of more indirect and subtle means of intervention, both within the legislative and administrative branches. Such mechanisms are often specific to individual legal systems, working to establish accountability within the bureaucracy and thus dealing with failure when it arises.[19] Within the legislative branch, too, there are indirect powers of accountability, for example through budgetary control over government spending, which parliaments may use to increase leverage over the executive branch. Here, too, though, the scope and impact of such powers will depend on the specific legal and constitutional context.[20] And as we have seen, some constitutions explicitly provide federal governments with powers to intervene in individual states under certain circumstances or contain emergency clauses that shift powers to the executive branch in some situations, which I address briefly in Section 1.2.3.

1.1.3 Summary and Consequences

This brief overview shows that there is a range of formal and informal mechanisms to respond to failure by exchanging personnel or by intervening directly through mechanisms of oversight and control. Yet, it is also easy to see how some cases of failure or dysfunction might slip through the cracks. Not all available mechanisms will be adequate to all kinds of failure, and some may not themselves be working, for pragmatic or structural reasons. This is especially true for the kind of failures that are not likely to be remedied by exchanging officeholders but are

[19] For the United States, see for an overview A. Bernstein and C. Rodríguez, 'The Accountable Bureaucrat' (2023) 132 *Yale Law Journal* 1600.

[20] L.-M. McCarthy-Cotter and M. V. Flinders, 'Accountability in Liberal Democratic, Parliamentary Systems', in E. Ongaro and S. Van Thiel (eds.), *The Palgrave Handbook of Public Administration and Management in Europe* (Palgrave Macmillan, 2017); F. Meinel, 'Confidence and Control in Parliamentary Government: Parliamentary Questioning, Executive Knowledge, and the Transformation of Democratic Accountability' (2018) 66:2 *The American Journal of Comparative Law* 317.

structural or systemic in nature. Addressing these often requires significant efforts, including coordination between multiple branches. Not surprisingly therefore, administrators and politicians have sometimes sought to take over issues and deal with them *outside* of those legally prescribed channels. Doing so, of course, then implies a certain degree of legal flexibility.

1.2 Necessity and Effectiveness in Public Law

There are three main frameworks that serve this purpose: first, arguments about implied powers or indeed the need for the effective realization of certain rights/values/goals; second, arguments from failure; and third – at the other end of the scale – full-throated emergency arguments. All three are driven by an overarching logic of efficiency and output legitimacy, albeit that the outputs pursued may be something like the effective realization of human rights. They are also closely related to each other and may blur into each other. All of these different arguments, however, enter the picture only when the standard constitutional and legal mechanisms set up to deal with crises and disasters do not seem to be sufficient to respond to a problem. Accordingly, often (though not always) there will be no textual basis for them in existing laws.

1.2.1 Arguments from Failure

A prototypical example for a rare legalized argument from failure is rules on federal coercion, such as Art. 356 of the Indian Constitution. India is not an outlier in this regard. Rules for federal coercion exist in a host of states, sometimes framed in more explicit, sometimes in less explicit terms, allowing federal states to intervene in cases where sub-national units such as states fail to fulfil certain duties.[21] My own home country, Germany, provides for this possibility in Art. 37 of the German Basic Law:

1. If a Land fails to comply with its obligations under this Basic Law or other federal laws, the Federal Government, with the consent of the

[21] For instance, Art. 34 of the Brazilian Constitution permits federal intervention in cases in which national unity, the federal structure or the functioning of public institutions is threatened. In Canada, Section 90 of the Constitution Act 1867 allows for the Governor Central to disallow provincial laws that are inconsistent with federal interests or constitutional principles. Likewise, Art. 52 of the Swiss Federal Constitution, Art. 100 of the Austrian Federal Constitution and Art. 6 of the Constitution of Argentina contain similar provisions, allowing central governments to take measures to uphold the constitutional order within their federated states or provinces.

Bundesrat, may take the necessary steps to compel the Land to comply with its duties.

2. For the purpose of implementing such coercive measures, the Federal Government or its representative shall have the right to issue instructions to all Länder and their authorities (official translation).

Translated by Professor Christian Tomuschat, Professor David P. Currie, Professor Donald P. Kommers and Raymond Kerr, in cooperation with the Language Service of the German Bundestag.

This rule has a considerable tradition in German constitutional history, going back to the German Empire.[22] The takeover of the Prussian government by the federal German government under Chancellor Franz von Papen in 1932, the so-called coup or putsch in Prussia (*Preussenschlag*), represents an infamous example for the exercise of that power. It led to a prolonged legal battle in court (*Staatsgerichtshof*), which ultimately upheld the measure, albeit with some modifications.[23] The measure was based on the second paragraph of Art. 48 of the Weimar Constitution, which concerned cases of the disturbance of public order and security, and thus somewhat differs from Art. 37 of the Basic Law. But Art. 48 allowed intervention also in cases where states did not fulfil their duties towards the *Reich*, and, perhaps surprisingly, this provision survived National Socialism. Both provisions essentially constitutionalized arguments from state failure to the benefit of the respective federal governments. However, unlike in Spain, where the federal government made use of the similarly phrased – and German-inspired – Art. 155 of the Spanish constitution to take over the Catalan government in the wake of its secessionist actions in 2017,[24] in Germany, this

[22] F. Shirvani, 'Die Bundes - und Reichsexekution in der neueren Deutschen Verfassungs geschichte' (2011) 50:1 *Der Staat* 102.

[23] The take-over of the Prussian government by the federal German government under Chancellor Franz von Papen, the so-called coup or putsch in Prussia (*Preussenschlag*) in 1932, represents an infamous example for the exercise of that power, albeit in response to disruption of public order, not strictly speaking failure that was listed as additional grounds for intervention under Art. 48 of the Weimar Constitution; see *Preussen contra Reich vor dem Staatsgerichtshof, Stenogrammbericht der Verhandlungen vor dem Staatsgerichtshof in Leipzig vom 10. bis 14. und vom 17 Oktober 1932* (J.H.W. Dietz Nachf., 1933). On the legal theoretical underpinnings of the arguments presented, see D. Dyzenhaus, 'Legal Theory in the Collapse of Weimar: Contemporary Lessons?' (1997) 91:1 *American Political Science Review* 121.

[24] M. J. García Morales, 'Bundeszwang und Sezession in Spanien: Der Fall Katalonien' (2019) 1 *Die öffentliche Verwaltung* 1. The drafting was influenced by Art. 37 of the German Basic Law; see H. Bauer, 'Der Bundeszwang in der bundesstaatlichen Ordnung des Grundgesetzes' (2019, special issue) *Revista Catalana de Dret Públic* 1.

provision has never been used in the post-war era, perhaps due to its abuse in the Weimar Republic.[25] India's Art. 356, by contrast, has been relied on in many controversial cases, with the Indian Supreme Court declaring some instances unconstitutional, in spite of claiming only (limited) powers of review.[26]

Beyond cases of federal coercion, where we typically have a legal basis for intervention, there are many further examples for arguments from failure in a number of different contexts. They range from arguments for why courts need to undertake structural reform and intervene in expansive ways in failing institutions to examples for triggering intervention by different international bodies and organizations, among many other contexts and areas.

Both the reasons for failure and its magnitude, however, may be very different. Sometimes, the original design may have been faulty from the start. Sometimes, institutional inertia blocks necessary adaptation, or institutions are captured by influential groups. Sometimes there may be coordination problems between different offices that need to work together. Failure can be limited to concrete instances of regulatory oversight, or it can be of longer duration. In the latter case, it often makes more sense to speak of dysfunction, though I use both terms interchangeably here. Sometimes, it arises because legislators or administrators actively want to harm certain groups, or because they do not care, since those groups lack political power; sometimes because they are unsure what to do to address a problem or feel they do not have the means to address it. Arguments from failure or dysfunction appear in all of these different circumstances, as a rhetorical device to justify expansions of authority – 'power grabs' – in certain exceptional situations. And while they are often blurred with arguments about implied powers or emergencies, they are not identical with either, nor should they be treated as if they were.

1.2.2 Teleological Interpretation and Implied Powers

Arguments about implied powers are, strictly speaking, one important example of a purposive or teleological approach in interpreting

[25] Bauer, 'Bundeszwang', 1 at 8–9.

[26] See, e.g., *S. R. Bommai v. Union of India* [1994] 2 SCR 644; AIR [1994] SC 1918; [1994] 3 SCC 1, where the Indian Supreme Court tried to regulate the use of emergency powers under Art. 356 of the Indian Constitution. See also for a broader discussion Sagar, 'Emergency Powers'.

institutional competences. As such, they share the broader problems associated with purposive or teleological interpretation. Those problems are exacerbated when dealing with the interpretation, not of rights, but of competences. Teleological interpretation entails an interpretation of law in light of the key purpose or *telos* of the specific rule, which is typically deduced not from the historical drafter's original intent, though such intent may play a role, but from a broader reading of the respective norm in its legal and political context. Thus, while teleological interpretation seeks to realize the primary aim or goal associated with a specific norm, there is always a risk of such an interpretation going considerably beyond the legal text. For example, the European Court of Justice has used the doctrine of the so-called *effet utile* to justify a 'functionalist' reading[27] of many Treaty provisions in ways that have dramatically strengthened individuals' economic rights under the Treaty, as well as the scope of Union law more broadly. This has sometimes occurred in a context of perceived political failure where the Court has felt it necessary to step in.

While such teleological arguments are primarily or ostensibly about the realization of certain rights (under a constitution or treaty), they often have significant and sometimes unintended consequences for our understanding of institutional roles and competences, which can be far-reaching. They may also blur into more specific arguments about the roles of particular institutions, for example in the context of structural reform litigation, where courts are called upon to ensure the effective protection of rights.

In other cases, the argument is more explicitly about the scope of the competences or jurisdiction of specific institutions. This complicates matters insofar as such competences are meant from the outset to be limited by the constitutional framework.[28] Nevertheless, public lawyers have often adopted broad approaches to the interpretation of competences as well, where this has seemed necessary to exercise governmental functions, for example, by developing the doctrine of implied powers. Today perhaps most commonly used in the realm of international law, the doctrine was originally developed by the US Supreme Court in

[27] T. Isiksel, *Europe's Functional Constitution: A Theory of Constitutionalism Beyond the State (Oxford Constitutional Theory)* (Oxford University Press, 2016).

[28] Of course, the difference between the two scenarios may not be as big as it may seem at first glance. Today, many will accept that rights that are real require governmental action and intervention as much as non-action and restraint – a position I share, but my argument here is not dependent on it.

McCulloch v. Maryland, an early decision discussing whether the federal government had the power to establish a (second) federal bank for the United States, in the context of a state's efforts to undermine this effort by taxing the bank.[29] The US Supreme Court famously argued that while the power to establish a bank was not a power specifically enumerated in the US Constitution, it was implied by others that were. The general clause entitling the federal government to make 'all laws which shall be necessary and proper for carrying into execution the foregoing powers' therefore provided it with such power.[30] Similarly, albeit in slightly different terms, the German Constitutional Court has developed the concept of federal competence in those cases where the issue to be regulated is per se a federal concern (*Kompetenz qua Natur der Sache*) – and many other courts have come up with similar ideas.[31] In international and European law, too, ideas of implied or inherent powers play an important role.[32]

Arguments about implied powers are sometimes blurred with emergency arguments (which I will discuss below). This is regrettable because the two are ultimately based on different rationales. Not infrequently, such a blurring of argumentative frames indicates that we are really dealing with a case where an argument from failure would be most appropriate. This becomes clear once we understand the purpose of implied powers arguments. That purpose is to read competences into an institution's governing framework, 'not in order to modify it or add to the members' burdens, but in order to give effect to what they agreed by becoming parties to the constitutional treaty'.[33] Giving effect to what the parties agreed on may imply filling in some gaps, but only where this is

[29] *McCulloch v. Maryland*, 17 US 316 (1819).

[30] Ibid., p. 17.

[31] BVerfGE 3, 407 (422); 22, 180 (217 f.); 84, 133 (148); for a (German) discussion, see, e.g., K. Harms, 'Kompetenzen des Bundes aus der "Natur der Sache'?" (1994) 33:3 *Der Staat* 409.

[32] See, e.g., for the ICJ *Reparation for Injuries Suffered in the Service of the United Nations* (Advisory Opinion) [1949] ICJ Reports 198 and *Certain Expenses of the United Nations (Article 17, Paragraph 2, of the Charter)* (Advisory Opinion) [1962] ICJ Reports 153; for the CJEU Case 22/70, *Commission of the European Communities v. Council of the European Communities(ERTA)* [1971] ECR 263; N. M. Blokker, 'International Organizations or Institutions, Implied Powers', in A. Peters and R. Wolfrum (eds.), *The Max Planck Encyclopedia of Public International Law* (Oxford University Press, 2008–) https://tinyurl.com/8wu8z5fe.

[33] K. Skubiszewski, 'Implied Powers of International Organizations', in Y. Dinstein and M. Tabory (eds.), *International Law at a Time of Perplexity: Essays in Honour of Shabtai Rosenne* (Martinus Nijhoff Publishers, 1989), p. 860.

possible in light of the overarching framework in place rather than providing a new mechanism to deal with unforeseen events, such as emergencies. In other words, in cases of emergencies and indeed when we encounter arguments from failure, the special powers sought are typically not already provided for by the existing legal materials. This is different from arguments about implied powers, which are geared towards giving effect to the original purpose of the existing *text*, albeit by interpreting it in a broad manner.

In contrast, the less we can draw on text and standard interpretative methods, the more we move into the realm of failure and emergency arguments, where we will typically encounter efforts to distinguish the situation from other, more 'normal' ones and appeals to necessity. Moving in that direction means moving into a grey area of legality. Whereas implied powers and teleological interpretation are today widely relied upon and accepted as 'legal' methods/doctrines, the same is not true for arguments from failure and indeed emergency arguments, unless they are explicitly provided for in the legal text. As we have seen in the introduction, failure in particular seems too vague a notion, too politically and ideologically polarizing to count as a legal concept as opposed to a convenient rhetorical trope.

1.2.3 Emergency Arguments

Perhaps we should thus simply understand arguments from failure as a specific case of emergency arguments and defend them in those terms.

Contemporary constitutions today routinely include emergency clauses. These typically transfer powers to the executive and often allow for the abridgement of certain constitutional rights in cases of emergency. The database of the Constitute Project lists emergency provisions in 180 constitutions.[34] Indeed, the US Constitution is today an outlier in not providing a specific regime of emergency powers, but here too a set of constitutional doctrines and statutory provisions lay down specific rules to apply in different kinds of emergencies. Many modern constitutions include emergency provisions in the text itself. Consider, for example, the Indian Constitution (Art. 352 ff.), the South African Constitution (Art. 37) and the Colombian Constitution (Art. 212 ff.), all of which transfer certain competences to institutions that do not normally hold

[34] See www.constituteproject.org.

them. The Colombian Constitution stands out insofar as it endows the president with emergency powers not only in the standard cases of war or internal violence but also in situations that 'disrupt or threaten to disrupt in serious or imminent manner the economic, social, or ecological order of the country or which constitute a grave public calamity' (Art. 215).

But even where such explicit rules are lacking or indeed unclear, we may encounter emergency arguments seeking to defend acts that would otherwise be illegal in terms of necessity.

Indeed, several authors defend a specific category of failure arguments, namely arguments for certain kinds of structural judicial intervention, in terms of a response to an emergency. Thus, in his work on the separation of powers, after criticizing courts that initiate judicial proceedings by themselves, as happens in some cases of public interest litigation, Christoph Möllers argues:

> To be sure, as we know from Indian constitutional law, there may be cases of such a flagrant violation of human rights that the intervention of a court may be the only morally permissible solution. But instead of finding a further constitutional justification for such an intervention, it seems more plausible to concede that this kind of argument ends at this point. In cases of moral emergency, procedural arguments from constitutional theory lose their appeal.[35]

Möllers' framing suggests that we may be moving outside of the realm of constitutional law in such cases and instead be operating within the realm of morality, albeit that it is unclear in what kind of cases this verdict might apply and whether it is confined to cases where judges initiate proceedings on their own.

Möllers is not alone in invoking an emergency argument in this context, though his qualification of the practice as extra-legal is not widely shared. Thus, in his work on the separation of powers and the role of courts, Dimitrios Kyritsis approaches failure as a case of emergency, but one that can be accommodated as legal under certain conditions:

> We can imagine extreme situations where it would arguably be appropriate for another state organ to step in and take the requisite measures beyond its jurisdictions. Perhaps, a political standoff has crippled the competent organ's capacity to govern or an urgent measure is persistently

[35] C. Möllers, *The Three Branches: A Comparative Model of Separation of Powers* (Oxford University Press, 2013), p. 146.

> vetoed by a powerful faction. This is one way to conceptualize the controversial activism involved in the desegregation cases for example. Clearly, it is not the courts' job to design school bus routes. Nonetheless, if nobody else will do it in a non-discriminatory way, then the courts' reasons for abstinence may plausibly be said to be overridden by the urgency of doing justice under the circumstances. Still, the mere fact that it would be permissible to disregard the division of labour in an emergency does not ordinarily undermine the force of the rule.[36]

These arguments are not surprising. Arguments from failure share an argumentative structure with emergencies and can accordingly be hard to separate from the latter. As Christian Kreuder-Sonnen argues in his book on international emergency powers, 'the state of emergency can be understood as a legal institution regulating the suspension of (certain provisions of) the normally applying constitutional order – the state of normalcy'.[37] Kreuder-Sonnen argues that exceptional cases in this sense presuppose two things: First, there needs to be a 'constitutionally deviant expansion of political power for executive actors increasing the reach and/or the intrusiveness of authority (i.e. the adoption of emergency powers)'; and second, this expansion of powers will be justified in terms of 'necessity'.[38] Moreover, emergency clauses typically respond to anticipated failure or at least inefficiency of the institution ordinarily responsible by delegating power to another institution.

This closely parallels the kind of arguments we encounter in cases of institutional failure, and it is therefore no surprise that the two are often blurred and confused. However, there are several reasons why we should treat arguments from failure as distinct from emergency arguments.

First, unlike emergency arguments, arguments from failure are in practice not always or necessarily geared towards increasing executive power. Indeed, quite a few of the cases discussed in this book involve shifting powers away from the executive branch. To be fair, this difference would not seem decisive if we are trying to justify failure as an emergency insofar as shifts to other branches may be normatively less problematic. In other words, we might think that if we accept unwritten emergency powers for the executive branch, we should have even less of a

[36] D. Kyritsis, *Where Our Protection Lies: Separation of Powers and Constitutional Review* (Oxford University Press, 2017), pp. 46–7.

[37] C. Kreuder-Sonnen, *Emergency Powers of International Organizations: Between Normalization and Containment* (Oxford University Press, 2019), p. 29.

[38] Ibid., p. 30.

problem with granting emergency powers to other, less dangerous branches and institutions.

Emergencies also often involve the suspension, or at least significant limitation, of individual rights, whereas arguments from failure are often directed towards better protecting individual rights, as we will see in later chapters. Once again, however, this would presumably be an argument for rather than against defending arguments from failure. More importantly though, while emergencies are notoriously difficult to define in advance, they are typically characterized by two qualities: scale and urgency.[39] Urgency, however – that is, a rapidly escalating situation where things will get significantly worse unless speedy action is taken – will not always and not necessarily be present in cases where we encounter arguments from failure. As we will see in the course of this book, arguments from failure are often arguments about governmental omissions over a certain time period. Accordingly, the situation is often much less urgent, in the sense of not arising suddenly and requiring an immediate response to ward off further damage, leaving no time to reflect.

Moreover, the existence of unwritten emergency powers as such is already a highly problematic proposition and their legality is heavily contested in public law.[40] While there are some who assert the need for such powers and defend them in terms of unwritten rules or indeed on the basis of a non-legal concept of emergency powers, following Carl Schmitt,[41] many scholars are rightly sceptical, given the high risks of abuse.[42] A range of theorists have emphasized how the toggle-switch paradigm of the emergency as an exception as opposed to a state of normalcy neither fits the very different realities of the cases that arise (ranging from natural disasters to terrorist attacks to cases of war and

39 N. C. Lazar, *States of Emergency in Liberal Democracies* (Cambridge University Press, 2009), p. 7.

40 For a survey of the international discussion in the wake of the 'war on terror', see W. E. Scheuerman, 'Survey Article: Emergency Powers and the Rule of Law After 9/11' (2006) 14:1 *Journal of Political Philosophy* 61.

41 E.g. O. Gross, 'The Prohibition on Torture and the Limits of the Law', in S. Levinson (ed.), *Torture: A Collection* (Oxford University Press, 2004), p. 239, drawing on C. Schmitt, *Politische Theologie: Vier Kapitel zur Lehre von der Souveränität* (Duncker & Humblot, 1922).

42 E.g. Scheuermann, 'Emergency Powers', 61; see also for a legalization of emergency powers with an aim of confining their abusive potential B. Ackerman, *Before the Next Attack: Preserving Civil Liberties in an Age of Terrorism* (Yale University Press, 2007); J. Ferejohn and P. Pasquino, 'The Law of the Exception: A Typology of Emergency Powers' (2004) 2:2 *International Journal of Constitutional Law* 210.

martial law) nor indeed provides a normatively convincing template to deal with them in terms of public law.[43] What we need, therefore, are differentiated responses to different problems, and this entails recognizing arguments from failure as a category of their own, as opposed to treating them in terms of a dichotomous emergency framework.

Moreover, the general risks associated with emergency powers are heightened if we rely on them to address institutional failure. Crisis and failure are, as we know, hard to measure objectively. Blurring failure and emergency arguments plays into the hands of populists, emphasizing the 'out of the ordinary "character"' of events in order to justify radical breaks with existing rules. Famous examples include the fire of the German parliament, allowing a further clamp-down on political opponents by the German National Socialists in the 1930s, as well as the more recent military coup and its suppression by the Turkish government and its role in the installation of a new, more authoritarian constitution.[44] Crises and their performances are important instruments in the emergence and strengthening of populist movements, as Moffitt shows drawing on Laclau's work.[45] Consider in this context also Bhuwania's troubling account of Indian Public Interest Litigation, which he argues has enabled a form of judicial populism (see Chapter 4).[46]

Such risks of abuse loom especially large because the central justificatory framework when it comes to emergency arguments is necessity: Something truly dreadful will happen if the executive does not seize extraordinary powers to act. This also implies that the greater the danger, the more can be justified – opening up a dangerous slippery slope that may justify the adoption of authoritarian measures whenever a transgression of legal competences seems warranted as a matter of output. If we are seeking to 'abuse-proof' legal doctrines, adopting an emergency framework is therefore clearly the wrong way to go.

43 K. L. Scheppele, 'Small Emergencies' (2005) 40 *Georgia Law Review* 835; K. Loevy, *Emergencies in Public Law: The Legal Politics of Containment* (Cambridge University Press, 2016); Lazar, *States of Emergencies*.

44 P. U. Murphy and P. Pasquino, 'Long Lasting State of Emergency in Turkey and the Recent Constitutional Amendments Under Its Shade' (2023) 10:2 *International Journal of Human Rights and Constitutional Studies* 99.

45 B. Moffitt, 'How to Perform Crisis: A Model for Understanding the Key Role of Crisis in Contemporary Populism' (2013) 50:2 *Government and Opposition* 189; with references to E. Laclau, *On Populist Reason* (Verso, 2005).

46 A. Bhuwania, *Courting the People: Public Interest Litigation in Post-Emergency India* (Cambridge University Press, 2017), p. 142 and elsewhere.

Finally, the emphasis placed on necessity in emergency arguments only partly captures what is going on in arguments from failure, which are, inter alia, concerned with inter-institutional relationships or at the very least *should* be understood in these terms (see more below). Thus, while considerations of necessity are hardly irrelevant to arguments from failure, they should not be understood as their animating spirit. The term *failure* – which is irrelevant to a straightforward emergency argument – emphasizes that.

1.3 Conclusion

Together with arguments about implied powers and emergency arguments, arguments from failure provide some flexibility to state actors in the interest of dealing with problems in other parts of the state. Yet, they should also be treated as distinct from those two more established public law concepts.

Start with their rationale, which is to step in for other institutions that are failing – for whatever reason – to do their job and deal with a problem. This rationale is different to both implied powers arguments and emergency arguments. First, there is the idea of other parts in the system not working properly and 'stepping in for others', which goes beyond the straightforward necessity argument we find in emergency contexts. Second, the idea of failure also signals that the standard expectations of a well-functioning system do not apply, and there is a need for a deviation from existing rules – thus typically going beyond implied powers arguments, which predominantly seek to unearth already present, albeit not textually explicit, competences.

If this speaks to why we should want to treat arguments from failure as a distinct idea, it is not yet clear that we should treat them as a *legal* doctrine or concept. In particular, we may worry that the risks associated with the idea of unwritten powers are simply too great to defend arguments from failure, under any circumstances. And indeed, even where we have a basis in law for arguments from failure, for example in some constitutions providing for federal coercion, such clauses open up wide room for abuse. At the same time, as we have seen above, there are often limited ways and means to address failure even in well-functioning constitutional democracies, and this makes arguments from failure a tempting tool to respond to dysfunction in different forms.

What, in light of these competing considerations, are we to do?

2

Safe, Legal and Rare

The Case For and Against Arguments from Failure

In August 2023, just an hour after the election results were announced in Gabon confirming previous president Ali Bongo Ondimba as the winner, a group of military leaders assembled to announce their take-over of power. An officer reading out a statement justified the coup as a response to the 'serious institutional, political, economic and social crisis' Gabon had been experiencing:

> We are therefore forced to admit that the organisation of the general elections of 26 August 2023 did not meet the conditions for a transparent, credible and inclusive ballot so much hoped for by the people of Gabon (...) Added to this is irresponsible and unpredictable governance, resulting in a continuing deterioration in social cohesion, with the risk of leading the country into chaos (...) People of Gabon, we are finally on the road to happiness.[1]

The Gabonese coup is only one among several recent coups in Africa. Here and elsewhere, military leaders have invoked the failure of elected governments to deal with ongoing crises, giving rise to a discussion in the literature if there might be such a thing as a 'good coup'.[2] None of this is surprising. States and governments have long depended on their ability to achieve certain things – security first and foremost, but also, more broadly, the welfare of their populations. In his recent monograph *All Is Well: Catastrophe and the Making of the Normal State*, Saptarishi Bandopadhyay argues that disaster management became a core function of eighteenth-century states, whose governments sought to reframe disasters and emergencies as something to be managed, guarded against and administered rather than viewing them as natural events or indeed divine

1 'A "Coup" in Gabon: Who, What and Why?', *Al Jazeera*, 30 August 2023, www.aljazeera.com/news/2023/8/30/a-coup-in-gabon-who-what-and-why.

2 N. Okechukwu, 'The Fragility of the African Governance Agenda: A Crisis of Legitimacy', *European Centre for Development Policy Management*, 30 October 2023, www.ecdpm.org/work/fragility-african-governance-agenda-crisis-legitimacy.

punishments.[3] By demonstrating their ability to grapple with disasters and restore normalcy, states and rulers asserted their legitimacy and to that purpose began building modern ('rational') bureaucracies, staffed with experts.

But it is one thing to seek to design the government to be effective and another to then argue for departures from the existing legal framework in cases of supposed or real failure. As we saw in Chapter 1, such arguments come in different forms and contexts. Sometimes they have a basis in law, but more often this is not the case. They often challenge key constitutional principles, such as the separation of powers, the rule of law, constitutionalism, federalism and, not least, democracy.

I start this chapter by spelling out these normative stakes more clearly, albeit briefly. Next, I turn to theoretical resources in the literature on the separation of powers, including in systems of 'transformative constitutionalism', and on democratic experimentalism, that offer a defence of arguments from failure. Some of these are more convincing than others, as we will see. These resources nevertheless suggest that a principled defence of arguments from failure as legal is possible in some cases. In other words, reiterating the introduction – the challenge is to make sure that arguments from failure are safe, legal and rare.

2.1 Normative Stakes

Not all arguments from failure come with the same normative stakes.

Whenever arguments from failure are not explicitly legalized – which means in most cases – they will raise questions about the rule of law and constitutionalism. State institutions exercising power over citizens must be established by law and only exercise their powers as circumscribed by the law. This core principle of constitutionalism, however, is put at risk if existing rules and competences can be simply expanded in the interest of better results. If institutions are free to fix problems arising in response to the failure of others, this may lead to what Alexander Somek labels in the context of the European Union 'governance by situations'.[4] To Somek, the 'normativity of distress demanding that something be done in the face of security hazards, pandemics, collapsing banks, volatile financial markets, high sovereign debt, or terrorist activity' constitutes a threat to

[3] S. Bandopadhyay, *All Is Well: Catastrophe and the Making of the Normal State* (Oxford University Press, 2022), p. 173.

[4] A. Somek, *The Cosmopolitan Constitution* (Oxford University Press, 2014), p. 222.

the traditional understanding of constitutionalism and legality, which presuppose that any exercise of public authority is based on law.[5] Arguments from failure may hence feed into an ultimately authoritarian paradigm. Within this paradigm, democracy, too, takes a backseat as legality is no longer understood in terms of acting in accordance with a power authorized by the people, but rather in the interest of bringing about certain results. This begs the question if arguments from failure ultimately pave the way for a triumph of utilitarianism, for what is 'good' over what is 'right', opening the door to any number of rights abuses in the name of collective welfare as associated with many totalitarian regimes.[6]

Second: democracy. Whatever our understanding of democracy entails, democratic principles are at stake first and foremost when arguments from failure sanction the expansion vis-à-vis parliaments of the powers of actors such as courts or other institutions that do not have the same kind of democratic legitimacy. Structural reform litigation is the most straightforward example for this practice when it sees judges intervening not just in administrative processes, but in the kind of lawmaking that remains the domain of legislatures. But as we have just seen, democracy is also indirectly at stake in other cases, simply because the relevance of democratic authorship recedes in the interest of effective problem-solving.

Third, arguments from failure may run counter to the principle of the separation of powers if institutions exercise powers normally reserved for another branch. This is true whether we are dealing with a system where the separation of powers is applied relatively strictly or more loosely. Arguments from failure challenge the principle of functional integrity, traditionally considered an important aspect of the separation of powers, which in turn constitutes a key principle of constitutionalism and is of relevance at the international level as well.[7] It entails the idea that each of the three branches of the government exercises a distinct task, sometimes put forward in the strict form of a 'one branch-one function' view.[8] Functional integrity requires mutual respect: As different branches fulfil their tasks, they must not encroach on each other's spheres and competences.

[5] Ibid.

[6] H. Arendt, *The Origins of Totalitarianism* (Harcourt Brace & Company, 1973), p. 299. See also Conclusion.

[7] I. Venzke and J. Mendes, 'The Idea of Relative Authority in European and International Law' (2018) 16:1 *International Journal of Constitutional Law* 75; see more in Chapter 7.

[8] I borrow the term from A. Kavanagh, 'The Constitutional Separation of Powers', in D. Dyzenhaus and M. Thorburn (eds.), *Philosophical Foundations of Constitutional Law* (Oxford University Press, 2016), pp. 221 ff.

But why is functional integrity important and what does it mean? Eoin Carolan argues that the distinctness of the three branches reflects the autonomy of the individual citizen as the core value.[9] Individual autonomy, according to Carolan, is not only protected by individual rights or in individualized procedures. Individuals also have an interest in the collective good. The key yardstick for Carolan is that decision-making procedures are non-arbitrary, which implies that they must be designed to fit their (different) purposes. The different branches realize these purposes (setting out collective policies, local application, ensuring fairness in individual cases) in different ways, which reflect their institutional capacities.[10] Similar to Carolan, Christoph Möllers seeks to root the separation of powers in autonomy, more precisely in individual autonomy to make our own life choices and collective autonomy to decide together how we want to live in a society and state. Möllers accordingly doesn't distinguish the different branches in terms of their reasoning, but instead as a matter of institutional set-up. This set-up has to match their function. Hence, legislatures decide collective issues prospectively and in collective procedures. In contrast, '[c]ourts adjudicate individualized cases on external initiative, retrospectively'.[11] Different institutions and different institutional processes thus ensure that both individual and collective autonomy can be realized. This also means, however, that even standard practices such as constitutional review pose a challenge to Möller's conception, because they allow judges to 'make decisions of a scope that would typically require democratic legitimacy'.[12] It is easy to see how arguments from failure that allow institutions to take over the functions of another branch, albeit temporarily, may fall short of these requirements.

Finally, arguments from failure in the context of federal coercion may undermine federalism. How important federalism is depends on context; that is, on the purposes federal arrangements serve in concrete cases. Federalism can be an essential tool to achieve integration within a nation while preserving space for diversity, granting a degree of regional autonomy to those concerned.[13] The stakes involved are therefore often high – as enduring conflicts in many countries, such as Spain, Canada, Britain

[9] E. Carolan, *The New Separation of Powers: A Theory for the Modern State* (Oxford University Press, 2009), p. 134.

[10] Ibid., p. 124.

[11] C. Möllers, *The Three Branches* (Oxford University Press, 2013), p. 89.

[12] Ibid., p. 128.

[13] For a broader overview, see E. Bulmer, 'Federalism: International IDEA Constitution-Building Primer 12', 2nd ed., *International Institute for Democracy and Electoral Assistance*, 2017, www.idea.int/sites/default/files/publications/federalism-primer.pdf; see

and Ireland, Kenya, South Africa, India, the United States and others, demonstrate. Other advantages of federalism may be that it allows for regional experimentation and limits the risks of abuse of political power by dividing it. Federalism, thus, typically creates further veto players,[14] which can be a good thing, but also problematic when major reforms are necessary. In the more recent literature, federalism has also been advocated by some as enhancing democracy overall by allowing citizens to exercise more power over regional/local matters directly and thus stabilizing democratic regimes.[15]

More could of course be said here with respect to all these principles. But ultimately the details will depend on the concrete case and institutional and legal context. Often, several principles will be involved, and sometimes it will be hard to distinguish between them. Thus, for example, the separation of powers serves the goals of enabling individual as well as collective autonomy, and thus democracy, and is also often considered an important part of the rule of law. It is therefore not surprising that insofar as specific uses of arguments from failure are debated in the existing literature, authors often engage with different principles at the same time.

2.2 Theoretical Resources

Once we start engaging more deeply with the constitutional theory literature, however, we can see that there is space for defending arguments from failure, at least in some forms and some cases. In what follows, I try to bundle some of the different strands in the literature into what seem to me the most important theoretical approaches to deal with arguments from failure. The first of these is the more recent literature

also A. Benz, 'Demokratisches Regieren im Föderalismus: Neue Literatur zu einem alten Thema' (2019) 64 *Neue Politische Literatur* 513.

14 G. Tsebelis, 'Decision Making in Political Systems: Veto Players in Presidentialism, Parliamentarism, Multicameralism and Multipartyism' (1995) 25:3 *British Journal of Political Science* 289.

15 However, such claims are contested; ultimately, their persuasiveness will depend on context. For more on this, see R. Inman and D. L. Rubinfeld, *Democratic Federalism: The Economics, Politics, and Law of Federal Governance* (Princeton University Press, 2020). For a more critical take, see C. Sharman, 'Parliamentary Federations and Limited Government: Constitutional Design and Redesign in Australia and Canada' (1990) 2:2 *Journal of Theoretical Politics* 205; for a generally more sceptical take on the relationship between federalism and democracy, see S. Brenton, 'Does Federalism Enhance Representative Democracy? Perpetual Reform and Shifting Power in a Divided Belgium' (2022) 31:2 *Journal of Contemporary European Studies* 500.

on the separation of powers, both in Europe and in the Global South, where it often appears under the label of transformative constitutionalism; the second is the literature on democratic experimentalism. Both literatures occasionally overlap, but each offers important tools and ideas to address the normative stakes involved with arguments from failure, even though we may be sceptical of some of their claims.

2.2.1 *Rethinking the Separation of Powers*

The more recent literature on the separation of powers takes an approach that is more flexible than both the traditional model – which emphasizes that each branch of the government must exercise a distinct task – and Christoph Möller's autonomy-based conception. More recent writing often starts from a critique of the traditional model, which has indeed never prevailed in theory or practice in a pure form.[16] It places emphasis on the need for the separation of powers principle not just to constrain power and secure individual liberty by creating checks and balances, but to bring about a rational and efficient ordering of the state.[17] Indeed, this 'effectiveness rationale' itself is nothing new in many ways, but in fact goes back a long way, and is discussed in such canonical sources as the Federalist Papers.[18] Placing emphasis on considerations of effectiveness opens the door to theories of inter-institutional comparison, which ask which institutions are best able to fulfil certain functions as a basis for allocating legal authority. This in turn opens the door to arguments from failure – albeit without presupposing the need for them. It may be the case, after all, that more rigid conceptions will provide a better basis for an effective government. However, as soon as we accept effectiveness as a central consideration, the debate changes and starts being about degrees of flexibility and rigidity, rather than about clashes of principle.

[16] Thus, even early authors such as James Madison recognized in the Federalist Papers that a total separation of the different was not in fact possible or for that matter desirable, e.g. J. Madison, 'Federalist Papers No. 47 and 48', in A. Hamilton, J. Madison and J. Jay, *The Federalist Papers*, C. Rossiter (ed.) (Dutton/Signet, 2012); for a discussion of the Federalists' approach to the separation of powers, in particular with regard to efficiency, see T. Isiksel, *Europe's Functional Constitution: A Theory of Constitutionalism Beyond the State* (Oxford University Press, 2016), pp. 46 ff.

[17] Kavanagh, 'Separation of Powers', and id., *The Collaborative Constitution* (Cambridge University Press, 2023), as well as N. Barber, *The Principles of Constitutionalism* (Oxford University Press, 2018), p. 79.

[18] Federalist Papers No. 68; Isiksel, *Europe's Functional Constitution*, p. 48.

2.2.1.1 Transformative Constitutionalism

Challenges to the traditional model have come in particular from scholars writing on the Global South, who sometimes formulate their arguments in fairly radical terms. A range of scholars have criticized the traditional 'liberal' conception of constitutionalism as overly preoccupied with securing individual freedom as opposed to bringing about real transformation.[19] Pointing to the need for different state institutions to realize constitutional values and emphasizing the shortcomings of existing political processes, they have argued that we need to rethink the meaning of constitutionalism and the separation of powers. In particular, they have contended that a strict model of the separation of powers does not work in many Southern contexts. Instead, they have argued for a degree of flexibility and creativity, including, in some cases, the creation of new 'fourth branch' institutions to complement other branches and ensure good governance.[20] Such approaches are not confined to scholarship either. Thus, the South African Constitutional Court has adopted a flexible approach to the separation of powers and stressed the need for responsiveness between the different branches. Quoting Sandy Liebenberg's concept of a dialogic relationship of the different branches, the Court has suggested that 'the limits of each branch's institutional power will be continually defined and redefined as they respond to the multifarious challenges of South Africa's evolving constitutional democracy'.[21]

Unsurprisingly, the details of different proposals vary though. Some authors have adopted what David Landau calls a 'constitutional realization' model, which seeks to endow courts with a more active role in the

[19] See, e.g., K. E. Klare, 'Legal Culture and Transformative Constitutionalism' (1998) 14:1 *South African Journal on Human Rights* 146 at 153; S. Sibanda, 'Not Purpose-Made! Transformative Constitutionalism, Post-Independence Constitutionalism and the Struggle to Eradicate Poverty' (2011) 22:3 *Stellenbosch Law Review* 482.

[20] D. Bilchitz and D. Landau, 'Introduction: The Evolution of the Separation of Powers in the Global South and Global North', in id. (eds.), *The Evolution of the Separation of Powers: Between the Global North and the Global South* (Edward Elgar Publishing, 2018), pp. 1 ff.; see also F. Mahomed, 'The Fourth Branch: Challenges and Opportunities for a Robust and Meaningful Role for South Africa's State Institutions Supporting Democracy' ibid., pp. 177 ff., generally and in particular on the role of fourth branch institutions in South Africa; for an early account, see F. Vibert, *The Rise of the Unelected: Democracy and the New Separation of Powers* (Cambridge University Press, 2009), chapter 8, pp. 114–28.

[21] *Mwelase and Others v. Director-General for the Department of Rural Development and Land Reform and Another*, CCT 232/18 [2019] ZACC 30 (20 August 2019) (South African Constitutional Court), at 46 and 47, citing S. Liebenberg, 'Socio-Economic Rights: Adjudication Under a Transformative Constitution' (2010) 24:2 *European Journal of International Law* 739.

context of realizing 'transformative constitutionalism' as a countermodel to the traditional liberal understanding.[22] Though it remains impossible to define clearly what exactly transformative constitutionalism encompasses[23] – the early definition of Klare described the South African Constitution as 'social, redistributive, caring, positive, at least partly horizontal, participatory, multicultural and self-conscious about its historical setting and transformative role and mission'[24] – it seems clear that it requires the state to pursue the transformative vision the constitution lays out.[25] The constitutional realization model thus seeks to relax traditional understandings of the separation of powers and give courts a broader role in order to realize core constitutional values.[26]

Consider, for example, a 2016 article on the separation of powers by Dennis Davis, a prominent South African judge and academic commentator. Davis suggests that the separation of powers should be 'developed to accommodate a variety of social, political and economic challenges', given that 'the core object of the Constitution which is relevant to this discussion is that a participatory democracy is incompatible with poverty or stark inequality'.[27] Similarly, another South African commentator, Tim Fish Hodgson, argues that '[A]ny interpretation of the separation of powers doctrine within South Africa's specific constitutional design must be oriented towards the purpose of eliminating inequality and eradicating poverty'.[28] From that understanding, Hodgson argues, several consequences follow, among them that courts must have a role to play in cases

[22] D. Landau, 'Institutional Failure and Intertemporal Theories of Judicial Role in the Global South', in David Bilchitz and David Landau (eds.), *The Evolution of The Separation of Powers: Between the Global North and the Global South* (Edward Elgar Publishing, 2018), pp. 31–56.

[23] For an overview and further references, see M. Hailbronner, 'Transformative Constitutionalism: Not Only in the Global South' (2017) 65:3 *American Journal of Comparative Law* 527, but the debate has since progressed; see, e.g., J. Fowkes, 'Transformative Constitutionalism and the Global South: The View from South Africa', in A. von Bogdandy, E. Ferrer, M. Morales and F. Piovesan (eds.), *Transformative Constitutionalism in Latin America: A New Latin American Ius Commune* (Oxford University Press, 2017), pp. 97 ff.

[24] Klare, 'Legal Culture', 146 at 153.

[25] Hailbronner, 'Transformative Constitutionalism', 527.

[26] Landau, 'Institutional Failure', p. 45.

[27] D. M. Davis, 'Separation of Powers: Juristocracy or Democracy' (2016) 133:2 *South African Law Journal* 258 at 270.

[28] T. Fish Hodgson, 'The Mysteriously Appearing and Disappearing Doctrine of Separation of Powers: Toward a Distinctly South Africa Doctrine for a More Radically Transformative Constitution' (2018) 34:1 *South African Journal on Human Rights* 57 at 75.

where legislative tools of holding the executive accountable are not employed and that there cannot be a political question doctrine excepting certain kinds of question a priori from judicial review.[29]

These statements are part of broader critiques of constitutionalism's liberal bent, as well as of transformative constitutionalism itself, which is by now the subject of strong attacks as unable to deliver real change in South Africa.[30] This connection between the need for change and specific outputs and constitutionalism was spelt out explicitly and early on by Sanele Sibanda, who suggested that:

> Put differently, in the South African context the failure to more directly and concretely connect the goals the Constitution's transformative vision with ideals of delivering truly egalitarianism outcomes and poverty eradication creates room for a charge to be levelled that asserts that as currently conceived constitutionalism is viewed as an end in itself, rather than as a means to an end.[31]

This approach opens the door to arguments from failure quite widely – and in many ways understandably so. In focusing on socio-economic inequality, it is addressing longstanding blindspots of liberal constitutionalism. If our key focus must be on realizing a constitution's transformative vision in bringing about equality, and existing mechanisms and allocation of competences are failing to achieve this goal, then the overarching importance of realizing that vision suggests a flexible approach to those competences.

2.2.1.2 Recent European Scholarship

Interestingly, European scholarship has moved in a similar direction in recent years, albeit in a less radical key. In particular, Aileen Kavanagh has recently set out a more collaborative understanding of constitutionalism, requiring institutions to work together in a way that ensures '1) mutual responsiveness; 2) mutual respect and support; and 3) a commit-

[29] Ibid., at 76–8.

[30] See, e.g., J. M. Modiri, 'Conquest and Constitutionalism: First Thoughts on an Alternative Jurisprudence' (2018) 34:3 *South African Journal on Human Rights* 300; T. Madlingozi, 'Social Justice in a Time of Neo-Apartheid Constitutionalism: Critiquing the Anti-Black Economy of Recognition, Incorporation and Distribution' (2017) 28 *Stellenbosch Law Review* 123; S. Sibanda, 'When Do You Call Time on a Compromise? South Africa's Discourse on Transformation and the Future of Transformative Constitutionalism' (2020) 24:1 *Law, Democracy & Development* 384.

[31] Sibanda, 'Not Purpose-Made', 482 at 498.

ment to the joint enterprise as a "shared cooperative activity"'.[32] Ideally, Kavanagh argues, each institution will perform the tasks it can do best and support other institutions in their respective roles.[33] Thus, while each branch plays a 'distinct role' in modern constitutional states, functions may be shared among them. The question is how far this reaches and what it requires in terms of the distinctiveness of the different roles of different branches. Kavanagh argues that even where institutions exercise functions shared with other branches, they will nevertheless perform their roles in different ways – and this ensures distinctiveness. For example, she readily accepts that courts may make law, too, but points out that they do so 'in different ways' to the other branches, more 'piecemeal and incremental'.[34]

Even earlier, Nick Barber put forward a similarly flexible conception of the separation of powers rooted in an idea of the state that is not merely a threat to individual liberty but provides a foundation for efficient government.[35] Though Barber acknowledges that the division of labour brought about by the establishment of different branches may be important, he argues against treating this division too rigidly. In particular, Barber suggests that institutional roles should be understood as interdependent, arguing explicitly that 'where one institution is failing, the other needs to accommodate this'.[36] Barber thus views the separation of powers not as an absolute principle but would allow for limitations in what are essentially cases of dysfunction or failure. Even more explicitly, he argues that:

> An extreme activist court may emerge to compensate for an exceptionally supine legislature; a competent executive may dodge enforcing the rulings of a corrupt judiciary. If the compensating institution is reformed, and brought back in line with the requirements of the separation of powers, the problem within the constitution may be exacerbated. Whilst in these systems the separation of powers should be worked towards, it should be applied carefully: the failing institution may need to be reformed first.[37]

It is easy to see that from this perspective arguments from failure can be legitimate tools as part of a broader, more flexible approach to institutional competences. The advantage of this kind of more flexible

[32] Kavanagh, *Collaborative Constitution*, p. 5.
[33] Ibid., Introduction (and elsewhere).
[34] Kavanagh, 'Separation of Powers', p. 232.
[35] Barber, *Principles*, chapter 3.
[36] Ibid., p. 76.
[37] Ibid., p. 79.

approach put forward by Barber and Kavanagh is not only that its understanding of the separation of powers arguably better captures constitutional reality, but also that it is normatively attractive. This is true in particular if we focus on the need to realize certain constitutional goals or values in political systems that function less than well. It also speaks to the kind of argument for judicial intervention put forward first by David Landau[38] and most comprehensively in terms of responsiveness by Rosalind Dixon,[39] which I discuss in more detail in Chapter 5.

2.2.2 *Democratic Experimentalism*

The democratic experimentalism literature culminated in a series of publications in the first decade of the 2000s. This work applied the concept of democratic experimentalism in a variety of different settings, but with a particular emphasis on structural reform litigation and administrative processes, as well as EU governance issues. It is related to the broader governance discourse,[40] which set out to describe changes in the processes of how states governed, emphasizing public-private cooperation, decentralization and a shift away from a command-control mode, all against the background of the 1990s' turn to neoliberalism.[41] With this literature, democratic experimentalists share the belief in the need for decentralization and collaboration among multiple – public and private – players, but take a more normative position as compared to most strands of the governance literature.

Democratic experimentalists often understand their approach to be in line with a pragmatist conception of democracy that emphasizes

[38] D. Landau, 'Political Institutions and Judicial Role in Comparative Constitutional Law' (2010) 51:2 *Harvard International Law Journal* 319.

[39] R. Dixon, *Responsive Judicial Review: Democracy and Dysfunction in the Modern Age* (Oxford University Press, 2023).

[40] G. de Búrca and J. Scott, 'Introduction', in id. (eds.), *Law and New Governance in the EU and the US* (Bloomsbury Publishing, 2006), pp. 1 ff.; see also M. C. Dorf and C. F. Sabel, 'A Constitution of Democratic Experimentalism' (1998) 98:2 *Columbia Law Review* 267; C. F. Sabel and J. Zeitlin, 'Learning from Difference: The New Architecture of Experimentalist Governance in the European Union' (2008) 14:3 *European Law Journal* 271.

[41] M. Bevir, 'Governance', *Encyclopedia Britannica*, 22 December 2021, www.britannica.com/topic/governance; D. Levi-Faur, 'From "Big Government" to "Big Governance"?', in id. (ed.), *The Oxford Handbook of Governance* (Oxford University Press, 2012), p. 3; A. Pagden, 'The Genesis of "Governance" and Enlightenment Conceptions of the Cosmopolitan World Order' (1998) 50:155 *International Social Science Journal* 7.

epistemic uncertainty. With that comes the need for constant learning and experimentation as a key democratic virtue. Simon Sabel and Joshua Cohen in particular have developed a concept of 'directly-deliberative polyarchy', which they describe as a 'radical, participatory democracy with problem-solving capacities useful under current conditions and unavailable to representative systems'.[42] Apart from Dewey, intellectual support for such ideas is drawn from a wide variety of sources, including business modernization literature, for example, on the so-called Toyota model,[43] as well as the work of Roberto Unger. In a famous paper titled 'Destabilization Rights', Simon and Sabel build on arguments developed by Roberto Unger in his 1987 book *False Necessity*[44] to defend structural reform litigation.[45] Unger put forward a broader argument for democratic experimentation in an attempt to find a path beyond Marxism with its rigid understanding of history and emphasis on structural conditions, on the one hand, and social democracy with its acceptance of capitalism and its resulting inequalities, on the other.

More recent authors writing along similar lines, such as Roberto Gargarella, have moreover drawn on work by Jürgen Habermas on deliberative democracy.[46] Gargarella argues for the introduction of more participatory elements in certain political systems where elites block real democratic participation through representative processes and defends judicial intervention to that purpose, including in cases of structural reform litigation.[47]

In the context of structural reform litigation, the key point of this line of thought is that the legitimacy of structural intervention by judges depends less on the 'who and why'-question than the 'how'-question.

[42] J. Cohen and C. F. Sabel, 'Directly-Deliberative Polyarchy' (1997) 3:4 *European Law Journal* 313.

[43] W. H. Simon, 'Toyota Jurisprudence: Legal Theory and Rolling Rule Regimes', in G. de Búrca and J. Scott (eds.), *Law and New Governance in the EU and the US* (Bloomsbury Publishing, 2006), p. 37; Dorf and Sabel, 'Democratic Experimentalism', 267.

[44] R. M. Unger, *False Necessity: Anti-Necessitarian Social Theory in the Service of Radical Democracy* (Cambridge University Press, 2001 (1st ed. 1987)).

[45] C. F. Sabel and W. H. Simon, 'Destabilization Rights: How Public Law Litigation Succeeds' (2004) 117 *Harvard Law Review* 1016.

[46] R. Gargarella, *Latin American Constitutionalism, 1810–2010: The Engine Room of the Constitution* (Oxford University Press, 2013) and id., *The Law as a Conversation Among Equals* (Cambridge University Press, 2022), p. 41 (and elsewhere) with reference to J. Habermas, *Between Facts and Norms: Contributions to a Discourse Theory on Law and Democracy* (MIT Press, 1996).

[47] Gargarella, *Latin American Constitutionalism*, e.g. p. 190.

In other words, what matters is not so much under what conditions judges intervene in administrative or legislative processes, but *how* they do it. Thus, as long as judges act in an inclusive and participatory manner that is open to later correction – as opposed to issuing commands from the bench – their justificatory burden for acting in the first place is significantly reduced. While failure therefore plays a role in some theories that adopt an experimentalist approach, such as Simon and Sabel's concept of destabilization rights, this is often not where the emphasis lies.

But democratic experimentalism goes beyond defending a particular 'experimentalist' style of structural reform litigation. It also plays a role in conceptualizing (and ratifying) the interplay of different state and supranational actors as well as private actors in the context of policymaking in the European Union – in particular, the Commission's White Paper on Governance of 2001[48] and the so-called open Method of Coordination. These sources provided a framework for developing soft-law policies on particular issues and should thus be understood as part of a broader move towards more flexible understandings of competences in the European Union. Subsequently, the concept has been broadened to encompass the relationships between different courts, such as national constitutional courts and the CJEU. These are understood as a form of experimentalist governance, insofar as they involve a series of judgments where courts shape their jurisdiction in a mutually interdependent manner, leading to the creation of a polyarchic and pluralist structure where no one institution has the last word.[49] More recently, the concept of experimentalism has also been employed by Gráinne de Búrca in a human rights context as a way of describing how different local and global bodies, both public and private, are involved in the process of creating new human rights through political struggles as well as implementing such rights on the ground.[50]

Such ideas can help accommodate and justify arguments from failure. They shift the key challenge not towards defending intervention in the first place, but rather towards evaluating and designing responses in a

48 European Commission, European Governance, White Paper, COM 2001 [428].

49 M. Kumm, 'Constitutionalism and Experimentalist Governance' (2012) 6:3 *Regulation & Governance* 401.

50 G. de Búrca, *Reframing Human Rights in a Turbulent Era* (Oxford University Press, 2021); see also G. de Búrca, 'Human Rights Experimentalism' (2017) 111:2 *American Journal of International Law* 277.

way that is sufficiently open and participatory. And they suggest that if the response to failure consists in opening up avenues for participation and experimentation, perhaps we should understand this as an improvement of democracy, rather than as a problem.

2.3 Discussion

These different strands in the literature have in common that they provide some room to argue for expanding existing powers of state institutions in cases of failure, at least in certain circumstances. The more recent European and South African literatures on the separation of powers and constitutionalism stress the need for legal flexibility. They emphasize the importance of enabling different institutions to collaborate to achieve key constitutional goals – in a South African context in particular the eradication of poverty and the achievement of a more equal society. The democratic experimentalism literature adds a concern with procedures, suggesting not just the *ends* to which institutions exercise their powers matter, but also the *ways* in which they do so, stressing the importance of inclusivity and participation. Both strands of literature, however, also raise important questions that we need to address.

2.3.1 Separation of Powers and Transformative Constitutionalism

The literature on transformative constitutionalism and the new separation of powers, with its focus on effectiveness, comes with significant risks of enabling a slide towards authoritarian modes of governing. The more we focus on output rather than input as a standard of public legitimacy and legality, the more we enable governance unrestrained by legal and democratic safeguards.

This risk strikes me as particularly prevalent in some of the more radical South African critiques that treat constitutionalism only as a value insofar as it furthers certain substantive aims, that is the eradication of poverty and the construction of a more equal society. Somewhat ironically, this kind of outcome-focused style of argument strongly recalls similar purposive arguments in an EU context, though deployed there to bring about the common market, rather than equality. This speaks not only to the ideological malleability of such arguments but their authoritarian underpinnings. We can see glimpses of that already in an EU context,[51] but for a different picture of where such an approach can lead, we might also consider India's experience with Indira Gandhi's emergency regime from 1975 to 1977, in which arguments from the failure to bring about a more equal society played a central role.[52] Indira Gandhi's political campaign was based precisely on the eradication of poverty in India. She used this as an argument to resist the threat of the Indian judiciary and in particular the Supreme Court in blocking her political agenda.[53] In particular, she blamed India's Anglo-Saxon legal system for being insufficiently attuned to the needs of the 'poor and weak', which in turn fed into her broader attack on the judiciary as a guardian of this outdated concept of law – foreshadowing contemporary critiques of constitutionalism as insufficiently decolonialized.[54] Framing this as a 'conspiracy' due to her introduction of 'certain progressive measures of benefit to the common man and woman in India', as a result of which '[d]uly elected governments have not been allowed to function', she invoked the constitutional emergency clause to suspend a range of rights as well as democracy. Before it ended, 11 million Indians were sterilised (as part of the plan to eradicate poverty) and 110 000 people jailed.[55] India's story is not, of course, an outlier; authoritarian regimes have served different political guises, some furthering not only left-wing but also right political agendas.

That said, transformative constitutionalism as a concept is committed to legal and constitutional means of change. (And this is why those who adopt a more radical approach, are increasingly critical of transformative constitutionalism, which they view as an insufficiently decolonialized project.[56]) African comparative scholarship on the separation of powers,

[51] M. A. Wilkinson, *Authoritarian Liberalism and the Transformation of Modern Europe* (Oxford University Press, 2021).

[52] On this, and the economic and social drivers of her emergency regime, see C. Jaffrelot and P. Anil, 'A Constitutional Dictatorship', in id. (eds.), *India's First Dictatorship* (Oxford University Press, 2021), pp. 23 ff.

[53] Ibid. Her campaign slogan was 'Garibi Hatao', that is eradicate poverty.

[54] Sibanda, 'When Do You Call Time on Compromise?'; Madlingozi, 'Social Justice in a Time of Neo-Apartheid Constitutionalism'; Modiri, 'Conquest and Constitutionalism'.

[55] Jaffrelot and Anil, *India's First Dictatorship*, p. 17.

[56] Sibanda, 'When Do You Call Time on Compromise?'; Madlingozi, 'Social Justice in a Time of Neo-Apartheid Constitutionalism'; Modiri, 'Conquest and Constitutionalism'. For an engagement with this literature, see T. Roux, 'Grand Narratives of Transition and the Quest for Democratic Constitutionalism in India and South Africa' (2024) 57 *Verfassung in Recht und Übersee/World Comparative Law* 5.

in contrast, often still takes a more traditional liberal approach.[57] And even where constitutional realization approaches are popular, as in South Africa, they will not necessarily be dominant in judicial practice. The South African Constitutional Court has accepted the need for collaboration among the different branches, in particular with an eye to 'fulfilling practical constitutional promises to the country's most vulnerable'.[58] At the same time, it has also often been more careful and cautious than many of its academic commentators would like it to be when it comes to involving the court in the details of policy-making.[59]

In Europe too, the call for flexible responses and collaboration comes with limitations. Thus, Nick Barber emphasizes the need to reform institutions rather than take over their powers in the long run.[60] Aileen Kavanagh puts forward a more explicit argument about how courts should approach situations when other branches are unwilling to do their job. She argues that political deadlock or legislative inertia does not allow for judicial intervention in all cases, both because judges cannot actually fix all problems and because their doing so would not be legitimate.[61] Ultimately, for Kavanagh, whether judicial intervention in cases of legislative inaction is legitimate depends on a range of factors, including the

> urgency of resolving the particular dispute before them, the severity of the alleged interference with rights, and concerns about the appropriate division of labour in the constitutional scheme. Timing is also important. If the legislature is the best-qualified and most legitimate branch of government to tackle a particular issue, then it should be given time and opportunity to do so.[62]

This is fairly close to the model I propose below, but some further qualifications are necessary. Courts cannot always wait for legislatures

57 See, e.g., the contributions in C. M. Fombad (ed.), *The Separation of Powers in African Constitutionalism* (Oxford University Press, 2016).

58 *Mwelase and Others v. Director-General for the Department of Rural Development and Land Reform and Another*, CCT 232/18 [2019] ZACC 30 (20 August 2019) (South African Constitutional Court), at 46.

59 For a discussion of that literature and defence of the Court, see J. Fowkes, *Building the Constitution: The Practice of Constitutional Interpretation in Post-Apartheid South Africa* (Cambridge University Press, 2016); T. Roux, *The Politics of Principle: The First South African Constitutional Court, 1995–2005* (Cambridge University Press, 2013). See also Chapter 4.

60 Barber, *Principles*, p. 79.

61 Kavanagh, *Collaborative Constitution*, p. 324.

62 Ibid., p. 325.

to act, and there are other factors we need to take into account. It also matters whether courts expand their powers to protect and fulfil rights and alleviate poverty or whether administrators do so in the interest of, for example, realizing the common market in the European Union, even though both discourses open up risks of a slide towards authoritarianism. Most importantly, however, this literature suggests the need for clearer legal categories that cash out limits to the role of effectiveness arguments in public law – and thus the need for the project taken up in this book.

2.3.2 Democratic Experimentalism

The democratic experimentalism literature suggests a way of mediating some of these issues. One way to respond to the inherent authoritarian drift of arguments from failure is by insisting on inclusiveness and participation. It is therefore important to think about *how* institutions should intervene, in particular in the context of structural reform litigation, which I discuss in Chapter 5. Yet, while the focus on inclusive procedures and experimentation is important, they are not a solution to all problems. Indeed, they also create some problems of their own.

Start with experimentation. Roberto Unger himself argued that in order to enable experimentation, citizens must be able to rely on the existence of a certain safety net, protected in the form of 'immunity rights'.[63] Immunity rights 'protect the individual against oppression by concentrations of public or private power, against exclusion from the important collective decisions that influence his life, and against the extremes of economic and cultural deprivation', giving him 'the justified confidence of not being fundamentally endangered by the expanded conflicts of an empowered democracy'. Healthcare, housing and education[64] – all major fields of public law litigation in the United States as well as in the Global South – therefore all fall within the scope of immunity rights, whose realization Unger thinks must be guaranteed as a matter of course. Immunity rights are not predicated upon their effect on others and thus must not be balanced against other interests or rights. They are absolute, circumscribed in bright and clear lines. In all of these fields, including freedom from governmental and private(!) oppression[65], Unger therefore discouraged experimentation, because he thought that

63 Unger, *False Necessity*, pp. 524 ff.
64 Ibid., p. 528.
65 Ibid.

even within the empowered democracy citizens must be safe in the sphere circumscribed by immunity rights. In fairness to Simon and Sabel, Unger himself is not clear what precisely would be covered by immunity. He refers to judicial intervention in schools or electoral organization as an example of institutional destabilization, as Simon and Sabel rightly point out.[66] Nevertheless, experimentalism should clearly not be without limits and these limits thus need to be spelt out.

Second, developing participatory practices and encouraging negotiation and collaboration may be misplaced in some cases. For example, as Katie Young and Sandy Liebenberg have emphasized in the context of socio-economic rights litigation, collaboration and engagement are all very well if all parties of the conversation hold roughly equal power. But they are likely to generate unfair outcomes where significant imbalances of power, often affected by wealth, exist.[67] This argument would seem to apply beyond the realm of structural reform litigation in other contexts involving collaborative structures of governing.

Most importantly though, we should not mistake 'stakeholder democracy' for democracy. This applies especially where final decision-making powers do not lie with state institutions, such as courts. Nor do public hearings provide a substitute for parliamentary debate and decision-making. Even where courts or the EU Commission bring in new voices, forcing governmental officials and/or legislators to sit down with civil society representatives to set out a path for structural reform together, the group selected will necessarily be just that: selected and selective. It will not represent a majority of citizens, not in either a formal or an informal sense. In other words, participation does not mean democratic accountability, whatever other values, such as transparency, reason-giving and judicial scrutiny, it may serve. Democracy also includes the voters' ability to throw the rascals out. Where policymaking is conducted in complex multilevel networks, including private and public actors, accountability can be difficult to achieve. No one can be voted out of office in the next elections. And whatever else democracy entails, this idea is at the heart of the prevailing conception of democracy in nearly all democratic states as well as part of Dixon and Landau's concept of a

66 Sabel and Simon, 'Destabilization Rights', 1016, Fn. 123.

67 S. Liebenberg and K. G. Young, 'Adjudicating Social Rights: Can Democratic Experimentalism Help?', in H. Alviar García, K. Klare and L. A. Williams (eds.), *Socio-Economic Rights in Theory and Practice: Critical Inquiries* (Routledge, 2015), p. 237.

democratic minimum core, building on a wide range of democratic scholarship and practice.[68]

Of course, representative democracy may itself not be all that we make it out to be. With its emphasis on the value of participation in local units and experimentation, democratic experimentalism connects to moves in the more recent radical democracy literature, seeking to go beyond representative democracy.[69] For example, Helen Landemore has recently put forward proposals for greater openness in democracy, suggesting the creation of mini-publics consisting of individual citizens randomly selected by lottery to be involved in deliberating policy and in law-making over a limited time period.[70] How much room there is for such arguments will depend on the broader constitutional framework in place; some constitutional systems like Germany are based on a firmly representative concept, while others are more open in this respect. Yet, regardless of these details, democratic accountability will remain a key concern as elections remain the central mechanism for securing it.[71] If democratic experimentalists shift power to fora and procedures that are lacking in this regard, this requires justification, even if those fora may be inclusive or participatory. As it stands, such justifications often involve claims of failure, as we have seen, whether this is a specific institutional failure or a wholesale democratic failure.

This is not to say that democratic experimentalism is not a useful descriptive and normative frame. It is, and indeed there is much to like about it. By focusing on enabling political participation of citizens in the policy-making that affects them, and drawing attention to institutional dysfunctionalities that target minorities, democratic experimentalism is not just another neoliberal governance theory. However, unless its proponents spell out more clearly its relationship with the rule of law and democracy, it risks becoming just that. Experimentation must take place within certain legal parameters if it is to respect the equal dignity and

68 R. Dixon and D. Landau, *Abusive Constitutional Borrowing: Legal Globalization and the Subversion of Liberal Democracy* (Oxford University Press, 2021), chapter 3.

69 On the contested nature of democracy and different theoretical strands see F. Cunningham, *Theories of Democracy* (Routledge, 2002), pp. 3 ff.

70 H. Landemore, *Open Democracy* (University of Princeton Press, 2020), pp. 13 ff.

71 See, e.g., Rosalind Dixon and David Landau's outline of a democratic minimum core as well as Tom Ginsburg's and Aziz Huq's work, encompassing (1) free and fair multiparty elections, (2) political rights and freedoms and (3) core elements of the rule of law; T. Ginsburg and A. Z. Huq, *How to Save a Constitutional Democracy* (The University of Chicago Press, 2018), pp. 10 ff.

voice of participants. It must ensure the accountability of the central actors involved. Democratic experimentalism is also not the only problematic concept in this regard, of course. This applies more broadly to other theories that sideline central constitutional principles in favour of an emphasis on networks[72] and collaboration.

2.4 Working Out a Framework

In light of the above, the best response to the risks and challenges that come with arguments from failure is to take them seriously as a legal argument and be as clear as possible as to what they are and what they are not and under what conditions they might be legal.

This means, first and foremost, that we need to distinguish arguments from failure from other, more standard arguments about the need for purposive interpretation and the effective realization of rights and other constitutional values or goals, as I have argued in chapter 1. It is therefore crucial to remember that arguments from failure – unlike such broader arguments about updating constitutional norms and effective realization – are geared towards justifying a temporary exception from existing competences as they are commonly understood, rather than providing arguments for updating certain competences and for bringing about permanent changes. However, in practice, we often combine and blur them with other arguments into a broader functionalist approach to legal interpretation. This is precisely what we need to avoid. Such an approach feeds into an effectiveness paradigm of public law where each institution is accorded the power to do whatever it can to maximize output. Once this happens, we are not far from Somek's dystopian depiction of 'governance by situations'[73] where legality in its traditional sense has ultimately disappeared.

We also need to say more about its prerequisites: Under what conditions might one institution step in for another? What institutions are we talking about? What constitutes failure, and how can we distinguish it from political disagreement? And how can we make sure that allowing for such arguments does not pave the way for a new paradigm of public law, rooted in effectiveness and further removed from any democratic legitimation?

In what follows, I endeavour to answer these questions. Doing so means engaging with the central normative stakes and the literatures

[72] E.g., E. L. Rubin, *Beyond Camelot* (Princeton University Press, 2007).
[73] Somek, *The Cosmopolitan Constitution*, p. 222.

discussed above, which come with certain implications for the legality and legitimacy of arguments from failure. Together, these implications add up to a framework, albeit one that consists of a set of questions to ask whenever we encounter such arguments, rather than a set of ready-made answers. I will put some more flesh on this skeletal framework in the following chapters, where I address a range of typical settings and situations for arguments from failure.

2.4.1 Constitutional Authority in Context

The first requirement for arguments from failure is that we must be operating within a political and legal context where expectations of mutual collaboration and responsiveness prevail. Arguments from failure are not just devices for self-help,[74] but are rooted within a broader legal framework that envisages different institutions to work together.

Within domestic constitutional systems, this is usually the case. Most constitutional democracies typically subscribe to some version of the separation of powers. It is also clearly the context in which Kavanagh's theory is meant to apply.[75] That said, some legal systems are more open to this kind of flexible approach than others. It is not accidental that Kavanagh herself writes from a background in the United Kingdom, a stable democracy based on the principle of parliamentary supremacy, without a strict understanding of the separation of powers. Some other contemporary constitutions already come with a thick normative agenda obliging the state to pursue certain goals, such as a transformative constitution. That, too, can readily ground a constitutional imperative to collaborate to achieve the shared goal. Yet, even absent such more obviously legally friendly environments, most constitutional democracies should be open to arguments from failure in principle, albeit some in much more limited ways than others. This is because even in systems where more emphasis is placed on constraining state power and preserving individual liberty understood in a traditional way, we will find expectations of cooperation and of effective government. This is not to say, however, that arguments from failure can be defended in all circumstances.

Things become more difficult in the realm of international law, where such expectations will not always hold. There is typically no traditional

[74] D. E. Pozen, 'Self-Help and the Separation of Powers' (2014) 124:1 *The Yale Law Journal* 2.

[75] Kavanagh, *Collaborative Constitution*.

separation of powers in this context, even within specific treaty regimes, and this begs the question how to assess arguments from failure in that context – a question I address in Chapter 7.

2.4.2 *Legalizing Failure*

To evaluate arguments from failure, it also matters how existing competences are formulated in the legal text – and in particular whether they are clearly framed in a broad and flexible manner or in a narrower manner and whether they set out a comprehensive framework or not. It also matters what other legal mechanisms exist to address failure. Finally, we need a clearer sense as to what constitutes failure – a question which I have bracketed so far. While it would be impossible to put forward a definition of failure to fit all circumstances where arguments from failure come into play, as I argued in the introduction, we can still give some more content to the idea to get a better grip on it.

2.4.2.1 A Violation of Law

First, our failure should normally be anchored in some breach of law. In other words: While the failure or dysfunction itself may involve issues that are hard to capture in legal terms, such as the capture of an institution by external interests or problems of institutional design, we should understand *in legal terms* either the inaction or the problem that needs resolving. We should understand them, in other words, as a violation of law. While this is usually a relatively straightforward issue, it can be tricky to determine in individual cases if legal rules have been violated. That said, this kind of question is of course the bread and butter of courts.

2.4.2.2 Inability and Resistance

Thinking about the problem that needs fixing in terms of a violation of law makes clear that the failure in question must be understood in terms of the inability and/or unwillingness of the responsible institution to remedy that violation. The distinction between problems of capacity/inability and unwillingness/resistance has been emphasized in the literature on structural reform litigation, with some authors calling for more robust intervention in the latter case.[76] However, we should not exaggerate that difference. In reality, if we encounter an argument from failure,

[76] E.g., K. Roach and G. Budlender, 'Mandatory Relief and Supervisory Jurisdiction: When Is It Appropriate, Just and Equitable?' (2005) 122:2 *South African Law Journal* 325.

there is always at least a degree of unwillingness/resistance. This is because complete governmental inability would imply that no intervention can fix the problem, including interventions by other institutions that try to step in. What appear as cases of inability are therefore usually cases that will require multi-institutional coordination or oversight and/or involve higher costs. Those needs are not easy to meet. They therefore typically involve intervention at higher levels of government that has not already been forthcoming, because of negligence and/or resistance.

2.4.2.3 No Comprehensive Framework

The more there is already a set of checks and mechanisms of control provided for within existing institutional arrangements, the less room there is to invoke failure as a basis for acting outside or in addition to those arrangements. In other words, there exists typically a gap in the law when it comes to remedying failure, that is existing rules do not provide means to address the situation. We can borrow here from earlier writings on state necessity prerogatives, which similarly presuppose that there are gaps in the law in the sense that there are no explicit legal rules to address cases of emergency.[77] Thus, for example, if state practices lead to a massive and enduring violation of human rights/constitutional rights, we must ask if and to what degree there already exist mechanisms and institutions to tackle the problem.

If we seek to determine whether the existing constitutional rules are comprehensive, it also matters if a constitution is old and hard to change, as is the case for the US Constitution and many international treaties, or if it is more recent and perhaps easier to change. Where formal constitutional change is in practice almost impossible, arguments for a purposive interpretation as well as arguments from failure are more likely to be convincing.

And in consideration of alternatives, the legitimacy and capacity of the institutions involved also matter. Some institutions may be better suited to deal with the problem, and some may enjoy a greater degree of legitimacy. For example, when courts prescribe detailed policies from the bench, akin to a legislator, this is likely to be more problematic than when they interfere with the administration. Democracy will be at stake in the former case, but much less so in the latter. This in turn has implications for assessing which institutions may put forward arguments from failure more broadly.

[77] A-B. Kaiser, *Ausnahmeverfassungsrecht* (Mohr Siebeck, 2020), explicitly p. 342.

2.4.2.4 Judicial Review

Given the associated risks of abuse, any exercise of power on the basis of arguments from failure should moreover be considered justiciable. As with many legal issues, analyzing arguments from failure will involve a more stringent judicial control in some respects – for example when it comes to identifying a violation of rules giving rise to the central problem – and a more restrained approach to other aspects. But this poses no uniquely difficult challenge. Many of the considerations relevant to failure involve fairly standard legal questions that judges can realistically be expected to grapple with, some vagueness notwithstanding. Of course, where courts themselves intervene, this can be difficult. But even here, unless the highest courts are themselves involved, appeal procedures provide some measure of control.

2.4.2.5 Further Considerations

It bears emphasizing that not all problems disappear in those cases where there is a legal basis for institutions to step in when others are failing. The standard example for such explicit failure provisions is clauses allowing for federal coercion, as briefly discussed in Chapter 1. Though this book is primarily concerned with the expansion of powers on the basis of failure *without* a specific basis in law, the frequently vague framing of such provisions leaves lawyers to fill in the details and in doing so to work to minimize the risks of abuses. In engaging with such written powers, the first task of any lawyer will of course be to grapple with the legal text itself. However, the considerations discussed in this book should be considered relevant in such cases, too. While there can of course be no question with regard to the existence of a gap in the law, the requirement of some legal anchor in the form of a violation of law together with an assessment of functionality, necessity and costs, as discussed in Chapter 2, should be understood to play a role here too.

2.4.3 Managing Risks

However, in light of our discussion above and the literature survey, there will be some cases where arguments from failure should not be considered permissible, in light of the grave risks to democracy they would entail.

2.4.3.1 Military and Presidential Rule

To begin with, some institutions in constitutional democracies should never be allowed to step in, even where others are failing, because their intervention would be at odds with core principles of constitutional democracy. The most important example of this is the military. Military takeovers or coups often involve claims of taking over responsibility for the public welfare, sometimes in response to real problems as in Gabon,[78] Niger[79] or, indeed, Thailand.[80] This is because military coups do not simply stretch existing competences, but rather replace democracy with an authoritarian system wholesale, albeit for a temporary period (or so their defenders typically claim). This is distinct even from very activist courts seeking to address specific problems in light of persistent political failures to do so.

A more difficult question is whether executive interventions on the basis of failure should similarly be considered incompatible with constitutionalism. Consider intervention by presidents through emergency decrees or other executive decrees as an example. Thus, in the US arguments about congressional dysfunction and gridlock have long played an important role in justifying an expansive use of presidential powers including issuing executive orders, though arguably we are dealing with an expansive use of existing powers here rather than an assumption of new ones, and thus are outside the scope of arguments from failure.[81] Generally, the answer will have to be more nuanced here. In some systems, such as Germany, where presidents only hold a ceremonial role – in response to the Weimar practice of governing through emergency decrees – we should similarly reject intervention in such cases. The Basic Law was explicitly designed not to repeat the lessons of Weimar, and there is accordingly no gap in the system to be filled. In presidential systems without a comparable history, however, the situation is less clear. Here, too, though, the risks for abuse are considerable. It matters therefore if we are dealing with one specific targeted intervention in an individual case or rather a shift to a broader, albeit temporary, presidential rule by decree. The latter case involves another

[78] N. Okechukwu, 'The Fragility of the African Governance Agenda: A Crisis of Legitimacy', *European Centre for Development Policy Management*, 30 October 2023, www.ecdpm.org/work/fragility-african-governance-agenda-crisis-legitimacy.

[79] Ibid.

[80] A. Croissant, 'Thailand: The Vicious Cycle of Civilian Government and Military Rule', in id. (eds), *Comparative Politics of Southeast Asia* (Springer, 2nd ed., 2022), pp. 315 ff.

[81] R. Aldana, 'Congressional Dysfunction and Executive Lawmaking during the Obama Administration' (2016) 91 *Chicago-Kent Law Review* 3 and the further articles in the same issue dealing with specific policy areas.

wholesale change of constitutional regime and thus falls outside of the scope of failure arguments – and this takes me to the next point.

2.4.3.2 Democratic Failure

Can arguments from failure justify interventions in response to democratic failure as such, rather than some more narrow instance of failure? This question partly goes back to the democratic experimentalism literature. If politics in a particular country are highly elitist, if the parliament is de facto unable to reach decisions on most issues because of a high degree of political fragmentation and/or polarization, if the electoral process is skewed by money and/or tailored to preserve the power of those inside the system, we may ask if and to what degree democratic procedures and institutions still deserve respect. Thus, David Landau has argued that where the democratic system in place is deeply dysfunctional, courts may step in to address important social questions.[82] Similarly, Roberto Gargarella has emphasized the dysfunctionalities plaguing a range of Latin American democracies and called not just for reforms in the 'engine room', that is in the political organization, but on that basis also defended judicial intervention, particularly where it has come in participatory forms.[83]

I broadly agree with these approaches. However, with regard to arguments from failure, I would insist on proceeding on a case-by-case basis. In other words, democratic failure as such should not be taken as a justification for institutional expansion and should only be considered relevant insofar as it affects specific problems – for example because it means that certain violations of law will likely persist. The reasons for my more cautious approach lie once again in the risks that come with such general assessments of democracy.[84] What constitutes an improvement of one meaning of democracy may well constitute an infringement according to others.[85] Should, for example, the fact that certain minorities or indeed women are not statistically adequately represented in parliaments and face structural hurdles in the political arena lead us to consider a democracy insufficiently open and thus ultimately

[82] Landau, 'Political Institutions'.

[83] Gargarella, *Latin American Constitutionalism.*

[84] E.g., see M. Hailbronner, 'Combatting Malfunction or Optimizing Democracy? Lessons from Germany for a Comparative Political Process Theory, (2021) 19:2 *International Journal of Constitutional Law* 495.

[85] For an early version of the argument see M. Hailbronner, 'Political process review: Beyond distrust' (2020) 18:4 *International Journal of Constitutional Law* 1458.

insufficiently democratic? Should we therefore adopt laws compelling parties to draft electoral lists that are equally representative, or are such rules in turn incompatible with democracy and the freedom of voters and political parties? Or consider the influence of money in politics. Do such influences at some point turn the system into a plutocracy no longer deserving of democratic respect, and if so, what point is that? And so on.

What is 'democratic' and what isn't is thus not an easy question to answer, even within a specific domestic constitutional system. And the risks of allowing arguments from democratic failure are enormous.[86] This is not to say that there is no way to identify cases of democratic malfunction; indeed, sometimes it may be obvious that the democratic system is not working well. But in many others, it will not be.[87] Permitting this kind of general assessment invites not just over-generalizations and clichés, but it also opens the door to populists seeking to portray the political system as hijacked by elites disconnected from the real people. Thus, in Germany today, far-right supporters sometimes argue that there is no real democracy in the country, comparing the contemporary German governments to the former GDR.[88]

We might ask if those risks can be contained if we were to restrict this kind of argument to institutions outside of the fray of party politics, such as courts. But courts and judges are hardly apolitical. Judges, too, may engage in judicial populism, portraying themselves as the 'true friends' of the people in contrast to corrupt political elites.[89] Generalized distrust is strongly linked to personal ideological preferences, and this makes it a suspicious ground for judges to expand their power. That said, there are some situations where dysfunctionality is not a matter of contest but rather common knowledge, and international courts or organizations may have assessed the situation in similar terms. It is largely this kind of situation that both Landau and Gargarella have in mind and where accordingly we can see the importance of such a broader assessment.

[86] Consider again Indira Gandhi's twisting of the meaning of democracy in justifying her emergency regime, as detailed in Jaffrelot and Anil, *India's First Dictatorship*.

[87] E.g., see Hailbronner, 'Combatting Malfunction', 495.

[88] E.g. J. Merkel et al., 'Wie die AfD mit deutscher Geschichte Politik macht', *MDR*, 12 August 2024, https://tinyurl.com/y2evmv8u.

[89] D. Werneck Arguelhes, 'Judges Speaking for the People: Judicial Populism beyond Judicial Decisions', *Verfassungsblog*, 4 May 2017, https://tinyurl.com/32uud729; see also A. Bhuwania, *Courting the People: Public Interest Litigation in Post-Emergency India* (Cambridge University Press, 2017).

Nevertheless, arguments from failure should still focus on more specific cases of inaction or enduring violations of law by state institutions rather than be deployed in response to democratic failure as such, albeit the existence of the latter may have consequences for the former in concrete cases. This follows not least from their purpose: to allow only for *temporary* deviations from standard rules.

2.4.3.3 Disagreements, Legislative Failure and the No-More-Democratic-Means-Test

In many cases, different institutions and actors will disagree – both about what the law is and about what should be done to comply with it. And this is likely to give rise to accusations of failure. Where some will see a fraudulent election, others will suspect a sore loser. Where some see a violation of social rights, others will point out that governmental capacity and funds are finite. Can we meaningfully distinguish such disagreements from failure? The correct answer to these questions will depend on the case and institutions involved.

If we take representative democracy seriously when it comes to arguments from failure, we will be particularly worried about accusations of legislative failure offered to justify intervention by other, less democratic institutions, such as courts or governmental or administrative officials. It is easy to see how accusations of failure in this context may simply be opposition rhetoric, deployed by actors seeking to expand their own powers. This risk will be particularly high in presidential systems when the government is divided into different institutions that may be held by opposing political parties as is often the case in the United States. But disagreements about what constitutes adequate performance may arise in other contexts as well. Though this was not the actual legal justification offered, when the UK government under Johnson prorogued parliament, some commentators defended this as a necessary response to parliament's refusal to fall in line with the government's Brexit proposals and thus in terms of a kind of parliamentary failure.[90] As it was, the UK Supreme Court did not accept the government's approach – and for good

[90] V. Bogdanor, 'Parliament had failed on Brexit long before this prorogation', *The Guardian*, 29 August 2019, www.theguardian.com/commentisfree/2019/aug/29/parliament-brexit-prorogue-mps-alternative-no-deal; for an academic take and defence of the House of Commons M. Russell, 'Brexit and Parliament: The Anatomy of a Perfect Storm' (2021) 74:2 *Parliamentary Affairs* 443.

reasons.[91] Accusations of failure may play a role in other contexts as well. There are plenty of instances, for example, where governments have attempted to put pressure on courts in legally doubtful ways, often in response to previous jurisprudence, which governments consider to be judicial overreach.

The first and most obvious point to make in response is to recall that arguments from failure presuppose a violation of law. Constitutional norms sometimes stipulate legislative or parliamentary obligations, as do other statutes or indeed internal parliamentary rules. In other words, by not acting or acting inappropriately, parliament can sometimes be understood to violate its legal obligations. However, if parliamentary action or omission is considered to violate not constitutional but statutory law, this should generally be considered insufficient as a basis for intervention, given that parliament is violating rules authored by itself, which it may change. Thus, the mere refusal to deal with an urgent political problem – for example Brexit – without a constitutional basis for compelling such action should not be considered sufficient to warrant intervention by others unless such an omission violates norms of a higher status.

Insofar as there is a serious disagreement, it will thus have to be a disagreement either about the meaning of constitutional norms or about what to do with respect to a violation of constitutional norms, that is about how to remedy it. In this situation, a lot depends on which institution is seeking to step in. For example, when a court steps in to deal with rights violations according to its view, but not according to the government's view, scope for governmental disagreement is usually limited, as I argue in Chapter 5. Courts are meant to have the last word on how to interpret legal rules, at least in most cases in most systems.[92] By contrast, if the executive or a president seeks to intervene on the basis of her understanding of rights, which is different from parliament's, and/or we are dealing with a disagreement about how to respond, the

[91] *R (on the application of Miller and another) (Respondents) v. Secretary of State for Exiting the European Union (Appellant)*, 24 Jan 2017, [2017] UKSC 5; *R (on the application of Miller) (Appellant) v. The Prime Minister (Respondent)*, 24 September 2019, [2019] UKSC 41.

[92] Exceptions are countries where courts either have no such final say or no power to declare laws invalid or where parliaments retain a right to pass countervailing legislation, such as Australia and New Zealand, the UK or Canada. See, e.g., S. Gardbaum, *The New Commonwealth Model of Constitutionalism: Theory and Practice* (Cambridge University Press, 2013).

situation is more difficult. Here, too, the principle of democracy suggests that, generally speaking, parliaments as representative institutions are better suited than the executive branch to develop and act on their own understanding of the constitution and to decide what needs to be done to respect, protect and fulfil them. In most countries, therefore, interventions by executive officers seeking to take over parliamentary tasks should as a default be considered illegal, with only some narrowly tailored exceptions to that rule, for example where the political party system and accordingly, the parliament have been clearly dysfunctional for a long time, as in Landau's Colombian example.[93]

And this leads us to a broader point I want to make: namely the need for a no-more-democratic-means-test for arguments from failure. In other words, institutions may only expand their powers to deal with a problem where there are no other more democratic means that would address the problem with comparable efficiency. Of course, such an analysis may be difficult to conduct, and in many cases, the fact that massive rights violations have persisted over a long time will have to suffice as an indication that no other more democratic means are likely available. In other cases, however, there may be significant political mobilization around the issue in question; there may be an ongoing parliamentary debate, and so on. If so, we should leave room for disagreement to unfold within the ordinary democratic channels. In such cases, stepping in will typically not be the appropriate response. In contrast, where parliaments step in to deal with issues traditionally reserved for other branches, we should be more open towards such interventions.

2.5 Conclusion

This chapter has shown how arguments from failure play a role in a range of existing debates on constitutional theory. In particular, recent scholarship on the separation of powers with its emphasis on effectiveness and the need for collaboration and the literature on democratic experimentalism open up space for such arguments. However, such approaches often come with high risks of opening the doors too widely to a general logic of efficiency, with potentially disastrous consequences for democracy and the rule of law.

[93] Landau, 'Political Institutions'.

The first and most important conclusion to draw from this, then, is that arguments from failure need to be as clearly delineated as possible if they are to be considered legal. It also means that arguments from failure presuppose a certain legal context where expectations of institutional collaboration are appropriate. Moreover, intervention can only ever be legitimate if the existing legal framework cannot be understood as comprehensive. Failure should be understood to stem from an inability or unwillingness to remedy rights violations and accordingly be considered justiciable. In addition, arguments from failure can only justify interventions in concrete cases or instances, rather than justifying a wholesale shift of power within the political system at large. And finally, the democratic stakes matter, and any intervention requires that there are no other more democratic ways to end the violation of law: It must pass the no-more-democratic-means-test.

3

Proportionality

3.1 Introduction

Today, it is no longer contested that the United Nations has a mandate to deal with domestic human rights violations. There are international treaties on human rights, in particular the two International Covenants, as well as an institutional infrastructure to help enforce the rights contained therein, albeit imperfectly. But in the 1950s, this was not true. Fears of the potential of human rights to undermine states' sovereignty played an important role in discussions about human rights protection in the United Nations, leading initially to the adoption of only the non-binding Universal Declaration.[1] Human rights were mentioned in the UN Charter, of course, such as in the Preamble. Art. 62 of the Charter charged the Economic and Social Council (ECOSOC) with the responsibility to 'make recommendations for the purpose of promoting respect for, and observance of, human rights and fundamental freedoms for all'. Art. 68 explicitly provided that this task included setting up a human rights commission. Yet, the powers of this Commission beyond the drafting of the Universal Declaration were unclear. It did not initially deal with reports of concrete rights violations, even though it almost immediately received hundreds of individual communications from individuals complaining of rights abuses.[2] Instead, the Commission followed a policy Howard Tolley describes as 'self-denial', deciding that it lacked authority to take action regarding concrete complaints about human rights violations.[3] In the mid-1960s, however, this changed – and it

[1] For a comprehensive historical account of the drafting history, see J. Morsink, *The Universal Declaration of Human Rights: Origins, Drafting, and Intent, Pennsylvania Studies in Human Rights* (University of Pennsylvania Press, 1999), pp. 15 ff.

[2] H. Jr. Tolley, *The U.N. Commission on Human Rights* (Westview Press, 1987) and id., 'The Concealed Crack in the Citadel: The United Nations Commission on Human Rights Response to Confidential Communications' (1984) 6:4 *Human Rights Quarterly* 420.

[3] Tolley, 'The Concealed Crack', 420 at 422.

changed due to the recognition that some kinds of human rights abuses could simply not be ignored by the United Nations. Justifying this expansion of its mandate, the Commission and its Sub-Commission sought (albeit with moderate success) to distinguish 'ordinary' rights violations from other, more systemic ones, and in doing so essentially developed an argument from failure.

The empowerment of the UN Commission of Human Rights and its Sub-Commission is interesting here because it involves an attempt to cash out more explicitly the kind of failure that would lead to an expansion of the United Nations' mandate on human rights. While this attempt is set in a specific context and deals with international rather than domestic constitutional law, we will see that the criteria developed here strongly resemble what we encounter in the context of structural reform litigation – and they can still provide guidance for dealing with arguments from failure today. The story of the UN Human Rights Committee also shows how attempts to categorize failure in legal terms will typically give rise to contestation. Such contestation takes place within broader legal and constitutional structures, shaped by the interests of those in power. But even while this is true, our example also shows that this may nevertheless serve as a tool for empowerment in some cases.

The expansion of the Human Rights Commission's mandate represented an important success for many newly independent Southern states' efforts at the United Nations. These states began to use human rights as part of their broader struggle against colonialism and racial oppression. In the 1960s, Apartheid South Africa became a subject of nearly constant human rights criticism in UN institutions.[4] It was in this broader context of de-colonisation that ECOSOC started to push for the Human Rights Commission 'to consider the question of the violation of human rights and fundamental freedoms, including policies of racial discrimination and segregation and of apartheid, in all countries, with particular reference to colonial and other dependent countries and territories'.[5] The Sub-Commission, consisting of a panel of experts, first considered setting aside the principle of non-intervention

[4] Tolley, 'The Concealed Crack', 420 at 426 ff. For a comprehensive account of the role of former colonial states in the human rights movement, see S. L. B. Jensen, *The Making of International Human Rights: The 1960s, Decolonization, and the Reconstruction of Global Values* (Cambridge University Press, 2016).

[5] E.S.C. Res. 1102, 40 U.N. ESCOR Supp. (No. 1) at 6, U.N. Doc. E/4179 (19), quoted according to Tolley, 'The Concealed Crack', 420 at 426.

in domestic affairs in cases where, as a draft by the US representative suggested, 'a consistent pattern' of rights violations existed. This language subsequently made its way to the Human Rights Commission, which adopted Resolution 8 (XXIII). The Resolution asked ECOSOC to expand its mandate to study and investigate concrete rights violations in situations where a consistent pattern of human rights violations appeared and suggested that the Sub-Commission bring such cases to its attention, including 'policies of racial discrimination, segregation and apartheid'.[6]

Unsurprisingly, the language was deliberately chosen so as not to raise concerns among the representatives of powerful states. Thus, during the debates, Mr Waldron-Ramsey, a Tanzanian delegate, reassured US and UK colleagues: 'Obviously the Commission had no need to concern itself with any regrettable violation of human rights in the United Kingdom itself, or in the United States, since those were attributable to individuals and did not stem from the official policy of government in power.'[7] Waldron-Ramsey was of course very much aware that the proposed course of action might well have implications for these powers, as his references to the US civil rights movement and the continuing legacy of British imperialism demonstrated. Indeed, while he explicitly recognized the US federal government's efforts to address racial discrimination at home, Britain came in for critique for its colonial legacy as well as its ongoing protection of African states that practised apartheid. In legal terms, the challenge was to balance sovereignty and human rights. The United Nations was after all not a 'world government', as the British delegate Sir Samuel Hoare pointed out.

The aim then was to identify cases such as Apartheid South Africa and distinguish them from others arising in powerful Western states. The Commission's request to ECOSOC was successful. ECOSOC followed up with Resolution 1235 (XLII), conferring on the Commission the task to analyze 'situations which reveal consistent pattern of violations of human rights'.[8] While careful not to tread on the sensitivities of powerful Western states, this concept clearly had subversive elements, being

[6] UN Human Rights Commission Resolution 8 (XXIII), see 42 ESCOR, Suppl. No. 6 (E/4322), pp. 80–146. My account largely follows Medina, see C. Medina Quiroga, *The Battle of Human Rights: Gross, Systematic Violations and the Inter-American system* (Springer, 1988), pp. 7 ff.

[7] Commission on Human Rights, Twenty-Third Session, Feb. 22, 1967, E/CN.4/SR. 898, 11.

[8] Economic and Social Council Resolution 1235 (XLII), 42 U.N.

directed against Apartheid South Africa, which was then still officially supported by the UK and US governments. However, it also reduced the threat to those governments of becoming targets themselves, by putting forward what was essentially a concept of failure in human rights.[9] As the later president of the Inter-American Court, Cecilia Medina Quiroga, argued in her Dutch dissertation in 1988, titled *The Battle of Human Rights – Gross, Systematic Violations and the Inter-American system*:

> [o]nly when national governments fail to give adequate protection to human rights, the international community is called to fill in the gap and lend some form of protection of the victim. It could thus be assumed that the international community starts from the premise that its task is subsidiary and that its purpose is to supplement an already existing national system for the protection of human rights.[10]

Newly endowed with its mandate, the Sub-Commission soon began to explore other cases such as Haiti and even situations in non-colonial settings, such as, most prominently, Greece, which had recently turned authoritarian. In debating these two cases, in both of which government representatives denied that human rights had been violated, delegates discussed what constituted a consistent pattern of rights violations.[11]

Perhaps unsurprisingly, the record shows that they disagreed about nearly everything in doing so. Some delegates argued that considerations of both the nature and the scale of the violations were relevant. Others sought to define the concept as 'implying the repeated occurrence of violations over a substantial period of time as a result of a deliberate governmental policy'[12]. Still others objected to the time component, connecting the term instead to the Security Council's authority to take action in cases of threats to international peace and security.[13] '[F]lagrant and systematic' human rights violations in their opinion were likely to lead to this situation.[14] It was also unclear how the Commission should react when it had identified a consistent pattern of human rights violations. Should it issue a condemnation, or was this not an adequate reaction given

[9] Commission on Human Rights, Twenty-Third Session, Mar. 8, 1967, E/CN.4/SR.918, 14.

[10] Medina, *The Battle of Human Rights*, p. 17.

[11] J. Carey, 'U. N. Response to Government Oppression' (1968) 3:1 *The International Lawyer* 102 and Tolley, 'The Concealed Crack'.

[12] U.N. Human Rights Commission's Report on the Twenty-Fourth Session, U.N. Doc. E/4475-E/CN.4/972 (1968), 69, para. 170.

[13] Ibid.

[14] Ibid., 70, para. 171.

that it was not a judicial body? In any event, Greece and Haiti were dropped from the agenda, ostensibly for lack of sufficient evidence but in truth for manifold reasons.[15] In response, the Sub-Commission began to use individual communications as evidence for their reports, much as the Inter-American Commission on Human Rights had already begun using such communications to start investigations in 1961.[16]

ECOSOC Resolution 1503 of May 1970 finally ratified and formalized the earlier practice, introducing with the so-called 1503 procedure the oldest human rights complaint mechanism in the UN system.[17] It authorized a working group of the Sub-Commission to consider all communications and bring to the attention of the Sub-Commission those that 'appear to reveal a consistent pattern of gross and reliably attested violations of human rights and fundamental freedoms within the terms of reference of the Sub-Commission'.[18] The 'consistent pattern' subsequently became a criterion for admitting individual communications, as did a requirement that victims must first exhaust domestic remedies. In the future, the Sub-Commission and the Commission would monitor cases, often on a confidential basis, communicating with governmental institutions sometimes over the course of several years. More rarely, statements and sometimes studies were released to the public in an attempt to put pressure on intransigent governments. However, the selection of cases continued to be challenging and led to accusations of the Commission's politicization. Ultimately, this led to broader institutional reforms, replacing the Human Rights Commission with the contemporary Human Rights Council, which would now scrutinize reports by all UN member states on a regular basis.

3.2 Proportionality

The attempt to define under what conditions UN bodies should be competent to deal with concrete rights violations in individual member states was ultimately an attempt to define failure in a specific human rights context – and it provides the main remaining puzzle piece for the framework developed here.

15 Ibid., 75, para. 192. For an overview, see Tolley, 'The Concealed Crack', 420 at 430 f.

16 Tolley, 'The Concealed Crack'; on the Inter-American system, see Medina, *The Battle of Human Rights*, pp. 71 ff.

17 United Nations Economic and Social Council, Res. 1503 (XLVIII): Procedure for Dealing with Communications Relating to Violations of Human Rights and Fundamental Freedoms, 27 May 1970.

18 The procedure has been revised as of 2000.

In the last two chapters, we have mainly engaged with institutional questions – who is acting, what are their competences, what is the basis for their legitimacy. Yet, to grapple with arguments from failure, it also matters what kind of failure we are talking about and what might be done about it. In other words, we need to continue the work of these UN institutions in thinking about what makes a consistent pattern of rights violations, as a prerequisite for intervention. We need to consider the proportionality of the intervention, in light of the problem to be resolved.

That proportionality is a necessary puzzle piece in a framework to evaluate arguments from failure hardly comes as a surprise. It is the standard test when it comes to the exercise of emergency powers and also plays an important role in the more recent literature on structural reform litigation.

Thus, Art. 4 (I) ICCPR, Art. 15 (I) ECHR and Art. 27 (I) IACHR all allow for the suspension of certain human rights in cases of emergency, but require any measures to pass a strict necessity test. It also features in the jurisprudence of the European Court of Human Rights[19] as well as the Inter-American Court on Human Rights.[20] Scholars, too, have routinely placed emphasis on necessity as a prerequisite for any exercise of emergency powers. Drawing on a range of sources, including Just War Theory, political theorist Kreuder-Sonnen argues for the adoption of a proportionality framework consisting of functionality, necessity and costs to evaluate the exercise of emergency powers in an international context.[21]

A similar proportionality framework not only recurs in standard domestic rights review but also when it comes to assessing judicial engagement in structural reform cases. Proportionality has been explicitly adopted by Kent Roach as a tool to evaluate which remedies are appropriate in a given case, in particular with an eye to structural remedies.[22] Similar considerations appear in the Colombian Court's

19 *Mehmet Hasan Altan v. Turkey*, Case No. 13237/17; *Şahin Alpay v. Turkey*, Case No. 16538/17; *Kavala v. Turkey*, Case No. 28749/18; *A. and Others v. the United Kingdom* [GC] Case No. 3455/05, para 182 ff. (ECHR).

20 Advisory Opinion OC-8/87 of January 30 1987 (Inter-American Court of Human Rights).

21 C. Kreuder-Sonnen, *Emergency Powers of International Organizations: Between Normalization and Containment* (Oxford University Press, 2019), p. 61; however, note that this is not in fact the key object of Kreuder-Sonnen's monograph but rather its relevance to the question whether the emergency powers exercised will likely be entrenched in the future (ratchet effect) as so often or whether they will be rolled back.

22 K. Roach, *Remedies for Human Rights Violations: A Two-Track Approach to Supranational and National Law* (Cambridge University Press, 2021), Introduction and elsewhere.

doctrine of the 'unconstitutional state of affairs', which seeks to qualify certain rights violations as distinct and requiring specific judicial action – quite similar to the attempts to define a consistent pattern at the United Nations.[23] While I discuss the latter two approaches later in Part II when I turn to analyzing structural reform litigation, it is important to note the overlap between international and domestic standards in this regard as well as the fact that considerations of necessity are not exclusively tied to an individual rights framework.

Proportionality is thus the final hurdle arguments from failure must clear. In many ways, this is foreshadowed already in the discussion in Chapter 2. There, I emphasized the need to evaluate an expansion of competences based on failure in the context of the broader legal and political framework, taking into account the democratic stakes of such arguments as well as other existing remedies available. Proportionality focuses our attention on the issue that has been left unattended as a result of existing failures or indeed been directly caused by such failures. Not any kind of violation of law warrants interventions beyond the routine channels provided. This is the lesson from the United Nations' moves to start scrutinizing human rights violations in specific countries. It also follows from the close relationship between arguments from failure and emergency arguments. However, I cannot emphasize often enough that it remains key not to treat proportionality as the only or even most important requirement when considering arguments from failure.

Since proportionality is a notoriously vague and problematic concept, in what follows I try to spell out a bit more what it should entail in the context of arguments from failure. In doing so, I build on Kreuder-Sonnen's framework, which distinguishes functionality, necessity and costs. As we will see, some of the considerations under such a framework closely parallel some of the arguments put forward in Chapter 2, while others supplement them.

3.2.1 *Functionality*

Functionality is a standard part of proportionality analysis nearly everywhere. It requires that the institution seeking to respond will be likely to resolve the problem at hand or at least contribute significantly to resolving it. Two related considerations are important in this regard. First, this

[23] Decision T-025 of 2004 (Colombian Constitutional Court).

involves thinking about what needs to be done to resolve the issue. Second, we need to assess the capacities of the institution seeking to respond.

What needs to be done is often not an easy question to answer. It depends on why state institutions are not acting to address the issue or indeed why they are causing it. Resistance in particular can be hard to overcome, particularly if important institutional actors are unwilling to do something. The same can be true for problems stemming from a mix of coordination problems, capacity issues and other structural factors. Overcoming what will often be entrenched dysfunction, due, for example, to corruption and capture of agencies, can be exceedingly difficult and sometimes impossible. In at least some cases, therefore, functionality will mean that arguments from failure cannot justify intervention by other institutions simply because there is no realistic chance of change. At the same time, the fact that it is not immediately clear what needs to be done is not a conclusive argument for doing nothing. But the remedy may not always lie in other institutions expanding their powers to take over. In some cases, the best strategy may lie in constructing so-called institutional bypasses that allow citizens to sidestep failing institutions by creating new channels and institutions rather than fixing the old ones. The idea – explored in more detail by Mariana Mota Prado and Michael Trebilcock in their pioneering work in this area – is that this can either exercise pressure on the old institution to reform or make the old ones superfluous in the long run.[24] And where new institutions are created, this is of course not necessarily an exercise of power that requires special justification.

In our context, we need to consider if the institution seeking to take over is itself institutionally suited to doing so. In many cases, this will be doubtful as institutions created for certain purposes will not have the necessary expertise or capacities to act on other issues. Some challenges in this regard will be more easily remedied than others. Thus, if expertise is the problem, the institution in question may bring in outside experts on specific questions. However, if the problem is of a strongly polycentric nature and we are dealing with a court considering to step in, it may not be amenable to resolution within the traditional bipolar structure of judicial trials, and courts then will have to decide whether to develop new procedures – as they often do in practice – or step back from the

[24] M. M. Prado and M. J. Trebilcock, *Institutional Bypasses: A Strategy to Promote Reforms for Development* (Cambridge University Press, 2019).

issue entirely. This is also where the literature on democratic experimentalism may show us the way to address structural problems in a creative and experimental manner.

3.2.2 *Necessity and Costs*

Necessity in our context must be understood both in terms of the legitimacy of the institution acting and the one seen to be failing – requiring us to conduct a no-more democratic means test – and as a qualifier when it comes to the problem that purportedly needs fixing.

On the first point, it bears emphasizing that it is not just the institutions that matter but the process too. Here, too, the democratic experimentalism literature offers important insights when it comes to favouring more flexible as well as participatory approaches over final dictates by individual judges. We must also address the question if the problem that has been left unaddressed due to the institutional failure is significant enough to warrant the intervention of an institution that ordinarily has no powers to address the issue in the way needed. What factors should matter in this context?

Recall the introduction to this chapter and the attempt by the UN Commission on Human Rights to carve out an exception to the standard practice of non-intervention for situations in which they encountered a consistent pattern of gross human rights violations. Spelling out what this meant was not an easy task. The Sub-Commission later asked a Russian expert, Dr. Stanislav Chernichenko, to prepare a paper inter alia to define what cases qualified.[25] This study was subsequently submitted to the Human Rights Committee. Chernichenko emphasized the difficulty of establishing clear criteria when it came to distinguishing 'gross', 'massive' or 'systematic' human rights violations both from each other and from other cases:

> One of the hardest problems is to draw the line between individual instances and massive violations of human rights. (. . .) It is also difficult to draw the line between minor and gross violations of human rights. This

[25] Economic and Social Council, Sub-Commission on Prevention of Discrimination and Protection of Minorities, Forty-Ninth session, Item 11 (c) of the provisional agenda, 28 May 1997, E/CN.4/Sub.2/1997/29, at 3. See also on this H. Rombouts, P. Sardaro and S. Vandeginste, 'The Right to Reparation for Victims of Gross and Systematic Violations of Human Rights', in K. de Feyter et al. (eds.), *Out of the Ashes: Reparation for Victims of Gross and Systematic Human Rights Violations* (Intersentia, 2005), p. 345.

> can be done only approximately. The same can also be said of systematic violations of human rights. In theory it is possible to conceive of systematic violations of the human rights of a particular person or small group of persons. A failure to nip them in the bud, however, would probably indicate a generally unhealthy human rights situation. (. . .) Attempts have been made to "measure" violations of human rights. One idea that merits attention is to use three indicators: the scope of violations, i.e. the degree of seriousness; their intensity, i.e. the frequency of their occurrence over a given period of time; and their range, i.e. the size of the population affected. One may object to the terms proposed. The intensity of human rights violations denotes less the frequency of occurrence than the degree of severity, or both. But in principle, "measuring" human rights violations like this is clearly the right way to go.[26]

Chernichenko also offered examples. According to his account, gross violations referred to a specific kind of human rights violation, for example cases of torture or arbitrary and protracted detention. They often led to 'massive' violations (understood in terms of range) such as genocide, disappearances, slavery-like practices, and mass and arbitrary executions, which also counted as gross violations at the same time. And though in principle open to measuring rights violations in some way, Chernichenko argued that the three factors to consider offered in the literature, namely 'the scope of violations, i.e. the degree of seriousness; their intensity, i.e. the frequency of their occurrence over a given period of time; and their range, i.e. the size of the population affected', were ultimately insufficient. In particular, when it came to economic, social and cultural rights, the problem was often going to be that governments simply did not have the means of improving things, and such cases thus typically should not be considered gross violations under the definition.

Though the efforts to define a consistent pattern were ultimately abandoned at the UN, Chernichenko was not the only one to attempt to define the term.[27] Similar to the three-factor test Chernichenko had discussed and dismissed, the Austrian scholar Ermacora suggested in 1974 that three elements had to be present: first, a time element in the

[26] *Excerpt from the expanded working paper submitted to the UN Human Rights Commission by Russian expert Dr. Stanislav Chernichenko, 28 May 1997,* Economic and Social Council, Sub-Commission on Prevention of Discrimination and Protection of Minorities, Forty-Ninth session, Item 11 (c) of the provisional agenda, 28 May 1997, E/CN.4/Sub.2/1997/29, para. 38.

[27] For an overview, see L. F. Damrosch, 'Gross and Systematic Human Rights Violations', *Max Planck Encyclopedia of Public International Law*, 2011, https://tinyurl.com/mr3uaetk.

sense of some continuity of the violations; second, a quality element that required violations to have a similar scope as apartheid and racial discrimination; finally, there should be a quantity element comprising a substantial number of cases and an expression of a broader policy or ongoing practice where no effective remedies existed within the state concerned.[28] These criteria lingered on in a later attempt at definition by US commentator Maxime Tardu. He added that there needed to be an additional element of planning or of sustained will on the part of the perpetrators, and that in considering the scope of violations, many thought that a degree of inhuman or degrading treatment should be required.[29]

The most comprehensive and convincing attempt at defining the term, however, was presented by Medina in her doctoral dissertation.[30] Based on her analysis of the UN developments and her reading of Ermacora and Tardu, Medina proposed a four-factor test for rights violations to count as gross, requiring (1) sufficient quantity, (2) a temporal element, (3) quality and (4) an element of governmental planning. While the first elements are fairly self-explanatory, it is less clear how to assess the quality of rights violations. Medina argued for an integrated approach which would consider the quality of the right or prohibition in question, the kind of violation, and the status of the victim. Regarding the quality of the right in question, she referred to the category of ius cogens offences, the categorization as international crimes or the fact that only some rights tend to be non-derogable in human rights treaties. The fourth and final element of planning is unfortunately not fleshed out much by Medina. She argued that violations cannot be committed 'at random' but must typically serve a specific goal and thus be part of a broader plan or policy. (This understanding, as we will see later, would make it very hard to capture socio-economic rights violations, today a major area of expansive action by domestic courts.) Summed up in one sentence by Medina:

> gross, systematic violations of human rights [are] violations, instrumental to the achievement of governmental policies, perpetrated in such a quantity and in such a manner as to create a situation in which the rights to life, to personal integrity or to personal liberty of the population as a

[28] F. Ermacora, 'Procedures to Deal with Human Rights Violations: A Hopeful Start in the United Nations?' (1974) 7 *Human Rights Journal* 670.

[29] M. E. Tardu, 'United Nations Response to Gross Violations of Human Rights: The 1503 Procedure' (1980) 20 *Santa Clara Law Review* 559.

[30] Medina, *The Battle of Human Rights*.

> whole or of one or more sections of the population of a country are continuously infringed or threatened.[31]

This analysis focusing on the quantity, duration and quality of rights violations has strong parallels to the doctrines we see in some courts today to deal with structural reform cases. This includes the Colombian Constitutional Court with its 'unconstitutional state of affairs doctrine,'[32] which I discuss in Chapter 4, as well as the European Court of Human Rights' pilot judgment procedure under Art. 61 of the Court's Rules of Procedure. In both courts, considerations of quantity and time are central to analyzing whether the cases they confronted warrant the application of the unconstitutional state of affairs doctrine or the pilot procedure – and thus an exceptional structural remedy.

Intent, on the other hand, usually plays a lesser role. In my view, it should not be taken as a requirement for intervention, which may appear necessary also in cases of incapacity or incompetence that do not include intent to violate, as the literature on structural reform litigation demonstrates. That said, intent can play some role as an additional argument for certain kinds of interventions.

Finally – costs. The costs of the respective intervention should ideally be understood to include both immediate costs as well as potential long-term consequences, which will often be harder to assess. They can accrue in relation to the institution failing to act as well as the one seeking to intervene or the broader public. Thus, it may be that an intervention will both remedy a pressing problem and help restore trust in the state and its institutions. However, the intervention may also contribute to fostering an abdication of responsibility by the institution in question and draw attention to dysfunctionalities in a way that damages public trust in institutions more permanently. Finally, as we know from the emergency literature, what starts as an intervention in an exceptional case may become normalized and entrenched in the longer run (the so-called ratchet effect),[33] extending the power of the institution to act in circumstances beyond the original case. In some situations, we may be able to take mitigating measures to lower the risks of certain negative consequences, but in others this may not be possible. Unfortunately, assessing

[31] Ibid., p. 315.

[32] See, e.g., Decision T-025 of 2004 (Colombian Constitutional Court).

[33] Kreuder-Sonnen, *Emergency Powers*, p. 44.

which of these consequences is most likely will often be difficult and involve prognoses with significant uncertainty.

3.3 Summary

With this, it is now time to gather the insights of our discussion in these first three chapters. In Chapter 1, we saw how arguments from failure overlap with existing arguments for institutional expansion but are also in important ways different from them. We saw that there are resources to justify intervention in cases of failure in the existing literature on the separation of powers and democratic theory, but also that such a flexible approach comes with risks.

Drawing on these debates, I propose that if we seek to evaluate arguments from failure from the perspective of comparative constitutional theory, we need to consider four different questions:

As a first step, we need to ascertain that we are operating within a context in which arguments from failure can generally have a place, that is within a system where expectations of mutual collaboration and responsiveness are appropriate. As I argued in Chapter 2, this is typically the case within standard constitutional democracies, but it may pose a more significant challenge in the international context (see more in Chapter 7).

Second, there needs to be a violation of law, with one exception, which I will discuss in Chapter 6. This, too, is typically a hurdle easily cleared. In the context of the UN bodies' involvement with human rights, the violation of law giving rise to accusations of failure would be the initial rights violations by the respective governments.

Third, it is important to take the existing institutional structures and legal frameworks seriously. This means that we need to consider whether existing frameworks should be understood as comprehensive. We also need to consider the legitimacy of the institutions involved, which includes a no-more-democratic-means-test, and distinguish cases of failure from those of disagreement.

Fourth, we need to assess the functionality, necessity and costs of the intervention proposed in light of the issue to be addressed.

These considerations necessarily provide only a rough guide to assessing arguments from failure in normative terms. The details will depend on the particular legal and institutional context in which the argument is put forward. Nevertheless, I believe that even the rough guidelines I offer here can be useful to help us think productively about arguments from failure rather than subsume them under existing doctrines of emergency powers or implied powers, or for that matter rejecting them altogether.

3.4 Case Study: The British Post Office Scandal

All of this is fairly abstract and vague. I, thus, want to turn to a real case, which is, I argue here, best understood and discussed in terms of an argument from failure. The case in question starts with the British so-called Horizon scandal from 1996 to the end of 2018, which ultimately saw legislation passed to quash the wrongful criminal convictions of postmasters, subpostmasters and other post office employees (in the following: postmasters) for offences including fraud, theft and false accounting.

3.4.1 Background

The events leading up to the passage of this legislation constitute one of Britain's major political scandals in the last ten years. They have been the subject of much public discussion as well as the release of a mini-series, titled *Mr. Bates vs the Post Office*.[34] In brief: From 1996 onwards, the British Post Office had piloted a new software called Horizon, designed by the Japanese company Fujitsu, to streamline accounting in its post offices. However, that software had serious flaws that were not public knowledge at the time. These led to the appearance of shortfalls in a range of post offices in Britain and subsequently to post office employees being investigated for a series of offences. As a result, many of those employees lost their jobs and their savings on account of having to make up for alleged shortfalls out of their own pockets. Four people killed themselves and hundreds ended up criminally convicted, with some serving time in prison. As the scandal slowly unravelled, the Post Office was shown to have ignored early warning signs about the software. More than that, the Post Office, which enjoys the legal power to conduct its own investigations instead of involving the British police, had not always conducted these investigations with the necessary care. It had sometimes only passed on

[34] On the background story, see S. Lipscombe et al., 'Post Office (Horizon System) Offences Bill', *House of Commons Library – Research Briefing*, 18 March 2024, www.commonslibrary.parliament.uk/research-briefings/cbp-9986/; S. Mason, 'The Post Office Horizon Scandal: A Brief Chronology' (2021) 18 *Digital Evidence and Electronic Signature Law Review* 1.

parts of the evidence to the state prosecutors, who subsequently brought the criminal charges against the employees. Efforts by the postmasters to uncover the truth were hampered for a long time by the Post Office's lack of cooperation, until they ultimately succeeded in the courts. In the landmark *Bates v. The Post Office* judgment, computer flaws were finally determined to be the cause for the alleged shortfalls.[35] Subsequently, a number of postmasters involved with the litigation successfully challenged their criminal convictions in the appeals courts, leading to a finding that not only had the defendants previously not received a fair trial, but also that the Post Office had acted to subvert the integrity of the justice system and undermine public confidence.[36]

However, it also became clear that there were hundreds of wrongful convictions still remaining on the books, leading to the question of how to deal with this situation. The normal route to challenging such convictions depends on where the original cases were tried and whether the individuals in question had pleaded guilty – which had often been the case, as many postmasters took deals to avoid prison time. Nevertheless, ultimately overturning convictions could only be done by the appeals courts, in some cases (especially after guilty pleas), only after a referral by the criminal cases review commission. However, given that some of the criminal convictions went back 20 years and evidence was not always still available, the process of overturning the convictions in the courts was neither straightforward nor fast, with each case requiring separate consideration. In other words, this route was quite burdensome and problematic. In response, the British government chose to draft legislation instead, quashing all convictions of post-office employees for certain offences falling within the prescribed time frame.

However, this legislation faced controversy among British public lawyers and judges. Some considered it an inappropriate intervention by the government into the judicial domain that interfered with the rule of law, the independence of the judiciary and, ultimately, the separation of powers. There have been more specific concerns about how to identify the people whose convictions would be quashed. Concerns about the legislation's legality have also been raised by the Chair of the Justice Select Committee in the House of Commons, Robert Neill, and by the United Kingdom's Chief Justice, who has challenged the claims that the justice system had not been able to process the appeals sufficiently,

[35] *Alan Bates and Others v. Post Office Limited* [2018] EWHC 2698 (QB).
[36] *Hamilton v. Post Office Ltd* [2021] EWCA Crim 577.

efficiently and swiftly.[37] That said, others defended the legislation as an appropriate use of parliamentary powers to address legitimate grievances within the British system of government, with its particular emphasis on parliamentary sovereignty. In this view, the legislation contributed to upholding the rule of law. It ensured that justice was done in a situation where many criminal convictions had been based on incomplete evidence.[38] In addition, the fact that the legislation targeted specific convictions meant, some argued, that it did not impinge on the rule of law or the separation of powers. Rather, it constituted an instance of parliament addressing a structural problem with corporate culture in the Post Office at the time and served to remind institutions with their own powers of investigation, such as the Post Office, of their duty to exercise these powers in a careful and impartial manner.[39]

While it, therefore, remains contested whether the separation of powers indeed allows for the passage of a statute quashing convictions, it seems fair to state that its passage involved an unconventional use of parliamentary powers. Thus, the official explanatory notes to the statute itself state under 'legal background' that '[t]his is an unprecedented and wholly exceptional legal solution to a miscarriage of justice of unparalleled scale and impact (. . .) The approach to quashing convictions in the Act does not set any constitutional precedent'.[40]

It seems to me that the postmasters statute is best understood in terms of an argument from failure, with the failure in question being the previous miscarriages of justice leading to hundreds of wrongful convictions and thus rights violations. Understanding the legislation in those terms makes clear that it does not involve an either-or-case, in the sense of parliament either having powers to quash convictions by legislative fiat or not. Rather, it is a case where such a power might be defended only in terms of the need to react to an exceptional situation by unconventional means and was not intended to set a precedent for the future.

[37] Lipscombe et al., 'Post Office Research Briefing', reference p. 36 with further references.

[38] R. Craig, 'The Constitutional Implications of Legislating to Exonerate the Post Office Sub-Postmasters', *UK Constitutional Law Association*, 16 January 2024, https://tinyurl.com/mrvyp3w8; see also K. Dewsnip, 'The Post Office Bill: Constitutionally Unusual, but not Inappropriate', *The Constitution Society*, 24 April 2024, www.consoc.org.uk/the-post-office-bill/.

[39] Craig, 'Constitutional Implications'.

[40] 'Explanatory Notes: Post Office (Horizon System) Offences Act 2024', www.legislation.gov.uk/ukpga/2024/14/pdfs/ukpgaen_20240014_en.pdf, n. 23 and 24.

As an argument from failure, we can then ask our set of questions. The first of these concerns the existence of a framework where there is a legal expectation of mutual collaboration and support. This is a hurdle easily cleared if we recall the broad basis for a collaborative understanding of constitutionalism in the United Kingdom, as argued convincingly by Aileen Kavanagh.[41]

The same applies to the requirement of a breach of law, which in this case was the miscarriage of justice involving criminal convictions on the basis of flawed evidence, as set out in the judgment of *Bates v. The Post Office.*[42]

The third concerns the question if we can indeed identify something like a gap in the law, in the sense of there being no comprehensive framework to deal with issues such as the one that has arisen. Here, things start getting trickier, given that there obviously is a process for overturning criminal convictions in place. The question then is to what degree we should understand this framework to be comprehensive. More particularly, we might ask if it is a framework that is geared to operate or can operate not just to deal with isolated wrongful convictions but rather with structural problems leading to hundreds of wrongful convictions, as in this case. This is where different understandings of the rule of law and the role of the British parliament start to matter. Given the principle of parliamentary supremacy and the traditional role of parliament in addressing grievances, it seems to me that there must be at least some room in principle for a parliamentary role in dealing with structural problems in the justice system as opposed to an isolated individual wrongful conviction – and this suggests that we should not view the existing judicial mechanisms as fully comprehensive. However, we should be mindful here that such an argument might be more difficult to make in other constitutional democracies where a stricter understanding of the separation of powers prevails.

Fourth, we will have to ask about the functionality, necessity and costs involved in quashing the convictions by legislative action. We, thus, need to answer the question if the legislation will actually remedy the problem. The main challenge in this regard will be whether it is possible to identify all the relevant post office employees. Some have argued that the framing of the statute is vague in places, thus making it difficult to identify with certainty all cases where criminal convictions should be

[41] Aileen Kavanagh, *The Collaborative Constitution* (Cambridge University Press, 2023).

[42] *Bates and Others v. Post Office.*

overturned.[43] Nor does the statute address the question of financial compensation, which is being addressed through additional legislation.

More difficult still is the question of necessity in the case at hand. For while it is clear that the Post Office scandal indeed involved a structural problem leading to miscarriages of justice in hundreds of cases with severe personal consequences, it is less clear that legislating to overturn previous convictions was necessary to restore justice. This question is perhaps the one that has loomed largest in the British debate, albeit in a rather freewheeling way that speaks to how we understand necessity to be a core requirement whenever we confront arguments from failure. The key question has been in particular whether the existing judicial process was indeed as slow as it was suggested, and if so, whether the best way to increase speed might not have been to increase funding for the Criminal Cases Review Commission instead. Like many British institutions, the Commission had suffered from severe cutbacks in the last fifteen years.[44] Others have, however, questioned if funding is the real or only problem. They have traced the very low success rates of appeals to the Criminal Cases Review Commission to the high statutory threshold for referring cases back to the appeals court, which requires a 'real possibility' of having the case overturned.[45] But whether funding or the current statutory framework is slowing things down, both could be addressed either by increasing funding or by changing the legislative framework.[46] It has also been pointed out that, currently, none of the people convicted are still serving prison sentences, and accordingly, the need for urgent action is less dramatic than it would have been some years ago. That said, previous criminal convictions of course continue to impact the lives of those concerned negatively in other ways. Overall, however, it seems that there is considerable scepticism within the British public law community as to whether legislation was necessary to deal with the situation. If the

[43] S. Tierney, 'The Post Office (Horizon System) Offences Act 2024: Necessary Remedy or Unwarranted Interference with Judicial Independence?', *UK Constitutional Law Association*, 3 June 2024, https://tinyurl.com/3jex8cmh.

[44] J. Robins, '#The Law is Broken', *New Law Journal*, 11 May 2018, www.newlawjournal.co.uk/content/law-broken.

[45] M. Naughton, 'What If the CCRC Had Unlimited Funding? A Submission to the Law Commission's Review of the Appeals System', *University of Bristol Law School Blog*, 23 January 2023, https://tinyurl.com/m4pejnte.

[46] D. Green, 'Why Legislating to Acquit Horizon Victims May Be Unnecessary in Practice and Wrong in Principle', *Prospect Magazine*, 18 January 2024, https://tinyurl.com/5yj2rmp9.

sceptics are right, the argument from failure would have to be rejected at this stage.

Lastly, when it comes to costs, additional problems surface. The legislation will likely exonerate some people whose criminal convictions were not based on flawed evidence. It will also lead to awkward results insofar as it excepts people who previously tried to challenge their convictions in the appeals court but were unsuccessful on the basis that their convictions were likely not based on the flawed Horizon evidence. Yet, this leads to a situation where people who would now have had their convictions purged under the more lenient statutory approach are excluded merely because they previously sought to use the ordinary appeals process to challenge their convictions. Most importantly, however, there is the risk of the legislation creating a precedent for other cases in which parliament might feel the need to overturn sets of judgments it considers problematic, albeit that the statute itself disavows that idea. On the other hand, there is a pressing need to bring about justice for hundreds of people whose lives had previously been turned upside down by wrongful convictions. All things considered, it would seem that the costs in this case are perhaps not the main challenge, but that it hinges on the question of necessity.

British public lawyers are far better qualified than I am to resolve that question, and I, accordingly, do not seek to provide a full answer here. My interest in this case is as an illustration of how treating the legislation quashing the convictions as an argument from failure provides a way to deal with the question of parliamentary overreach in a principled manner. As we have seen, evaluating the legislation in those terms means addressing many of the considerations already present in current British debates, but it does so within a broader theoretical and legal framework. That framework offers no straightforward answers. It also leaves plenty of room for discussion, as we have just seen. Context and the specifics of the local legal systems will have to be taken into account to come up with an answer. But the same is true for other approaches used in the existing debates, framed in terms of the scope of parliamentary sovereignty, or the somewhat free-floating references to necessity. Treating the legislation as an argument from failure at least means asking the right questions and thus provides an important step for ultimately developing a convincing answer.

II

Courts

4

Structural Reform Litigation in Domestic Courts

4.1 Introduction

In 2004, the Colombian Constitutional Court addressed the situation of displaced persons in Colombia, a result of the ongoing civil war. In its judgment, which has since become famous, the Court held that the situation qualified as an 'unconstitutional state of affairs'. The government had clearly been aware of the existing situation, but provided little in the way of a more comprehensive plan to improve the lives of displaced persons, millions of whom lived in dismal circumstances, without access to work, education or healthcare. The Court argued: 'Whenever a repeated and constant violation of fundamental rights is verified, which affects a multitude of persons, and whose solution requires the intervention of different entities to address problems of a structural nature, this Court has declared the existence of an unconstitutional state of affairs...'[1] The Court then issued a set of far-ranging structural interdicts, starting a multi-year process of developing and implementing a budget to address the situation while involving a range of state and civil society stakeholders in the ongoing reform processes to be supervised by the Court itself.

In 2013, a New York District Court found that the NYPD had followed an unconstitutional 'policy of indirect racial profiling', which the City and the NYPD had for a long time been 'deliberately indifferent' to.[2] Pointing out that she 'would have preferred that the City cooperate in a joint undertaking to develop some of the remedies ordered in this Opinion' but that it had declined to do so, the judge appointed an official

[1] Corte Constitucional [C.C.], Sentencia No. T-025/04 of 2004 (Colombian Constitutional Court).

[2] *Floyd et al. v. City of New York*, et al., 959 F. Supp. 2d 540 (S.D.N.Y. 2013) (US District Court), p. 184.

monitor to work with the NYPD to reform the stop-and-frisk procedures and report back to the Court. She also ordered the participants to involve community organizations in the reform process as well as to institute a pilot project with body cameras for police officers.[3]

Repeated and constant violations of fundamental rights, deliberate indifference, refusal to cooperate: What connects our two examples and many others is that these are not routine cases where the odd license or grant has been refused illegally, an isolated illegal arrest been made or a particular assembly been dissolved wrongfully by the police in violation of participants' constitutional rights. In other words, they do not represent the sort of thing that just happens sometimes even in the best of all possible democracies. Instead, they concern instances of broader failures to adequately respect or protect individual rights. And this is not the only thing the decisions above have in common. In both cases, courts respond to the situation in non-standard ways, making changes to existing procedures and/or remedies. They choose to stay involved in the issue even after announcing their judgment, to monitor compliance, and set out a series of detailed prescriptions governmental institutions have to follow. They also involve civil society actors and/or independent experts, such as a monitor or auditor, in the reform processes themselves.

None of this, as Abram Chayes famously remarked in the context of US structural reform litigation, constitutes traditional judicial activity.[4] Traditionally, courts are meant to decide cases in an individualized manner ex post and on the basis of legal norms, as distinct from considerations of policy. This or something like it represents the standard description of the judicial role in the literature, from Chayes to Christoph Möllers.[5] What we see in these cases, however, does not fit that template; indeed, it doesn't even come close. Yet, the 'phenomenon' (for want of a better word) is no longer new today – Chayes wrote his famous piece in the Harvard Law Review in 1976. Nor does it encompass only a few isolated cases. Instead, the practice, often labelled structural reform litigation in the United States, is today fairly commonplace both in the United States as well as in a wide range of Global South

[3] Ibid., Remedies Opinion.

[4] A. Chayes, 'The Role of the Judge in Public Law Litigation' (1976) 89 *Harvard Law Review* 1281.

[5] C. Möllers, *The Three Branches: A Comparative Model of Separation of Powers* (Oxford University Press, 2013), p. 98.

jurisdictions. It is also, as we will see, increasingly part of the jurisprudence of the regional human rights courts in Europe and the Americas.[6]

Arguments from failure play a central role in legitimizing this practice. In this chapter, I trace the development of this jurisprudence in a range of domestic courts in the United States, India, Colombia and South Africa. I have selected these four countries, which all count among the 'usual suspects' in comparative public law, for precisely that reason. All of them are known to have active courts that engage in structural reform litigation, which are well-researched in the academic literature. This matters because I am not only interested in what courts are doing and why but also in the accompanying scholarly discourses. Drawing mainly on this scholarship, I start with a survey of the development of structural reform litigation, teasing out some shared features as well as differences that have emerged in the jurisprudence of the different courts.

Note, however, that I will not provide a comprehensive comparative account of the legal frameworks and doctrinal concepts involved in individual systems. This is partly because these are often complex, and an attempt to summarize them far exceeds what is needed for my project. It is also because none of the courts I cover here – with something of an exception in the case of the Colombian Constitutional Court – works with a clear doctrinal concept, which then triggers a set of particular changes to the procedure or specific remedies.

Instead, courts generally operate with a host of different precedents and doctrines depending on the case and question at hand. Take as an example the United States. Class actions are an important tool in US structural reform litigation. A lawyer representing one or several plaintiffs approaches the court to litigate a case on behalf of a broader class of people for whom her plaintiffs are representative. However, there are different types of class actions.[7] In the context of public law litigation, two are particularly relevant: first, injunctive class actions, where the same remedy will necessarily apply to all members of the class, and second, those where this is not the case but where reasons of convenience suggest that a class action might be appropriate, sometimes

[6] A. Huneeus, 'Reforming the State from Afar: Structural Reform Litigation at the Human Rights Courts' (2015) 40 *Yale Journal of International Law* 1.

[7] See, e.g., for a discussion M. Carroll, 'Class Action Myopia' (2016) 65 *Duke Law Journal* 843.

called 'spurious class actions'.[8] They are employed, for example, if there are common questions of law or of fact that predominate, but also for reasons of efficiency insofar as class actions will offer a superior means to resolve the controversy in question. But class actions have recently been declining[9] and they are not the only relevant procedural tools. Nor are all class actions geared at structural reform litigation. Questions of procedure and evidence matter, too. Who can bring what evidence and at what point? What kind of witnesses and experts may be heard? Different rules on liability further complicate matters. Finally, there is the question of remedies, which is generally a matter of equity and judicial discretion, though certain criteria have emerged as a condition for permanent injunctions (orders prohibiting a party from engaging in a certain conduct after the trial, which are frequently used in institutional litigation).[10] First, plaintiffs must have suffered 'irreparable harm'. Second, other remedies such as damages must be inadequate to compensate for their injury. Third, the remedy must be appropriate considering the overall balance of hardships between the parties. Fourth, the remedy must serve the public interest.[11]

As this short and incomplete survey demonstrates, there are a host of different conditions and standards involved in cases of what I call, for simplicity, structural reform litigation. There is ample and often quite intricate doctrine surrounding individual cases, which I generally leave to one side here in order to consider a range of different jurisdictions. That said, I make one exception insofar as the Colombian Court has developed a more comprehensive approach with its unconstitutional-state-of-affairs doctrine, which I briefly discuss below.

4.2 Structural Reform Litigation in the United States

I begin with the United States because US developments mostly precede those elsewhere, influencing what is happening in other regions. The US case is also the best-researched one, even though recent scholarship on

[8] 1938 Rule 23 a *or b* 2 and 3.

[9] R. H. Klonoff, 'The Decline of Class Actions' (2012) 90 *Washington University Law Review* 729.

[10] *EBay Inc. v. MercExchange, L.L.C.*, 547 U.S. 388 (2006) (US Supreme Court). See also M. P. Gergen, J. M. Golden and H.E. Smith, 'The Supreme Court's Accidental Revolution? The Test for Permanent Injunctions' (2012) 112 *Columbia Law Review* 203.

[11] *EBay Inc. v. MercExchange.*

key Global South jurisdictions such as India, Colombia and South Africa is increasingly changing that.

4.2.1 Origins

That judges intervene in cases of institutional failure is not a given. Consider as an example the US Supreme Court's 1903 decision in *Giles v. Harris* on the disenfranchisement of black citizens in Alabama.[12] After the civil war, Southern states had to accept the Fifteenth Amendment and grant the right to vote to their newly minted black citizens, under the threat of Northern military supervision.[13] As a result, there were often initially quite a few black legislators in the parliaments of Southern states, in some cases even forming a majority. But by the end of the nineteenth and early twentieth centuries, this had changed. Southern states had implemented various mechanisms to keep their black citizens from voting and changed their imposed constitutions. For example, they introduced so-called grandfather clauses, which guaranteed voter registration to those entitled to vote before 1867 and their descendants, while making registration of all others conditional on further requirements. Those requirements typically provided (white) administrators with ample discretion to discriminate against black citizens wishing to register.[14]

In 1903, Jackson Giles, a literate black man and activist for the Republican Party, set out to challenge before the US Supreme Court the restrictions put in place by the Constitution of Alabama. He asked the Court to order the state to place him and other qualified members of his race on the voter roll of the state.[15] The Constitution of Alabama had been changed in 1901 to restrict voting, adding residency, educational and good character requirements, and poll taxes, with exceptions for ex-soldiers and their descendants. In an opinion written by none other than Oliver Wendell Holmes, the Supreme Court, however, declined to find a violation and make the order required.

12 *Giles v. Harris*, 189 U.S. 475 (1903) (US Supreme Court).

13 M. J. Klarman, *From Jim Crow to Civil Rights: The Supreme Court and the Struggle for Racial Equality* (Oxford University Press, 2006), pp. 28 ff.; J. C. Monnet, 'The Latest Phase of Negro Disfranchisement' (2009) 62 *Oklahoma Law Review* 407.

14 Ibid.

15 Secretly, the litigation was funded by Booker T. Washington; see R. H. Pildes, 'Democracy, Anti-Democracy, and the Canon' (2000) 17 *Constitutional Commentary* 295 at 304.

For this, Holmes offered two arguments. The first seemed plainly disingenuous. Given that the applicant had argued that the registration rules set up by the Constitution of Alabama itself constituted a fraud upon the US Constitution, Holmes argued that inclusion in the voter rolls under these rules would make the Supreme Court itself participate in the fraud in question. Second, and more importantly, Holmes argued that the Supreme Court could not make the order desired by the applicant because there would be resistance by the state of Alabama and because it would be impossible for the Court to actually enforce the order except by directly supervising Alabama's elections, a task considered obviously impossible as well as inappropriate:

> The other difficulty is of a different sort, and strikingly reinforces the argument that equity cannot undertake now, any more than it has in the past, to enforce political rights, and also the suggestion that state constitutions were not left unmentioned in § 1979 by accident. (. . .) The bill imports that the great mass of the white population intends to keep the blacks from voting. To meet such an intent something more than ordering the plaintiff's name to be inscribed upon the lists of 1902 will be needed. If the conspiracy and the intent exist, a name on a piece of paper will not defeat them. Unless we are prepared to supervise the voting in that state by officers of the court, it seems to us that all that the plaintiff could get from equity would be an empty form. Apart from damages to the individual, relief from a great political wrong, if done, as alleged, by the people of a state and the state itself, must be given by them or by the legislative and political department of the government of the United States.

Nowhere does Holmes address the question if the registration scheme of Alabama violated the Fifteenth Amendment, and thus if Southern institutions had actually failed to respect black citizens' voting rights. Nevertheless, the opinion reads in many respects as if he accepted that premise. As US commentators have pointed out, Holmes might well have been able to dismiss the case on the basis of mootness, as was common for dealing with comparable cases in the South, because the election in question had already taken place.[16] He could also have engaged with the substantive questions at stake, namely whether the grandfather clause of Alabama indeed constituted just a thinly disguised form of racial discrimination, and more generally what standard of proof should apply

[16] S. Brenner, '"Airbrushed Out of the Constitutional Canon": The Evolving Understanding of Giles v. Harris, 1903–1925' (2009) 107:5 *Michigan Law Review* 853 at 860 f.

when adjudicating claims of racial discrimination. More particularly, Holmes might have been able to shed light on the role of legislative intent in discrimination cases and the constitutionality of delegating wide discretion to registrars, such as with regard to the 'good character' of potential voters. As Klarman argues, all of these debates were very much open at the time – with precedents on both sides.[17] That Holmes did not engage with them at all, focusing instead immediately on the question of equitable remedies, suggests two things. First, he neither wanted to appear to give Alabama's voting procedure the Supreme Court's seal of approval by explicitly finding no violation, nor did he want to explicitly state that a violation had taken place, which the Supreme Court would then not be able to remedy and which also might have contributed to worsening race relations. Perhaps, as Klarman suggests, Holmes and his fellow justices also shared the growing sense among Northerners that the Fifteenth Amendment and voting rights for black people had been a mistake.[18] However, even if we accept that explanation, nothing suggests that Holmes and his colleagues did not in fact recognize that Alabama, like many Southern states, was de jure violating political rights on a massive scale. If Holmes and his colleagues decided not to act upon that recognition, it was most likely for the reasons stated in the judgment itself, namely the Court's limited power and authority to enforce such a judgment.

Today, we may be puzzled by Holmes' willingness to admit defeat and invoke the limits of judicial power before even engaging with the substantive question or with the political realities on the ground. Even if we are in principle open to strategic considerations about the limits of judicial power in the face of adverse political and elite opinion – as most US commentators are – we are likely to be suspicious of Holmes' one-dimensional assessment of the political situation in the South. As Rick Pildes has argued, a closer look at the political situation in Alabama at the time paints a nuanced picture. Opposition to black voting was by no means universal among Alabama's citizenry at the time. Only 57% of voters supported its disenfranchising Constitution, with 54 out of

[17] Klarman, 'Jim Crow'.

[18] Klarman, 'Jim Crow', pp. 37–8; Northern Republicans had often protected the right to vote of black citizens since black voters would reliably support Republican candidates, traditionally in a minority in the South. But electoral realignment in the South lessened Republican concerns and thus their willingness to protect the black vote, which many Northerners increasingly began to see as a mistake.

66 counties voting against it.[19] In light of this, it was much less clear than Holmes pretended how a contrary judgment by the Supreme Court would have been received and if and how it might have been enforced.[20]

And herein lies the broader lesson of *Giles v. Harris*. Though the literature of the past five decades has provided ample evidence for the limits of judicial power, we also know that courts have achieved successes where other institutions have previously failed, for whatever reason, including in cases where things have looked fairly bleak.[21] Those successes may have been limited and were typically conditional upon support by other actors: the broader population, organized civil society groups and political elites.[22] We also know that courts will sometimes fail and even face backlash, which may make things worse for the court itself and/or the groups involved in litigation.[23] But it will often not be easy to assess the situation in advance – and therefore, it will also be unwise for courts to admit defeat before the provisions and troops are counted and the positions and weaponry on both sides assessed.

But Holmes is not only concerned about what courts can do. He also worries about the appropriateness of judicial intervention: 'Unless we are prepared to supervise the voting in that state by officers of the court, it seems to us that all that the plaintiff could get from equity would be an empty form'. Supervising the conduct of state elections, so this passage suggests, is something out the question – and out the question presumably not just because such a task might prove difficult but also because it would be an inappropriate thing for a court to do.

This kind of argument about the judicial role, by and large, is still with us today. Consider as an example an earlier decision of the US Supreme Court on gerrymandering, which, albeit overruled today, is sometimes still invoked by the Court: its 1946 decision on electoral districting in *Colegrove v. Green*, written by Justice Frankfurter. Frankfurter explicitly

19 Pildes, 'Democracy', 295 at 316.

20 Ibid.; for a more skeptical take, see C. A. Heckman, 'Keeping Legal History Legal and Judicial Activism in Perspective: A Reply to Richard Pildes' (2002) 19 *Constitutional Commentary* 625–44; with Pildes replying R. H. Pildes, 'Keeping Legal History Meaningful' (2002) 19 *Constitutional Commentary* 645.

21 See, e.g., C. R. Epp, *Making Rights Real: Activists, Bureaucrats, and the Creation of the Legalistic State* (University of Chicago Press, 2009); see also some of the examples below.

22 Ibid.; see also C. R. Epp, *The Rights Revolution: Lawyers, Activists, and Supreme Courts in Comparative Perspective* (University of Chicago Press, 1998).

23 See, e.g., G. N. Rosenberg, *The Hollow Hope* (University of Chicago Press, 2008).

cited *Giles v. Harris*, putting forward a more elaborate argument about the judicial role and its limitations:

> In effect, this is an appeal to the federal courts to reconstruct the electoral process of Illinois in order that it may be adequately represented in the councils of the Nation. **Because the Illinois legislature has failed to revise its Congressional Representative districts in order to reflect great changes, during more than a generation, in the distribution of its population, we are asked to do this, as it were, for Illinois.** Of course, no court can affirmatively re-map the Illinois districts so as to bring them more in conformity with the standards of fairness for a representative system. At best, we could only declare the existing electoral system invalid. The result would be to leave Illinois undistricted, and to bring into operation, if the Illinois legislature chose not to act, the choice of members for the House of Representatives on a statewide ticket. The last stage may be worse than the first (. . .) Nothing is clearer than that this controversy concerns matters that bring courts into immediate and active relations with party contests. From the determination of such issues, this Court has traditionally held aloof. It is hostile to a democratic system to involve the judiciary in the politics of the people. And it is not less pernicious if such judicial intervention in an essentially political contest be dressed up in the abstract phrases of the law. (Emphasis by this author)[24]

Thus, unlike Holmes in *Giles*, Frankfurter explicitly denied in *Colegrove* that constitutional rights had been violated, given the vagueness of existing legal rules on districting. Yet, once again, his reasoning is instructive, insofar as he clearly assumes that the litigation presented the court with a case of political failure, namely the failure to revise Illinois' electoral districts. Yet, Frankfurter and his colleagues did not want to intervene in such a 'political thicket': 'The Constitution has many commands that are not enforceable by courts, because they clearly fall outside the conditions and purposes that circumscribe judicial action'.[25]

If *Giles* stands for the difficulties of judicial intervention in light of possible political resistance, *Colegrove* speaks to the broader debate about the role of courts in a democracy. Today, non-justiciability is no longer the key concern it used to be – and this is particularly true if we take a broader global perspective on the issue. We have not only seen a rise of constitutional review in global terms but also an increased willingness by courts to harness this power to a degree that the result is sometimes

[24] *Colegrove v. Green*, 328 U.S. 549 (1946) (US Supreme Court).
[25] Ibid.

described as a 'juristocracy'.[26] This is perhaps most visible in fields such as socio-economic rights, which were traditionally considered non-justiciable, but no longer are.[27] The contemporary jurisprudence of a wide range of courts in Southern and increasingly Northern jurisdictions shows that courts can develop legal mechanisms to enforce such rights – whether they consist in scrutinizing the consistency or reasonableness of governmental approaches or adopting a minimum core approach.[28] This is not to say that worries and concerns about justiciability have ceased to play a role, but rather that the ground here, too, has shifted. We no longer believe that questions of policy are sharply distinct from questions of law, even though the distinction as such continues to play a role.[29] This is also reflected in theories of judicial review, which typically operate today no longer by excepting certain issues or questions entirely from judicial scrutiny, but are instead about finding a balance between the courts and democratically elected actors.[30] In other words, the debate is one about the appropriate degree of judicial control rather than about setting sharp boundaries between law and politics. This is not to say that we are today comfortable with an idea of unlimited judicial power – we certainly are not – but that the relationship between courts and the other branches in most constitutional democracies today tends to be more complicated. As a result, judges today will find it less easy to turn away from cases of institutional failure than Justice Holmes did in *Giles*.

[26] R. Hirschl, *Towards Juristocracy: The Origins and Consequences of the New Constitutionalism* (Harvard University Press, 2009); for a recent analysis of this trend, see D. Lustig and J. H. H. Weiler, 'Judicial Review in the Contemporary World – Retrospective and Prospective' (2018) 16:2 *International Journal of Constitutional Law* 315.

[27] See, e.g., D. Landau, 'The Reality of Social Rights Enforcement' (2012) 53:1 *Harvard International Law* 190 at 190: 'For all practical purposes, the debate about whether to include social rights in constitutions is over.'

[28] For many see J. King, *Judging Social Rights* (Cambridge University Press, 2012); B. Ray, *Engaging with Social Rights: Procedure, Participation and Democracy in South Africa's Second Wave* (Cambridge University Press, 2016); S. Liebenberg, *Socio-Economic Rights: Adjudication Under a Transformative Constitution* (Juta and Company Ltd., 2010).

[29] See more below, Chapter 6.

[30] M. Tushnet, 'Law and Prudence in the Law of Justiciability: The Transformation and Disappearance of the Political Question Doctrine' (2002) 80 *North Carolina Law Review* 1203; see also with further references M. Hailbronner, 'Constitutional Legitimacy and the Separation of Powers in Africa: Looking forward', in C. M. Fombad (ed.), *The Separation of Powers in African Constitutionalism* (Oxford University Press, 2016), p. 385.

4.2.2 Development

Since *Colegrove*, the Supreme Court has changed its stance on redistricting, but even more so in other areas. It has addressed what were initially primarily problems of compliance, inaugurating what Abram Chayes in 1976 called the new model of public law litigation in the United States.[31] This new public law litigation, Chayes argued, broke with the traditional paradigm in several ways: First, the new cases had a 'sprawling and amorphous' party structure, no longer representing a bipolar conflict. This party-structure influenced the scope of the lawsuit, which was increasingly shaped by the court and the parties rather than corresponding to an established template of litigation. Suits were also no longer primarily retrospective and concerned with adjudicating past wrongs. Instead, they concerned future reforms, and the relief sought was no longer merely compensatory, but prospective, based on considerations of equity and often so broad as to affect others who were not party to the suit. Finally, and as a result, the trial itself increasingly involved negotiation and mediation among multiple stakeholders who worked out a consensual solution to a problem of public policy. In doing so, they were typically supervised by a managerial judge who directed and oversaw the reform process following the judgment, which often involved 'a wide range of outsiders – masters, experts, and oversight personnel'.[32]

Subsequent authors have pointed out that not all of these attributes were as new as Chayes made them out to be. Eisenberg and Yeazell have demonstrated how ongoing supervision of the implementation of judicial decrees, sometimes by judges and sometimes through other newly created institutions, was in fact a fairly routine matter in other fields of law, such as bankruptcy.[33] They argued that what was new about 'new' public law litigation was therefore less the form of the litigation than the kind of rights being enforced and issues tackled: clean sheets for mental patients or hearings for prisoners before parole could be revoked. This is not altogether surprising. Law develops incrementally, and even where there is noticeable change, that change itself is often rooted in some or other part of the established system. But even if certain elements of public law litigation in the United States thus have in fact a longer pedigree in

[31] Chayes, 'Role of the Judge'.

[32] Ibid. at 1284.

[33] T. Eisenberg and S. C. Yeazell, 'The Ordinary and the Extraordinary in Institutional Litigation' (1980) 93:3 *Harvard Law Review* 465.

US legal practice and culture, their combination and the extent of their use in public law litigation as it emerged in the 1960s was nevertheless something new.

The current form of this kind of litigation and its focus on the reform of public institutions developed during the Civil Rights Era. After the US Supreme Court in *Brown v. Board of Education* had famously judged segregated schools to be 'inherently unequal' and struck down segregation in education as unconstitutional, the question was what to do next.[34] In *Brown*, the US Supreme Court had not explained how one should remedy the situation nor indeed how fast. A year later, in *Brown II*, it clarified that desegregation should proceed 'with all deliberate speed'.[35] Political resistance in the South meant that in most areas little happened in response. Some years later, in *Cooper v. Aaron* it showed less patience towards attempts to further delay desegregation by the Arkansas School Board.[36] At the same time, it became clear that remedying segregation was not an easy task. It became patent that simply opening up former white schools to black students did not automatically lead to integration. The question was what to do then. Often faced with recalcitrant school boards, US federal courts first cautiously and later more assertively started to scrutinize school board desegregation plans.[37] Where such plans were found wanting, judges frequently became involved in developing substantive desegregation policies. Yet, even where detailed policies were developed in cooperation with a judge or directly ordered from the bench, they often met with resistance. Compliance was at risk. Judges thus increasingly stayed involved in those cases over longer time periods, supervising the reform efforts of school boards in response to the judicial decree. In this new role, they felt compelled first to order and then to supervise the redrawing of school districts, the reallocation of students, the establishment of remedial education programs and, not least, the particularly unpopular policy of busing students to particular schools to ensure de facto integrated educational facilities. All of this involved expansive and detailed judicial intervention, including, in some extreme cases, judicial orders to increase particular taxes to fund necessary

[34] *Brown v. Board of Education of Topeka*, 347 U.S. 483 (1954) (US Supreme Court).

[35] *Brown v. Board of Education of Topeka*, 349 U.S. 294 (1955) (US Supreme Court).

[36] *Cooper v. Aaron*, 358 U.S. 1 (1958) (US Supreme Court).

[37] See for a short history C. F. Sabel and W. H. Simon, 'Destabilization Rights: How Public Law Litigation Succeeds' (2004) 117 *Harvard Law Review* 1016; see also for individual accounts J. Bass, *Unlikely Heroes* (University Alabama Press, 1990).

improvements.[38] This style of judicial involvement subsequently spread to other areas of law where existing institutions were found in need of structural reform. Foremost among them were mental hospitals and prisons, the police, public housing and increasingly even private employers.[39]

But public law litigation or structural reform litigation encountered fierce resistance in some quarters and was decried as deeply inappropriate judicial activism. Indeed, by the time Chayes wrote his seminal Harvard Law Review foreword in 1976, some features of the new model were already being rolled back. The process gathered speed in the 1980s and thereafter under the influence of more conservative Supreme Court majorities. Such rollbacks concerned several areas of relevance to institutional litigation,[40] including questions of representation and thus the ability to bring class action suits, standing (public interest standing),[41] the ability to order broad remedies (since the *Milliken* decision in 1974)[42] and the temporal reach of injunctions (*Horne v. Flores* in 2009)[43]. Legislative changes further contributed to the trend towards judicial restraint. The Prison Litigation Reform Act of 1996, for example, required courts to grant relief only insofar as it constituted the least intrusive means to correct the violation of rights[44] – and thus makes for an explicit example of a proportionality approach to the choice of judicial remedies, as Kent Roach advocates more broadly today.[45]

Insofar as it persists as a tool for institutional reform for litigators in many state and federal courts in the United States, public law litigation has changed since the 1970s. As Simon and Sabel argued in their much-cited article 'Destabilization Rights', compared to earlier eras, public law

[38] *Missouri v. Jenkins*, 515 U.S. 70 (1995) (subsequently struck down) (US Supreme Court).

[39] Sabel and Simon, 'Destabilization Rights'.

[40] For a summary see M. Kelley, 'Saving 60(b)(5): The Future of Institutional Reform Litigation' (2015) 125 *The Yale Law Journal* 272–312. See also J. C. Coffee, *Entrepreneurial Litigation: Its Rise, Fall, and Future* (Harvard University Press, 2015) with regard to class actions in particular.

[41] *Lujan v. Defenders of Wildlife*, 504 U.S. 555, 112 S. Ct. 2130 (1992) (US Supreme Court), see on this C. R. Sunstein, 'What's Standing After Lujan? Of Citizen Suits, "Injuries," and Article III' (1992) 91:2 *Michigan Law Review* 163.

[42] *Milliken v. Bradley*, 418 U.S. 717 (1974), see *City of Los Angeles v. Lyons*, 461 U.S. 95 (1983); *Missouri v. Jenkins*, 515 U.S. 70 (1995) (US Supreme Court).

[43] *Horne v. Flores*, 557 U.S. 433 (2009) (US Supreme Court).

[44] Prison Litigation Reform Act (PLRA), 42 U.S.C. § 1997e.

[45] K. Roach, *Remedies for Human Rights Violations: A Two-Track Approach to Supranational and National Law (Cambridge Studies on Constitutional Law, Vol. 27)* (Cambridge University Press, 2021), Introduction.

litigation now follows less of a 'command-and-control model' and more of an 'experimentalist' one with regard to the remedies chosen.[46] This new experimentalist model involves greater reliance on negotiation among the stakeholders and the establishment of rolling rule regimes, leading to the setting of provisional rules only, subject to regular reassessment and potential revision and finally a higher degree of transparency.

4.2.3 *Framing and Scholarly Evaluation*

In spite of some scepticism, Chayes in 1976 offered a cautious defence of the public interest model.[47] Ultimately, he argued, the model enabled judges, endowed with professional authority and independence from bureaucracy and the political process, to give a voice to those aggrieved and tap energies outside of the government to solve pressing problems. In another now-canonical article in the Harvard Law Review, Owen Fiss set out to analyze and defend the new developments in even stronger terms. Fiss argued that the new model simply enabled judges to realize what had been their task all along: to articulate and implement constitutional values.[48] His was thus essentially an argument about implied powers of courts combined with a purposive approach to constitutional rights in the context of the emergence of large-scale organizations within modern societies.[49]

But not everyone supported the new trend as Chayes and Fiss did. Unsurprisingly, the scholarly community in the US has been and remains highly divided on the matter. Partly, this division is due to underlying ideological differences. Progressives sympathetic with the civil rights movement have tended to defend public law litigation, whereas conservatives have tended to be more sceptical for reasons of federalism, the separation of powers and the preservation of the capacity and independence of courts as neutral arbiters. But the lines were not always clear-cut. Among the critics, Lon Fuller's article 'The Forms and Limits of Adjudication' from 1978 turned out to be particularly influential, though it was written in the 1950s and didn't yet address US public law

[46] Sabel and Simon, 'Destabilization Rights', at 1016.

[47] Chayes, 'Role of the Judge'.

[48] O. M. Fiss, 'Foreword: The Forms of Justice' (1979) 93:1 *Harvard Law Review* 1.

[49] Ibid. at 36; another influential account was P. J. Mishkin, 'Federal Courts as State Reformers' (1978) 35:4 *Washington and Lee Law Review* 949.

litigation.[50] Fuller doubted the capacity of judges to adequately tackle structural reform issues, which he understood as polycentric matters not suitable for adjudication.[51] Problematizing the new 'managerial role' of judges in public law litigation, Judith Resnik drew attention to how considerations of efficiency had become increasingly important both during the trial and during the post-trial management. Judges now had to take into account not merely how to design a suitable remedy but how to assess the effect of their decisions on non-parties.[52] With the need for efficiency came a trend towards experimentation and more informal exchanges between judges and the parties, Resnik pointed out, thus challenging the traditional role of judges to serve as independent neutral arbiters. 'Seduced by controlled calendars, disposition statistics, and other trappings of the efficiency era and the high-tech age, managerial judges are changing the nature of their work,' Resnik concluded on a sceptical note.[53] At the same time, the increasing use of external monitors, masters and/or facilitators to supervise subsequent reform processes in US litigation responded partly to Resnik's concerns. By removing the judge from the day-to-day supervision of reform efforts, it is easier for her to preserve distance to the parties and remain an impartial arbitrator rather than an efficient manager of the process. That said, it is not surprising that US public law litigation remains contested and has been rolled back by conservative lawmakers and judges.[54]

What were the arguments for public law litigation? Since the early school desegregation cases, securing compliance under conditions where it could not be taken for granted has always been one prominent argument for structural reform litigation. As we will see below, this echoes more recent Global South approaches, in particular in South Africa. Another argument that played a role in the defense of public law litigation was narrower – and it too finds immediate parallels in contemporary discourse on Global South judicial activism. It was the idea, built on Carolene's famous Footnote Four,[55] that judicial scrutiny should be

[50] L. L. Fuller and K. I. Winston, 'The Forms and Limits of Adjudication' (1978) 92:2 *Harvard Law Review* 353.

[51] Ibid., at 371 and throughout.

[52] J. Resnik, 'Managerial Judges' (1982) 96:2 *Harvard Law Review* 374.

[53] Ibid., at 445.

[54] See, e.g., for a critical account R. Sandler and D. Schoenbrod, *Democracy by Decree: What Happens When Courts Run Government* (Yale University Press, 2003); see also Coffee, *Entrepreneurial Litigation.*

[55] *United States v. Carolene Products Company*, 304 U.S. 144 (1938) (US Supreme Court).

particularly searching when dealing with laws that either restricted the political process or displayed prejudice against 'discrete and insular minorities' that were not adequately represented in the ordinary democratic process.[56] As scholars noted, at least some of the early Warren Court's activism could be understood and defended in terms of Footnote Four, that is as judicial intervention in cases of 'legislative failure'.[57] However, this line of defence seemed hardly applicable for the range of new fields of judicial activity federal courts had started to embark upon by the late 1970s, as Owen Fiss remarked early on. But if legislative failure and the theory of representation fit badly with some of the new developments, the answer was not necessarily to turn towards a broader theory of adjudication, as Fiss suggested. Instead, it was possible to generalize the idea of legislative failure into a broader concept of institutional failure. In this vein, William Fletcher, then professor at Berkeley, today federal judge, argued in 1982 in the Yale Law Journal that the 'only legitimate basis for a federal judge to take over the political function in devising or choosing a remedy in an institutional suit is the demonstrated unwillingness or incapacity of the political body'.[58] Though generally sceptical of the wide discretion exercised by judges in the remedial phase of institutional reform litigation, Fletcher thought that an exception should apply in particularly egregious cases of political failure where no alternative to federal court intervention existed. In this case, and only this case, were judges justified in taking over political functions temporarily. Unfortunately, Fletcher did not set out to define more precisely what constituted an egregious political failure, pointing out that this would be a matter of subtle judgment, with many cases falling into a grey area.[59]

More than twenty years later, Simon and Sabel proffered a similar justification for their remedy of choice – institutional destabilization.[60] They advocated destabilization in those cases where an existing institution is 'failing to satisfy minimum standards of adequate performance and, second, is substantially immune from conventional political mechanisms of correction'. Unlike Fletcher, Simon and Sabel gave more thought to defining what constituted minimum standards of adequate

[56] J. H. Ely, *Democracy and Distrust: A Theory of Judicial Review* (Harvard University Press, 1980).
[57] Fiss, 'Foreword', at 6.
[58] W. A. Fletcher, 'The Discretionary Constitution: Institutional Remedies and Judicial Legitimacy' (1982) 91:4 *The Yale Law Journal* 635–97.
[59] Ibid., at 694–5.
[60] Sabel and Simon, 'Destabilization Rights', at 1062.

performance and immunity from the conventional democratic process. The failure to meet minimum standards, they thought, represented the least problematic element of their account, partly because in practice, state officials often acknowledged that problems existed, and partly because institutional performance could be measured against 'industry standards', for example performance standards, rules and guidelines developed by professional associations and within the administration itself. Immunity from the political process arose, they argued, in three cases: One concerned the case of majorities unresponsive to the demands of vulnerable and stigmatized minorities. The second case concerned situations where powerful concentrated groups exploited or disregarded the interests of diffuse majorities with individually smaller stakes, that is classical collective action problems as they arise in the case of regulatory capture of governmental agencies. The third example for immunity was the hardest to capture. Simon and Sabel referred here to 'the prisoner's dilemma, (where) groups are caught in a low-level equilibrium that is susceptible to beneficial improvement, but only through a kind of coordination that existing institutions are inadequate to induce'.[61] Their concern here is thus primarily with coordination problems, where multiple actors need to work together to induce change. Even though all may be broadly sympathetic to reform, the necessary coordination between them is not possible without some external push as provided by a court. Though their account is – in this regard – more normative than descriptive, we will see elements of these requirements for institutional destabilization recur both in the global literature and within the jurisprudence of certain courts.

4.2.4 Conclusion

In the United States, structural reform litigation emerged first in the context of resistance to the implementation of civil rights for black citizens. Over time, however, resistance was often no longer the key problem. Rather, as Charles Epp writes in *Making Rights Real*, in the later phase of structural reform litigation, officials often themselves recognized that existing problems constituted 'fundamental threats to their public and professional legitimacy', thus prompting them more often than not to cooperate in court-controlled reform projects.[62]

[61] Ibid., at 1065.

[62] Ch. Epp, *Making Rights Real: Activists, Bureaucrats, and the Creation of the Legalistic State* (Chicago University Press, 2009), at 1.

Courts thus often addressed cases of incapacity – resulting from different causes – rather than straightforward or pure cases of resistance.

4.3 Structural Reform Litigation Beyond the United States

The United States is no outlier when it comes to structural reform litigation. The list of jurisdictions in which this style of litigation has been making inroads is considerable. It includes not just domestic courts but international ones as well. Thus, the Inter-American Court of Human Rights, building on the work of the Inter-American Commission, is well known for its creative approach to remedies, including the long-term supervision of the implementation of its judgments.[63] And in the last twenty years, even the European Court of Human Rights has increasingly followed suit with its development of the pilot procedure and a more expansive approach to judicial remedies.[64]

In the jurisdictions I cover in this book, structural reform litigation routinely emerges in the context of broader political changes and against the background of a loss of trust in democratic institutions, whether justified or not.

Start by considering the South African case. In its early years, the South African Constitutional Court exercised its powers in a relatively balanced and often restrained manner, which drew a fair amount of criticism from South African commentators.[65] James Fowkes describes this line of jurisprudence as an exercise in constitutionalism based on the idea of building trust. In a newly emerging democracy, Fowkes argues, it is constitutionally ideal if courts can act in ways that express trust in other institutions to do their own jobs, which builds the constitution in a rich sense. It is when the basis for this trust weakens, and not merely when constitutional violations occur, that courts will have to intervene,

[63] T. M. Antkowiak, 'Remedial Approaches to Human Rights Violations: The Inter-American Court of Human Rights and Beyond' (2007), 46 *Colum. J. Transnat'l L.* 351.

[64] D. Kurban, 'Forsaking Individual Justice: The Implications of the European Court of Human Rights' Pilot Judgment Procedure for Victims of Gross and Systematic Violations' (2016) 16:4 *Human Rights Law Review* 731–69; Huneeus, 'Reforming the State' at 1.

[65] For the only two comprehensive assessments of the Courts jurisprudence over time, see T. Roux, *The Politics of Principle: The First South African Constitutional Court, 1995–2005* (Cambridge University Press, 2013) and J. Fowkes, *Building the Constitution: The Practice of Constitutional Interpretation in Post-Apartheid South Africa* (Cambridge University Press, 2016).

including using structural orders where necessary.[66] And indeed, in the last fifteen years, trust in the government has frayed considerably in South Africa, in light of widespread corruption under the Zuma administration from 2009 onwards and a sense of dysfunctionality in certain areas. In response to this situation, South African courts have increasingly criticized the government and started to experiment with more expansive remedies, some of which are familiar from the US and Indian context. They have inter alia issued increasingly detailed mandatory orders, provided for long-term supervision of reform processes, ordered the filing of regular reports, appointed external overseers, threatened contempt of court proceedings against individuals and – perhaps most creatively – remade the legal framework for implementing money orders against the state.

The Colombian Constitutional Court's jurisprudence developed in an even more extreme setting. It emerged against a background of the ongoing civil war and widespread violence in the country as well as a high degree of political polarization and fragmentation hampering the functioning of Colombian political institutions. In this situation, so commentators and the Court itself have argued, it fell to the Constitutional Court to realize constitutional values. Much like in India, Colombian jurisprudence is therefore shaped by a pervasive sense of generalized distrust in the political system, as David Landau in particular has emphasized.[67] The Indian story of the rise of public interest litigation (PIL) echoes this sense of rising distrust in India's political system, in response to Indira Gandhi's unpopular emergency regime, albeit with the particular twist of the Indian Supreme Court itself seeking rehabilitation after its failure to protect rights adequately during that time.[68]

Beyond those similar origins, there are also considerable differences between these jurisdictions, however. Though in most of them a range of factors are at play in driving the development of structural reform litigation, certain themes are more prominent in some than others. Thus, while arguments from failure play a role in all of these systems at some level, failure is sometimes understood more narrowly and sometimes more broadly. In South Africa, structural reform litigation, as it has

[66] Fowkes, *Building the Constitution*, Introduction (and throughout).

[67] D. Landau, 'Political Institutions and Judicial Role in Comparative Constitutional Law' (2010) 51:2 *Harvard International Law Journal* 319 at 319, and elsewhere.

[68] U. Baxi, 'Taking Suffering Seriously: Social Action Litigation in the Supreme Court of India' (1985) 6 *Third World Legal Studies* 107; S. P. Sathe, *Judicial Activism in India: Transgressing Borders and Enforcing Limits* (New Delhi/New York: Oxford University Press, 2nd ed., 2003), p. 12.

emerged to date, typically responds to concrete failures to implement specific previous judgments rather than in response to a general assessment of the political system as dysfunctional. This stands in some contrast to the Indian approach, which – while also targeting governmental lawlessness and problems with implementation – has long been embedded in a broader critique of Indian politics. Perhaps not accidentally, it is also in India where public reform litigation displays its most problematic side and has consequently received much criticism from academics.

4.3.1 Non-compliance in South Africa

Helen Taylor has described the threat of non-compliance as a key catalyst for remedial innovation in South Africa.[69] Mirroring Art. 142 of the Indian Constitution, Section 172 of the South African Constitution explicitly authorizes courts to 'make any order that is just and equitable' and thus provides a textual basis for remedial innovation. Yet, the South African Court has so far not interpreted this power as broadly as Indian courts have, though this may be changing.

The implementation of judgments has for some time been a matter of concern in South African jurisprudence. Somewhat ironically, the South African Constitutional Court's most internationally famous decision in *Makwanyane*, declaring the death penalty unconstitutional, was not implemented for a long time, because authorities failed to provide for the resentencing of those prisoners previously sentenced to death. In response, the South African Constitutional Court ultimately had to set out a structural interdict ordering the government to take a series of steps and report back to the Court, resolving the case successfully in the end.[70]

Threats of non-compliance with judicial orders have also played a role at the interpretive stage, shaping the deference accorded to a pre-

[69] H. Taylor, 'Forcing the Court's Remedial Hand: Non-compliance as a Catalyst for Remedial Innovation' (2019) 9:1 *Constitutional Court Review* 247; see similarly on non-compliance as a key factor in the South African jurisprudence S. Liebenberg, 'The Art of the (Im)Possible? Justice Froneman's Contribution to Designing Remedies for Structural Human Rights Violations' (2022) 12:1 *Constitutional Court Review* 137 at 149; G. Mukherjee and J. Tuovinen, 'Designing Remedies for a Recalcitrant Administration' (2020) 36:4 *South African Journal on Human Rights* 386 at 391 f.

[70] *Sibiya and Others v. Director of Public Prosecutions: Johannesburg High Court and Others*, CCT 45/04 [2005] ZACC 16 (7 October 2005) and *Sibiya and Others v. Director of Public Prosecutions*, CCT 45/04B [2006] ZACC 22 (30 November 2006) (South African Constitutional Court).

constitutional law that prohibited the attachment of state assets in judgments for money orders against the state as opposed to those against private persons. The plaintiff in that case, Nyathi, had been mistreated in a public hospital. He had sued successfully for the medical costs resulting from the care he subsequently required, but had not been paid fully, and as a result was unable to pay for his care and died.[71] Pointing to the 'systemic failure of state officials to perform their duties' and 'the (unacceptable) failure of the state to edify its functionaries about the very legislation which governs their duties,' as evidenced by some over 200 cases of non-payment of judgment debts (no precise number could be given),[72] the South African Court struck down the statute prohibiting the attachment of state assets as unconstitutional, albeit suspending the order to give parliament time to address the issue. It also ordered the government to draw up a list of all unsatisfied court orders to date and develop a plan to address their speedy settlement with the Court monitoring progress – a very expansive remedy, in what was formally an individual case dealing with one particular failure to pay, albeit a repeated failure. However, as the litigation demonstrated, the case was representative of a much broader pattern of non-compliance with monetary orders made by courts. The Court traced this pattern back to a broader failure of the government to establish an effective mechanism allowing for the payment of judgment debts even though '(t)here is a desperate need for legislation to be enacted that will specifically target the areas of concern outlined in this judgment. The apathy of state officials in their failure to pay judgment debts cannot be addressed unless progressive, targeted steps are taken towards solving these problems'.[73]

Problems with governmental payments have also been at the heart of a range of other cases, concerning the discontinuation of disability payments[74] and the refusal to pay arrears after reinstatement of

[71] *Nyathi v. Member of the Executive Council for the Department of Health Gauteng and Another*, CCT 19/07 [2008] ZACC 8 (2 June 2008) (South African Constitutional Court).
[72] ibid., para. 79
[73] ibid., para. 74.
[74] One such case (*Njongi v. Member of the Executive Council, Department of Welfare, Eastern Cape*, CCT 37/07 [2008] ZACC 4 (28 March 2008) (South African Constitutional Court)) eventually reached the Constitutional Court in 2008 which once again remarked in harsh words on the failure of the provincial government to administer the payments: 'All this speaks of a contempt for people and process that does not befit an organ of government under our constitutional dispensation. . . .The province's approach to these proceedings was contradictory, cynical, expedient and obstructionist' (ibid., para. 20).

welfare grants. In particular, the chronic mismanagement and dysfunction of the South African Social Security Agency (SASSA) led to a series of detailed and expansive judgments by an increasingly impatient and irate Constitutional Court.[75] In these and other cases, there is a clear trend towards broader arguments from failure, such as in the context of education, where institutional failure has been particularly rampant in South Africa, manifesting in the persistent lack of school buildings, furniture and teachers in some parts of the country.[76] South African legal NGOs have been litigating some of the worst cases with considerable success. Several of these cases resulted in settlements between the parties, which were subsequently incorporated into the judicial order. A number of these judgments have been quite expansive, with courts providing step-by-step instructions for necessary reforms, sometimes requiring regular reports to the court, sometimes involving external experts such as auditors and special masters.[77] One of the most far-reaching judgments that explicitly discussed the Court's role was *Mwelase*. This dealt with a case where plaintiffs claimed a violation of their constitutional rights because the government had failed to process their claims to be granted property rights as land tenants, as provided for in the respective statutory provisions. Given the government's failure to act for several years, the Land Claims Court had appointed a special master to help process the claims in question. This order was then overturned by the Supreme Court of Appeal on separation of powers

[75] *Allpay Consolidated Investment Holdings (Pty) Ltd and Others v. Chief Executive Officer of the South African Social Security Agency and Others* (*Allpay I*) CCT 48/13 [2013] ZACC 42 (29 November 2013); *Allpay Consolidated Investment Holdings (Pty) Ltd and Others v. Chief Executive Officer of the South African Social Security Agency and Others (Allpay II)* CCT 48/13A [2014] ZACC 12 (17 April 2014); *Black Sash Trust v. Minister of Social Development and Others (Black Sash I)* CCT 48/17 [2017] ZACC 8; 2017 (5) BCLR 543 (CC); 2017 (3) SA 335 (CC) (17 March 2017); *Black Sash Trust v. Minister of Social Development and Others (Black Sash II)* CCT 48/17 [2018] ZACC 36 (27 September 2018); *South African Social Security Agency and Another v. Minister of Social Development and Others (SASSA)* CCT 48/17 [2018] ZACC 26 (30 August 2018) (South African Constitutional Court).

[76] For an overview of the situation and ongoing litigation, see Legal Resources Center, *A Legal Resource for Realising the Right to Education*, 2015, https://lrc.org.za/fighting-to-learn/.

[77] Taylor, 'Forcing the Court's Remedial Hand'; see also Mukherjee and Tuovinen, 'Designing Remedies'.

grounds, but was restored by the Constitutional Court.[78] Tuovinen and Mukherjee show that the Court relied on a range of different factors in its judgment, that is the threat of non-compliance, the degree of harm by non-grant/consequentialism, the clarity of remedial steps, the underlying issue's salience and systematicity, the personal conduct of government officials, the extent of diffusion of powers in cooperative government, its institutional fit and epistemic superiority and the nature and functions of the invasive remedy.[79] While the Court thus argued that the separation of powers should not be understood to block courts from ensuring effective remedies,[80] which could be understood to drive a relatively free-wheeling attitude, it has overall adopted a nuanced and reflective approach. Expansive remedies require specific justification in individual cases rather than relying on a generalist critique of the government. In other words, where South African judges have set out structural interdicts, for example, they have routinely made the case that the situation is in some ways exceptional and thus merits a particularly intrusive remedy; in contrast, where this was not the case, they have been more restrained.[81] Like its Indian and Colombian counterparts, the South African Constitutional Court has also experimented with dialogic remedial approaches, developing in particular the so-called engagement remedy. Originally created to deal with eviction cases, it has the parties engage with each other in a meaningful way to come up with a mutually acceptable solution that will be subject to the Court's scrutiny.[82] Perhaps as a result of this careful approach, the South African jurisprudence is seldom criticized for going too far.

[78] *Mwelase and Others v. Director-General for the Department of Rural Development and Land Reform and Another (Mwelase)*, CCT 232/18 [2019] ZACC 30 (20 August 2019) (South African Constitutional Court).

[79] Mukherjee and Tuovinen, 'Designing Remedies'.

[80] *Mwelase*, para. 36.

[81] Fowkes, *Building the Constitution*, chapter 8 (in particular).

[82] E.g., Occupiers of 51 Olivia Road, Berea Twp. and 197 Main St. Johannesburg v. City of Johannesburg & Others 2008 (3) SA 208 (CC); Residents of Joe Slovo Cmty., Western Cape v. Thubelisha Homes & Others 2010 (3) SA 454 (CC); S. Liebenberg, 'Engaging the Paradoxes of the Universal and Particular in Human Rights Adjudication: The Possibilities and Pitfalls of "Meaningful Engagement"' (2012) 12 *African Human Rights Law Journal* 1.

4.3.2 *Failure and Good Governance in India*

Contrast this with the Indian case. Like US public law litigation, Indian PIL has shifted and developed over time. Indian commentators identify two or three phases of PIL. Key to the first phase were innovations in relation to standing, allowing publicly interested citizens to litigate issues on behalf of other citizens or the public good.[83] The idea behind this expansion of standing was initially to expand access to court and allow for judicial involvement on behalf of suffering marginalized groups, who would not normally approach the court on their own. Among those groups were, for example, prisoners, migrant labourers, pavement dwellers, children and mentally ill persons.[84] Though other procedural innovations accompanied the development of PIL – evidentiary standards were relaxed and the adversarial model disapplied in favour of a more collaborative process of problem-solving, often by involving other lawyers, technical experts and sometimes civil society activists in the judicial process – it is nevertheless important that PIL began with a concern for marginalized and vulnerable groups against the backdrop of concerns that their rights and interests were being persistently neglected by political actors. Thus, even at the beginning, Indian PIL responded to a broader political problem rather than individual instances of non-compliance with specific judgments.

This key feature of Indian PIL did not change in the second and third phases; indeed, if anything, failure assumed an even broader meaning here. According to the Indian Supreme Court, the second phase started in the 1990s, with a focus on issues such as the protection of the environment (clean air and vehicle regulation, pollution in forests and rivers) and historical monuments (such as the Taj Mahal). In a third phase, PIL increasingly deals with addressing broader good governance themes such as corruption and removal of illegal buildings, waste and slums.[85] In the literature, these latter two phases are often bundled into one and understood as the conservative turn in PIL, insofar as the kind of interests that

[83] A. K. Thiruvengadam, 'Swallowing a Bitter PIL? Reflections on Progressive Strategies for Public Interest Litigation in India', in O. Vilhena and others (eds.), *Transformative Constitutionalism: Comparing the Apex Courts in Brazil, India and South Africa* (Pretoria University Press, 2013), chapter 23, p. 519.

[84] Ibid., at 520.

[85] S. Muralidhar, 'Public Interest Litigation' (1997–1998) 33–4 *Annual Survey of Indian Law*, 525.

are litigated reflected more often than not middle-class concerns rather than those of particularly poor or vulnerable social groups.[86]

These developments were from the start accompanied by judicial and scholarly discourses of failure – indeed more so than in the other systems discussed here. Thus, Chief Justice Balakrishnan explicitly invoked state failure as a basis for the Court's increased activism in a speech in 2008:

> It is often argued that the Supreme Court should maintain restraint and should not violate the legitimate limits in the exercise of its powers. However, this argument fails to recognize the constant failures of governance taking place at the hands of the other organs of State, and that it is the function of the Court to check, balance and correct any failure arising out of any other State organ.[87]

Even in judgments themselves, references to governmental failures as a basis for judicial intervention abound. For example, in a 2016 judgment dealing with the response to a drought in many parts of India, the Supreme Court made a number of far-reaching orders, including the establishment of a National Disaster Response Force and Fund, which it justified in the following way:

> Public interest litigation presents the Court with an issue based problem concerning society and solutions need to be found to that problem within the legal framework. Sometimes, the cause of the problem is bureaucratic inactivity and apathy; sometimes executive excesses that cause the problem and sometimes the problem is caused by the ostrich-like reaction of the executive. These situations represent the broad contours of public interest issues brought to the notice of the Court, and these are the kind of issues for which we need to search for solutions.[88]

More often than not, however, the Indian Supreme Court confines itself to short remarks criticizing the government in harsh terms, as in a 2018 case concerning the preservation of the Taj Mahal, India's most famous historical monument: 'We wonder how the pristine beauty of Taj

86 Thiruvengadam, 'Swallowing a Bitter PIL?'; see also V. Gauri, 'Public Interest Litigation in India: Overreaching or Underachieving?' (2009) *The World Bank Policy Research Working Paper* 5109.

87 S. K. G. Balakrishnan, 'Address at Kerala Legislative Assembly, Golden Jubilee Celebrations 2007–2008', *Seminar on 'Legislature, Executive, and Judiciary'* (Apr. 26, 2008), quoted acc. to N. Robinson, 'Expanding Judiciaries: India and the Rise of the Good Governance Court' (2009) 8 *Washington University Global Studies Law Review* 1 at 17.

88 *Kalika Prasad Kala v. State of Uttarakhand and Others*, Writ Petition (PIL) No. 01 of 2015, para. 22 (Uttaranchal High Court, India).

Mahal as mentioned by the Standing Committee of the Parliament can ever be preserved or protected, if there is no willingness on the part of the concerned authorities to take any positive steps, but on the other hand, to take steps which appear to have more of a negative impact.'[89]

Academics have understood the Indian courts' activism in similar terms. Already in 1985, Upendra Baxi remarked that the new trend of PIL with its appeal to the people came at a time 'when other institutions of governance are facing a legitimation crisis'[90]. Yet, for Baxi the crisis was two-fold. First, there was the failure of liberal legalism to address and combat the oppression and exploitation of India's marginalized classes. Second, Baxi criticized the widespread practice of governmental lawlessness.[91] PIL, as it emerged, could be understood primarily as an attempt to address in particular the first kind of failure, by taking, as Baxi put it, the suffering of many Indian citizens seriously. In contrast, the later phases of PIL have been framed more broadly in terms of combating governmental lawlessness and governance failure, no longer necessarily tied to the protection of the rights of marginalized groups. Thus, according to Manoj Mate, '[j]udicial activism in the post-1990 era stemmed from a desire to address the Executive and Parliament's critical governance failures in the following areas: judicial administration, corruption, accountable environmental policy, and human rights'.[92]

Nick Robinson has similarly explained the Indian Supreme Court's activism as a response to the real and perceived shortcomings of Indian representative institutions, in particular the malfunctioning, fragmented and at least partly corrupt Indian parliament. He reads both the Court's development of the basic structure doctrine (safeguarding the unamendability of a core of Indian constitutional law) and its right-to-life jurisprudence as evidence of the Indian Court's self-understanding of its task as ensuring 'good governance'.[93] Another prominent commentator and constitutional scholar, Pratap Bhanu Mehta, has in this context spoken of a jurisprudence of 'exasperation': 'The function of law in this view is to express, both literally and figuratively, exasperation at the state of affairs. This is not a jurisprudence based on a concern for the formal

89 *M.C. Mehta (Taj Trapezium Matter) v. Union of India*, (1997) 2 S.C.C. 353 (Supreme Court of India).

90 Baxi, 'Taking Suffering Seriously', at 107.

91 Ibid., at 107.

92 M. Mate, 'The Rise of Judicial Governance in the Supreme Court of India' (2015) 33 *Boston University International Law Journal* 169 at 187.

93 Robinson, 'Expanding Judiciaries'.

allocation of powers. Nor does it consider carefully the actual consequences of law. Rather, it expresses a certain impatience with reality.'[94]

In addition, Anuj Bhuwania has demonstrated convincingly how Indian PIL is today not infrequently directed against the interests of those groups formerly meant to benefit from it, such as slum dwellers and other groups of urban poor.[95] He explains the Court's adoption of PIL as an imitation of the Indian government's populist style in the 1970s, showing how judges increasingly claimed to speak for the people, as opposed to elected politicians – a trend that can also be observed in other places, including notably in recent times in Brazil.[96]

Bhuwania's account in particular emphasizes the ideological malleability of arguments from failure. This malleability is not confined to the realm of international politics, as the Indian cases demonstrate, but rather is present even where we are dealing with courts enforcing individual rights. This is interesting and important because – as we will see more clearly in Chapter 5 – structural reform litigation is often understood and conceptualized as part of a progressive left agenda. That is, to be fair, where it generally originates, both in the United States as well as in India. Yet, the Indian story emphasizes that this association with a progressive political agenda is not a necessity or indeed fixed for all time. The theme of 'good governance' as it emerges in the 1990s and 2000s as an explanation for Indian judicial activism should be seen as part of the broader trend towards 'good governance' in institutions including the World Bank and associated neoliberal discourses, borne out by the subsequent development of PIL as a middle-class tool, sometimes employed *against* marginalized and vulnerable groups.

4.3.3 *Constitutional Justice in Colombia*

Concerns about compliance play a role in the Colombian story, too. But we also see relatively early signs of broader distrust in the government in the Colombian Court's jurisprudence, often coupled with a general

94 P. B. Mehta, 'Just Impatient: Can a Jurisprudence of Exasperation Sustain the Court's Authority?' *The Telegraph India*, 17 October 2005, https://tinyurl.com/3zun7y6z.

95 A. Bhuwania, *Courting the People: Public Interest Litigation in Post-Emergency India* (Cambridge University Press, 2017), p. 7.

96 D. Werneck Arguelhes, 'Judges Speaking for the People: Judicial Populism Beyond Judicial Decisions', *Verfassungsblog*, 4 May 2017, https://tinyurl.com/32uud729; see also for a broader discussion A. Bernstein and G. Staszewski, 'Judicial Populism' (2021) 106 *Minnesota Law Review* 283.

assertion of a broad role for the Court in realizing constitutional justice. Thus, in an early landmark case dealing with the public health impact of inadequate sewage provisions in nearby poor neighbourhoods, the Court already moved to define its role in the context of the constitutional imperative to realize its vision of justice, but also with reference to the 'dysfunction' of other institutions: 'But this intervention is not only manifest as a necessary mechanism to solve a dysfunction, but also, and above all, as an indispensable element to improve the conditions of communication between law and society, in other words, to favour the achievement of justice (. . .).'[97]

The Court noted that the fact that a sewage system had been planned but not completed indicated that the reason for the inaction was not likely to be due to a straightforward lack of funds. Rather, it pointed to the simple 'blatant neglect' of the issue by local authorities, who had not even bothered to explain their inaction to the Court.[98] In addition to emphasizing the inaction of local authorities, the Court also referred to broader political dysfunction in the legislature: 'The difficulties derived from the unchecked growth of the executive power in the interventionist state and of the loss of political leadership of the legislative organ, must be compensated, in constitutional democracy, by the strengthening of the judicial power (. . .).'[99]

This assessment of legislative dysfunction by the Court has since been bolstered in the academic writings on the subject.[100] Famous for its adoption of a new, less formalist and more teleological approach to interpretation, the decision draws both on the imperative of a transformative thick understanding of constitutionalism and institutional arguments about the dysfunction of political actors to justify robust intervention in the political and administrative process.

This development was also driven by increasing problems with case management that saw Colombian courts in the 2000s confronted with an enormous docket of individual complaints in the form of tutela (similar to the European Court of Human Rights around the same time). The tutela is special for its ease of use, in particular for foregoing

[97] Corte Constitucional [C.C.], Sentencia No. T-406 of 1992 (Colombian Constitutional Court) quoted according to M. J. Cepeda Espinosa and D. Landau, *Colombian Constitutional Law: Leading Cases* (Oxford University Press, 2017), p. 28.

[98] Ibid., p. 32.

[99] Ibid.

[100] Landau, 'Political Institutions'.

requirements of legal representation and for requiring judges to address tutelas within 10 days, thus giving them priority over other cases. Orders can be appealed in higher courts, and the Constitutional Court has discretion to take up any tutelas and address them in its jurisprudence.[101] Since their introduction in the 1991 Constitution, tutelas have become a major avenue for citizens to hold government responsible for a violation of their constitutional rights, in particular as the Colombian Constitutional Court has increasingly done away with the original confinement of tutelas to certain rights only – a process partly driven itself by arguments of governmental failure.[102] Ultimately, it led to the development of the unconstitutional state of affairs doctrine, designed as a way of dealing with hundreds of thousands of tutelas increasingly clogging the judicial system. The Court had already in its famous healthcare decision treated this situation as indicative of persistent governmental failure.[103] In response to that failure, the Court issued a set of individual and expansive structural orders, subject to further monitoring by the Court itself: 'For more than a decade, people have had to resort to tutela actions requesting legal intervention to solve controversies that could have been settled by competent regulatory bodies. This fact clearly points to regulatory failures in the health system, which in turn explains the general orders herein issued to correct them.'[104]

The Court issued a set of far-reaching orders demanding the redesign of the health system to address the problems and failures identified already in previous tutelas, such as clarifying coverage and ensuring access for all to essential medications and treatments while also preserving the financial sustainability of the health system. Moreover, authorities

[101] Cepeda Espinosa and Landau, *Colombian Constitutional Law*, p. 13.

[102] A. E. Yamin, O. Parra-Vera, and C. Gianella, 'Colombia: Judicial Protection of the Right to Health: An Elusive Promise?', in A. E. Yamin and S. Gloppen (eds.), *Litigating Health Rights: Can Courts Bring More Justice to Health?* (Harvard University Press, 2011), p. 103. The Court developed in its early cases what had become known as the 'connectivity doctrine', arguing in essence that where a violation of rights of a non-fundamental character endangered rights that were fundamental under the constitution or when particularly vulnerable persons such as children were concerned, they could nevertheless be enforced with the tutela where authorities had obviously failed to do so. Since then, however, the Court has further expanded the tutela to apply to the right to health independent of its connection to other rights; see Cepeda Espinosa and Landau, *Colombian Constitutional Law*, at 17: Sentencia No. T-706 of 2008.

[103] Cepeda Espinosa and Landau, *Colombian Constitutional Law*, at 170.

[104] Corte Constitucional [C.C.], Sentencia No. T-706 of 2008, cited acc. to Espinosa and Landau, *Colombian Constitutional Law*, at 175–6.

were ordered to involve patient and physician associations to participate in reform efforts, and the order provided for extensive long-term monitoring.[105]

Ultimately then, there are significant overlaps between the jurisprudence of the Colombian Constitutional Court with those of courts in the United States, South Africa and India. With the latter two, Colombia shares a strong transformative vision of constitutionalism, which drives some of the activism we see. But as in India – and increasingly South Africa – there is also a broader background of both general democratic dysfunction and more specific policy failures with regard to pressing social issues.[106] In those conditions, we encounter heightened distrust of political actors, and the failure of other institutions to fulfil their tasks is routinely invoked both by the Constitutional Court and scholars to justify expansive judicial action. However, unlike in South Africa, specific failures of individual officers or institutions seem to play a lesser role. The focus has shifted to broader structural problems, which have not been remedied in the past, but which are also often inherently difficult to remedy – such as the problems in the health system or the improvement of the lives of internally displaced persons (IDPs).

However, the Colombian approach is also more doctrinally structured. With the 'unconstitutional state of affairs' doctrine, the Colombian Court has developed a conceptual tool that has since been adopted by other Latin American courts, such as those in Peru[107] and Brazil.[108] An unconstitutional state of affairs in the jurisprudence of the Court describes the gap between the constitutional commitments and the reality on the ground, which must be so significant that the constitution essentially constitutes a 'dead letter'.[109]

The Court first developed the concept of an unconstitutional state of affairs in 1997.[110] It has since used it a number of times, with varying

105 Espinosa and Landau, *Colombian Constitutional Law*, at 176.

106 E.g. Mukherjee and Tuovinen, 'Designing Remedies'.

107 See TC Nº 3149-2004-AC/TC; Nº 06089-2006-PA/TC; Nº 00017-2008-PI/TC; Nº 03426-2008-HC/TC; Nº 05561-2007-PA/TC; Nº 04539-2012-PA/TC; Nº 00799-2014-PA/TC; Nº 00853-2015-PA/TC; Nº 02744 2015-PA/TC; Nº 00889-2017-PA/TC (Peruvian Constitutional Court).

108 See, e.g., E. A. B. de Oliveira, 'The Unconstitutional State of Affairs in Brazil's Prisons', in R. Becak and J. Lima (eds.), *The Unwritten Brazilian Constitution: Human Rights in the Supremo Tribunal Federal* (Lexington Book, 2021), pp. 233 ff.

109 Corte Constitucional [C.C.], Sentencia No. T-153 of 1998 (Colombian Constitutional Court).

110 Ibid.

degrees of success. Its most well-known application, however, came in what is probably the Colombian Court's globally most famous decision, referenced at the start of this chapter, that is on the rights of IDPs.[111] This concerned persons fleeing from the ongoing Colombian Civil War, whose number had risen to several million people and who largely lived on the outskirts of major cities, such as Bogota, in slums. Though the Colombian government had taken some measures, the number of tutelas seeking to enforce the rights of displaced persons had also risen steadily. In 2004, the Court bundled together 108 of these tutelas filed against different authorities, which primarily concerned issues such as access to housing, employment opportunities, healthcare and education.[112] After organizing several legislative-style hearings of affected persons and civil society groups and experts, the Court declared an unconstitutional state of affairs. In doing so, it set out a six-factor test, while emphasizing that all factors were only indicative. In its own words, these factors were:

> (i) a massive and generalized violation of several constitutional rights, which affects a significant number of people
>
> (ii) a protracted omission by the authorities in complying with their obligations to secure rights
>
> (iii) the adoption of unconstitutional practices, such as the incorporation of the tutela action as part of the procedure to secure the violated rights
>
> (iv) failure to adopt the legislative, administrative or budgetary measures required to prevent the violation of rights
>
> (v) the existence of a social problem whose resolution requires the intervention of several entities, demands the adoption of a complex and coordinated set of actions, and exacts a level of resources that implies an important additional budgetary effort
>
> (vi) if all the persons affected by the same problem were to resort to the tutela action in order to obtain the protection of their rights, a higher judicial congestion would be produced.[113]

This test raises several questions, but it notably includes an element of failure in the form of a 'protracted omission by the authorities in complying with their obligations to secure rights'. That said, the key emphasis is less on criticizing the government – though critique does

[111] Corte Constitucional [C.C.], Sentencia No. T-025 of 2004 (Colombian Constitutional Court).

[112] Espinosa and Landau, *Colombian Constitutional Law*, p. 179.

[113] Corte Constitucional [C.C.], Sentencia No. T-025 of 2004 (Colombian Constitutional Court).

play a role – and more on the structural reasons underlying the problem. In particular, the Court emphasized that 'the origin of such an infringement is not exclusively ascribable to the authorities accused, but also to structural factors' and pointed to the '[l]imited institutional capacity to implement policies and (ii) insufficient funds'. The Court also made clear that the concept of the unconstitutional state of affairs should be considered exceptional, transitory and limited in character ('*cuyo carácter es excepcional, intenso y transitorio*').[114]

If the Court does find an unconstitutional state of affairs, it will usually not only decide on the individual tutelas but issue structural orders to address the underlying broader problem, thus also working to reduce congestion within the judicial system.[115] Because an unconstitutional state of affairs will often require the cooperation of several institutions and actors, remedies will also often be complex and require the assistance and cooperation of multiple authorities and require significant expenditures. The Court has tried not to dictate sums from the bench but rather to ask authorities to set out budgets for specific issues on their own and report back to the court. Often the Court will combine a range of short- and long-term orders, including precautionary and immediate protective measures, while also trying to address the broader problem: by asking the government to set aside sufficient funds; work out the steps to be taken for addressing an issue; order specific agencies and actors, often including civil society actors, to co-operate to address a problem; provide victims with information on their rights; set out specific measures for particularly vulnerable groups such as children or the disabled, and, not least, report back to court regularly on progress achieved and the next steps to be taken.[116]

The supervision of the Court's judgment on internally displaced persons is still ongoing. In 2014, ten years after issuing its judgment, the Court pointed out that much progress had been made but that many problems remained unresolved. Its intervention has provided constant impetus to work towards improving the situation of IDPs in Colombia. Overall, however, scholarship indicates that its success has been mixed.[117]

[114] Corte Constitucional [C.C.], Sentencia No. T-774 of 2015 (Colombian Constitutional Court).

[115] Espinosa and Landau, *Colombian Constitutional Law*, pp. 182 ff.

[116] Ibid.

[117] C. Rodríguez-Garavito, 'Beyond the Courtroom: The Impact of Judicial Activism on Socioeconomic Rights in Latin America' (2011) 89 *Texas Law Review* 1669.

While its general activist approach has often received applause, particular concepts and decisions have been viewed more critically, and this is particularly true for the Court's concept of the unconstitutional state of affairs. Some scholars have pointed out that in transcending the protection of individual rights and allocating or directing the allocation of budgets, the Court assumes the historic role of a parliament and oversteps its own competences on the basis of a somewhat 'naïve' understanding of normativism.[118] Others have also accused the Court of judicial 'populism'.[119] Not least, there have also been concerns regarding the efficiency of the Court's interventions. However, given the alternative of deciding individual rights claims on a case-by-case basis, most attention tends to be directed towards identifying where the court can make a positive impact and in what forms, rather than on targeting the concept of the unconstitutional state of affairs itself on principle.[120]

In the English-language literature on the Colombian Court, two major strands of justification for the Court's interventions have emerged. The first line of thought, put forward most notably by David Landau, provides a general defence of the Colombian Court's activism – regardless of specific cases – as a response to the general dysfunction of the Colombian legislature and thus essentially of Colombian democracy.[121] Landau argues that Colombian political parties lack coherent ideological identities and are built around prominent individuals or families with highly clientelistic tendencies. This frequently makes it impossible to build policy coalitions around certain key issues in the legislature, rendering parliament largely dysfunctional. As a result, policy proposals only rarely come from parties, with the Colombian president instead seeking to legislate, often in the form of emergency decrees, to get things done. And even where coalitions are built to pass certain pieces of legislation, Landau argues, they are often not backed by and do not represent major social forces.[122] Landau also points out that the existence of the above-

[118] N. A. R. Páez, 'La doctrina del estado de cosas inconstitucional en Colombia: Novedades del neoconstitucionalismo y la "inconstitucionalidad de la realidad"' (2012) 1 *Derecho Público Iberoamericano* 243 at 259 f.

[119] N. Figueroa Garcia-Herreros, *A Critique of Populist Jurisprudence: Courts, Democracy, and Constitutional Change in Colombia and Venezuela*, PhD diss., The New School, 2016, pp. 175 ff.

[120] E.g., Rodriguez-Garavito, 'Beyond the Courtroom', at 1689.

[121] Landau, 'Political Institutions', at 335 ff.

[122] Ibid., at 337.

mentioned problems was one of the major drivers for constitutional reform and indeed for the creation of a constitutional court in the 1991 Colombian Constitution.[123] As a result, he argues that the Colombian Court's practice of 'legislative substitution' can be defended in this context.

Another major strand of justification as well as potential limitation of the Court's activism points to the dialogic character of many of the Court's interventions, echoing Simon and Sabel's work on destabilization rights in the United States. Indeed, the Colombian Court has often tried to avoid dictating detailed policy top-down from the bench and has instead sought to create a dialogue between the court and the state as well as plaintiffs and victims of human rights violations. In particular, Roberto Gargarella and Cesar Rodriguez-Garavito have put forward such arguments for dialogic intervention. They argue that by involving state agencies and civil society actors, the Court's interventions have been both more effective than more classical top-down one-time remedies[124] and more normatively defensible on democratic grounds by providing for deliberation and participation of different groups.[125]

4.4 Conclusion

The global expansion of rights and the role of courts have raised expectations of what courts can and should do that go beyond their traditional role. Today, the fact that rights are being violated in a grave manner will often prompt calls for courts to intervene, not just to declare rights violations, but where necessary also to intervene in more expansive ways, such as by actively pushing for structural reform. Such interventions may take the form of direct judicial step-by-step instructions, but they sometimes also take more flexible forms. Courts may either ask parties themselves to work out necessary reforms and/or bring in external supervisors or involve civil society stakeholders, with judges themselves

[123] Ibid., at 338 ff.

[124] Rodriguez-Garavito, 'Beyond the Courtroom'; see also C. Rodríguez-Garavito and D. Rodríguez-Franco, *Radical Deprivation on Trial* (Cambridge University Press, 2015).

[125] R. Gargarella, 'Dialogic Justice in the Enforcement of Social Rights: Some Initial Arguments', in A. E. Yamin and S. Gloppen (eds.), *Litigating Health Rights: Can Courts Bring More Justice to Health?* (Harvard University Press, 2011), p. 232. See also for an ultimately positive assessment of Colombia's model of 'judicial constitutionalism' C. Thornhill and C. Rodrigues de Araújo Calabria, 'Global Constitutionalism and Democracy: The Case of Colombia' (2020) 2 *Jus Cogens* 155–83.

supervising reform efforts at regular intervals. Such judicial interventions raise a host of normative and practical questions. Nevertheless, they have in the last two decades become accepted in a range of legal systems – sometimes more grudgingly than at other times – and have often been defended by both academics and judges themselves in terms of the failure of other institutions to respond appropriately and the need for courts to step in accordingly.

Problems with compliance with particular decisions often drive such developments in concrete cases. But judges engaging in structural reform may also be responding to broader political changes, sometimes self-consciously adopting a populist demeanour by criticizing political elites while styling themselves as the true public servants. In some systems, arguments for structural interventions on the basis of failure may also be combined with other broader arguments about the need for effective realization, sometimes in the context of transformative constitutionalism understood as a call for broader social and political changes. Thus, the more robust judicial interventions portrayed in this chapter speak not only to decreasing trust in state institutions but also to an increasing self-confidence of judges and a sense of optimism and hope for a better future.

5

A Framework for Structural Reform Litigation

5.1 Introduction

It was a cold December night when Cornelio McDonald, a middle-aged black man, was returning home after a visit to his mother. On his way, he had to cross a major road, and waited for a gap to do so. At this point, an unmarked red van pulled up suddenly in front of him, trapping him between two parked cars. The driver rolled down the window and started questioning Mr. McDonald about where he was coming from. When McDonald wanted to know why he was being stopped, the two plain-clothes police officers in the car got out, identified themselves and, without further explanation, began searching him. Asking why he was being searched, Mr. McDonald was informed that the officers wanted to ensure he did not have any weapons. Mr. McDonald objected. Together with eleven other plaintiffs, he subsequently sued the city of New York in a federal class action for its policy of 'stop and frisk', that is stopping and searching people on the street.[1] They argued that the New York Police Department's (NYPD) policy constituted an unconstitutional infringement of their civil rights, in particular, the Fourth Amendment, prohibiting unreasonable searches, and the Fourteenth Amendment, guaranteeing equal protection. Judge Shira Scheindlin at the New York District Court agreed, considering the NYPD's policy of stop-and-frisk an unconstitutional exercise in racial profiling.

So far, so conventional. Yet, the litigation itself was anything but conventional. In a nine-week trial, the District Court analyzed 4.4 million recorded stops by the NYPD between 2004 and 2012, on the basis of officers' reporting forms. It emerged that in spite of a much earlier report of New York's Attorney General, which had found that 15% of police stops in NYC were not based on reasonable suspicion, no action had been taken by the NYPD to change this; indeed, leading officers had not

[1] *Floyd et al. v. City of New York et al.*, 959 F. Supp. 2d 540 (S.D.N.Y. 2013).

even read the report. Instead, the introduction of a new statistics-based performance management system called Compstat had further increased pressure on officers to make a certain number of stops in order to obtain a positive productivity assessment. This was picked up in the media, and the ensuing criticism led to the introduction of a state law prohibiting quotas for stops within the NYPD. Yet, things had hardly changed thereafter. An official memo circulated to all officers made clear that the number of stops would continue to be relevant for their productivity assessment.[2] Considerations of efficiency rather than regard for the legality of stops also characterized further reforms within the NYPD, pointing to an almost complete lack of consideration in the NYPD for the legality of their stop-and-frisk policy. Based on this evidence, Judge Scheindlin concluded that the NYPD employed a policy of indirect racial profiling, which violated New Yorkers' constitutional rights under the Fourth and Fourteenth Amendments.

However, the case did not stop here. In a wholly separate opinion, joining the case with another one on New York police procedure,[3] Judge Scheindlin set out a series of expansive remedies in considerable detail. She ordered the NYPD to revise its existing policies and training in accordance with constitutional standards and New York state law and set out some standards to guide this work, including emphasizing that any stop must be based on individualized suspicion grounded on objective facts ascertained by the police. This explicitly included redrafting the existing forms. To contribute to the reform efforts and supervise them, Judge Scheindlin, moreover, appointed an official monitor who would have to report back to the Court every six months on the progress made. She also ordered New York City to institute a pilot project with body-worn cameras for police officers in parts of the city. Finally, Judge Scheindlin required the city and NYPD to involve community organizations in the reform process, announcing the appointment of a facilitator to that end and requiring that he or she hold 'town hall'-style meetings in the city to get feedback from stakeholders on the proposed course of action. As it stands, this supervision is still ongoing. Meanwhile, the number of stops made by NYPD's police force has decreased significantly without any relevant rise in crime.[4]

[2] *Floyd et al. v. City of New York et al.*, 959 F. Supp. 2d 540 (S.D.N.Y. 2013) at 77.

[3] *Ligon v. City of New York*, 538 Fed. Appx. 101 (2d Circ. 2013) (unpublished opinion, 2013).

[4] For an evaluation of the effects, see, e.g., M. D. White et. al., 'Federal Civil Litigation as an Instrument of Police Reform: A Natural Experiment Exploring the Effects of the Floyd

5.2 Stakes of the Argument

I contended in Part I of this book that arguments from failure may fill gaps by allowing institutions to react to a problem where other institutions are not responsive. Cases like *Floyd*, where there was clearly need for major reform, illustrate this – and accordingly, many progressives argue for judicial intervention in such cases. Ultimately, this is right. But to understand why, the stakes involved need more careful consideration than they often receive in that literature. In particular, we should not view expansive structural remedies simply as a way to provide effective protection of rights, requiring little further justification. Such an approach is too easy. To understand why, it is important to tease out briefly what precisely is normatively at stake in cases involving structural reform litigation along the lines of *Floyd*.

The answer is that it is no less than our core understandings of what a court is and does. Recall Chayes' description of traditional litigation as bipolar, party-initiated and party-controlled, retrospective as well as self-contained, with right and remedy interdependent.[5] Though this formulation breathes the spirit of US common law, with its traditional focus on party control, it is altogether not sharply distinct from Christoph Möllers' description of the judicial function as 'adjudicat(ing) individualized cases on external initiative, retrospectively'.[6] To Möllers, this feature of judicial procedures is key to preserving our individual autonomy, whereas we realize our collective autonomy in wider democratic procedures and institutions. This narrower view of resolving individual disputes, or something like it, encapsulates what both lawyers and laymen usually think of as the judicial function.

Cases like *Floyd* pose a challenge to this traditional idea. Where judges engage in structural reform, they address collective problems. As a result, the court will typically no longer be able to focus on the individual and her complaint as in ordinary judicial processes, where a particular individual and her specific situation and circumstances will be the focus of attention. If courts deal with a case involving hundreds of rights

Ruling on Stop-and-Frisk Activities in New York City' (2016) 14 *Ohio State Journal of Criminal Law* 9; see for regular updates on the ongoing case https://ccrjustice.org/home/what-we-do/our-cases/floyd-et-al-v-city-new-york-et-al.

5 A. Chayes, 'The Role of the Judge in Public Law Litigation' (1976) 89 *Harvard Law Review* 1281.

6 C. Möllers, *The Three Branches: A Comparative Model of Separation of Powers* (Oxford University Press, 2013), p. 89.

violations, the fact that the situation impacts person A in a slightly different way than person B will likely not be the focus of judicial attention. The effort must instead be to find a broader structural solution to the problem at hand. Moreover, as the mode of reasoning shifts to more general problem-solving, typically not fully provided for in existing doctrine or precedent, rights may turn into bargaining chips in policy debates, even if the ultimate aim remains to better realize or protect such rights. Not least, judges can no longer simply take a retrospective decision on whether rights have been violated in the past in such cases. They need to put forward a plan to remedy this situation for the future. As a result, judges will often act in ways that strongly resemble the approaches of legislators or administrators setting out policy.

One response to this might be that we simply need to revise our outdated ideas of judging and courts. Yet, we should resist such a conclusion, even though there is something to be said in favour of a more collaborative understanding of the separation of powers. Judicial intervention along the lines of *Floyd* and similar cases has its place, but should not become the new normal, justified simply in terms of 'making rights real'. For one thing, we should by no means take the effectiveness of judicially driven structural reform for granted. For another, we should be wary about the outcome-based logic at play and the democratic and rule of law stakes involved. As courts issue detailed remedies and/or supervise reform processes over longer time periods, our ability to collectively exercise our autonomy and determine ourselves how we want to live together in a democratic society is diminished. It also puts at risk the ability of judges to keep their distance from the parties and stay impartial, thus preserving their authority as independent dispute solvers. They increasingly risk turning into policy-makers who cannot avoid making political judgments, thus becoming the target of political criticism.[7] Finally, even the constraint that courts only operate on external initiative (from which some systems provide exceptions) – thus distinguishing them from legislators who may pursue their own agenda – may be compromised where judges monitor and evaluate progress on a constant basis. In the *Floyd* litigation, for example, Judge Scheindlin had suggested to litigants in a hearing on a prior case against the NYPD to bring new litigation instead.[8] She, thus, essentially prompted the litigation that followed, behaving more like a proactive administrator

[7] J. Resnik, 'Managerial Judges' (1982) 96:2 *Harvard Law Review* 374.

[8] *Ligon v. City of New York*, 538 Fed. Appx. 101 (2d Circ. 2013).

than an unbiased arbitrator. While *Floyd* was certainly an outlier in this regard and Judge Scheindlin was subsequently removed from the case for that reason,[9] the fact itself speaks to the changing role of judges who become 'managers' exercising significant control over the way the litigation unfolds. Where they seek to avoid this, for example by appointing independent third persons as masters or monitors as in *Floyd*, this provides only a partial fix. They nevertheless stay involved by supervising reform efforts (and these third persons) over longer time periods. Moreover, the holding of town hall meetings through a court-appointed 'facilitator' with 'stakeholders' speaks to the fundamental shift from the rights of individual plaintiffs to the broader interests of the community and stakeholders. And while such moves might have benefitted rights holders in the Floyd litigation, it is easy to see how things might not work out that way every time.

These are just the most important problems and risks associated with courts engaging in structural reform. Not all cases are prone to all of these risks and problems to the same degree. Some remedies are easier to defend than others, and sometimes, the issues at stake make us more willing to take them on. But this doesn't detract from the fact that structural reform should not be considered part of the ordinary arsenal of courts, as something 'normal'. This is true even where the practice may have become commonplace as a result of broad dissatisfaction and a lack of trust in the political system. Structural reform litigation needs to remain an exception, at the very least in normative terms – and this is why arguments from failure matter as a tool to both analytically capture what is going on and distinguish those cases where it provides the right approach from those where it does not.

5.3 Core Requirements

The framework we developed in Part I involved four core questions: (1) whether there is a broader legal framework in place that comes with expectations of mutual collaboration and support; (2) whether there is some violation of law, which has been allowed to persist; (3) whether there is a gap in the existing arrangements rather than a comprehensive framework of government; and (4) finally, a proportionality test. I will start here with the first three before turning to proportionality in Section 5.4.

[9] Ibid.

5.3.1 Collaborative Framework

The first hurdle is typically the lowest one, when it comes to structural reform litigation. At least where the litigation occurs in a domestic context rather than an international one, there is typically room for an argument about the need for collaboration and support.[10] The details will of course depend on individual legal systems, but it seems fair to say that in most constitutional democracies today, the separation of powers is no longer understood in a very rigid manner but in the sense of a broader system of checks and balances. With that comes a sense of mutual responsiveness. Sometimes, explicit constitutional principles such as comity provide broad support to concepts of collaboration. In other cases, a constitution's particular concern with realizing certain values and goals, as is the case in transformative systems, suggests the need for working together to achieve those goals. Yet, even more traditional liberal constitutions, such as the US text with its concern with controlling power, typically leave some room for arguments for responsiveness and collaboration.

This is particularly true when it comes to the role of courts, at least in many legal systems. Though all courts fulfil certain roles in democratic societies – including settling conflicts between private people on the basis of law – different societies and legal systems understand the role of courts differently. This is particularly true in public law, where some courts are a lot more restrained and deferential than others, for example when it comes to constitutional review. Thus, for example, if courts do not engage in constitutional review in a given legal system as a matter of principle, there will usually be no argumentative space for them to engage in structural reform, because their role is understood as narrower in general.

However, where courts routinely exercise constitutional review, their role is often understood to be responsive to the political branches.[11] Thus, Joseph Weiler and Doreen Lustig suggest that 'in some form or another the Ely thesis underlies many current regimes of judicial review within functioning democracies',[12] referring to the idea that courts

[10] On arguments from failure in an international context, see Chapter 7.

[11] R. Dixon, *Responsive Judicial Review: Democracy and Dysfunction in the Modern Age* (Oxford University Press, 2023).

[12] D. Lustig and J. H. H. Weiler, 'Judicial Review in the Contemporary World: Retrospective and Prospective' (2018) 16:2 *International Journal of Constitutional Law* 315, with reference to J. H. Ely, *Democracy and Distrust: A Theory of Judicial Review* (Harvard University Press, 1980).

should intervene when we cannot trust the democratic process. This claim is important in our context not because Ely defended structural reform litigation, but because his broader approach to judging provides a basis for such a defence, and has in fact been relied on to that purpose (see the discussion below in this section). Ely himself was concerned with arguing for a role for courts when it came to political malfunction, rather than institutional failure. He argued that only where democratic processes malfunctioned – because insiders were blocking the channels of democratic change for outsiders or because some outsiders (isolated and discrete minorities) had little chance to prevail in this process – should courts intervene. Ely's argument was very influential in the United States in spite of the criticism levelled against it. It has also proved influential elsewhere, and even where Ely has not been a direct influence, similar ideas are often central to justifying constitutional review.[13]

Ely was concerned first and foremost with political malfunction and the question whether to intervene in the first place, not how to intervene. More recent scholarship has taken a broader approach to the matter. Rosalind Dixon argues that responsive review implies courts should act to secure a democratic minimum core (if necessary, by robust means of intervention), but should also intervene in more routine cases of malfunction where democratic processes suffer from legislative blindspots or burdens of inertia.[14] Central to Dixon's account is her careful attention to tailoring remedies to respond to blockages and malfunction within the political system, ranging from weak form review in some cases to much more robust intervention in others. Similar to Dixon, David Landau has put forward what he describes as an intertemporal account of the judicial role, building on his previous work, defending the expansive jurisprudence of the Colombian Constitutional Court as a response to the dysfunctionality of Colombian democracy.[15] Another commentator, Stephen Gardbaum, not only argues for judicial intervention in cases

[13] R. Dixon and M. Hailbronner, 'Ely in the World: The Global Legacy of Democracy and Distrust Forty Years On' (2021) 19:2 *International Journal of Constitutional Law* 427 and other contributions in the same symposium.

[14] R. Dixon, *Responsive Judicial Review*, p. 3 and throughout; see earlier R. Dixon, 'Creating Dialogue About Socioeconomic Rights: Strong-Form Versus Weak-Form Judicial Review Revisited' (2007) 5:3 *International Journal of Constitutional Law* 391.

[15] D. Landau, 'Institutional Failure and Intertemporal Theories of Judicial Role in the Global South', in D. Bilchitz and D. Landau (eds.), *The Evolution of The Separation of Powers: Between the Global North and the Global South* (Edward Elgar Publishing, 2018), p. 31.

where there is a 'serious violation of one or more core democratic process values or their systematic undermining over time' but also proposes intervention in cases where legislatures fail to hold executives accountable or where independent institutions or the political processes are captured by special interests, as well as in cases of legislative failures to deliberate.[16] Katie Young has argued in the past that courts should act as catalysts, seeking to increase the capacity of political institutions, a thought picked up in recent work by Mark Tushnet and Madhav Khosla, who also advocate a broad role for courts that includes enhancing state capacity.[17] Add to this a host of scholarly voices who support structural reform litigation in certain cases,[18] some of them discussed in Chapter 4. Differences aside, this strand in the literature shares the view that courts should respond to malfunction, however defined. Ideas of broader political malfunction and more specific institutional failures are often blurred in this work – unsurprisingly so, since democratic malfunction may often lead to or at least enable institutional failure, even if they are not the same thing. And if we accept such a broader responsive role for courts, this opens a path for structural reform litigation, at least under certain conditions.

Moreover, as previously noted, in some jurisdictions, we will find clauses granting courts broad leeway in choosing appropriate remedies, which provides an opening for courts to choose expansive and non-conventional remedies where necessary. For example, consider Art. 142 of the Indian Constitution or Sec. 172 of the South African Constitution: 'When deciding a constitutional matter within its power, a court—... may make any order that is just and equitable...' or indeed Sec. 24 of the Canadian Charter, which states: 'Anyone whose rights or freedoms, as guaranteed by this Charter, have been infringed or denied may apply to a court of competent jurisdiction to obtain such remedy as the court considers appropriate and just in the circumstances.' The existence of broad remedial clauses like these provides an argument for judges to adopt structural remedies in the cases specified. However, their absence doesn't rule out such interventions either. And more than that: As such

[16] S. Gardbaum, 'Comparative Political Process Theory' (2020) 18:4 *International Journal of Constitutional Law* 1438.

[17] M. Khosla and M. Tushnet, 'Courts, Constitutionalism, and State Capacity: A Preliminary Inquiry' (2022) 70:1 *The American Journal of Comparative Law* 95.

[18] E.g., G. Mukherjee and J. Tuovinen, 'Designing Remedies for a Recalcitrant Administration' (2020) 36:4 *South African Journal on Human Rights* 386.

provisions are typically framed in a very open manner, they do not conclusively settle the issue of whether courts may step in where other institutions are failing to do their job, given that judicially driven structural reform is problematic not only for its more expansive approach to remedies, but effects broader changes to the judicial process. The existence of such clauses thus provides a path for courts to engage in structural reform, but it should not be understood as giving courts carte blanche for such interventions, independent of further considerations.

5.3.2 *Violation of Law or Democratic Dysfunction*

The second requirement too poses no major hurdle in most cases of structural reform litigation where we are typically dealing with a great number of rights violations. This may be different when it comes to defending the need for certain unconventional procedures deemed necessary to find out if there is a rights violation in the first place – for example, where courts are sending out a group of court-appointed experts to investigate a situation after receiving a newspaper clipping as a complaint. Insofar as the overall goal here is merely to establish the facts needed to make a finding that rights have been violated, this should, however, be understood as part of the judicial role, requiring no further justification in terms of failure, even where it involves some procedural innovations.

It is important to reiterate here, however, that the overall quality of the political system should not – absent a finding of a violation of law – constitute an argument for courts to engage in structural reform.[19] This is not to say that ideas of (broader) democratic failure or dysfunction may not have a role to play in theories of judicial review. But it is one thing to argue with Theunis Roux that judges need to take into account the 'quality of democracy in the society in which they are operating and adapt(ing) their role to changing democratic pathologies'[20] and another

[19] I would associate D. Landau's argument (id., 'Political Institutions and Judicial Role in Comparative Constitutional Law' (2010) 51:2 *Harvard International Law Journal* 319) with such a broader approach. This is not to say that the question whether and how to intervene for courts will trigger different answers of course. Often it won't, but this would be a good thing.

[20] T. Roux, 'In Defence of Empirical Entanglement: The Methodological Flaw in Waldron's Case Against Judicial Review' (2015) 73 *UNSW Law Research Paper*, available at https://papers.ssrn.com/sol3/papers.cfm?abstract_id=2712058; compare also D. Landau, 'A Dynamic Theory of Judicial Role' (2014) 55:5 *Boston College Law Review* 1501.

to issue a carte blanche for courts to engage in structural reform depending on their assessment of politics. Nor is it to say that courts might not intervene to remedy democratic problems in line with theories of responsive review in ordinary ways.[21] It is only an argument to suggest that courts should not adopt the kind of expansive remedies we see in structural reform cases on the basis *merely* of a general assessment of the democratic system. This is because such overall assessments open the door for judicial populism too widely, given the contested nature of democracy as well the fact that many judges will not have the necessary skills to make that kind of judgment (see already Section 2.4.3.2).

There may be some cases where the risks involved with this kind of overall assessment appear to be mediated by the fact that there are certain institutions outside of the fray of party politics that make such assessments, potentially on the international level, such as the Venice Commission. Yet, even such international institutions are not apolitical, and their assessments typically reflect the interests of powerful actors involved in them. Moreover, even where there is arguably a good case for generalized distrust, the question is still what this means for courts with regard to concrete cases. I believe the answer should be: not very much. Remedies should still be designed with an eye to the concrete case at hand rather than simply with regard to the overall quality of the democratic system. Thus, it may be that an overall breakdown of the system will significantly limit the chances that a specific judgment will be implemented in a particular case but that assessment needs to be made on a case-by-case basis. Add to this that judges intervening strongly in ordinary cases on the basis of a general systemic assessment are also likely to be subject to sharp criticism for overstepping their role and will potentially face political backlash. For all of those reasons, we should shy away from treating generalized distrust as a blank cheque for expansive judicial intervention, where the case at hand itself suggests little evidence for any kind of institutional failure. Instead, we might say that the question should be whether judges can trust other institutions *in concrete cases* to faithfully implement individual judgments and to remedy by themselves broader systemic problems that lead to rights violations, where the judgment identifies them, or whether such trust is not

[21] R. Dixon, 'The Core Case for Weak-Form Judicial Review' (2016) 38:6 *Cardozo Law Review* 2193; see also M. Hailbronner, 'Combatting Malfunction or Optimizing Democracy? Lessons from Germany for a Comparative Political Process Theory' (2021) 19:2 *International Journal of Constitutional Law* 495 at 19.

appropriate. Though generalized distrust will therefore necessarily and legitimately serve to put judges on alert to take their role seriously and interpret the law as the phrase goes 'without fear or favour', it should not serve as a basis for more expansive remedies without more.

5.3.3 *Non-exhaustiveness of the Existing Mechanisms*

Even where we accept that courts should be responsive to the political and legal context, this is not to say that they should be allowed to engage in structural reform litigation. We also need something akin to a gap in the system as opposed to a comprehensive regulatory framework that would exclude stretching existing competences. In particular, there should not be any other more competent and/or democratically legitimate institutions to deal with the issue (the no-more-democratic-means-test). This includes other watchdog institutions that might address the problem, such as Electoral Commissions, Public Ombudspersons, and so on.[22] If so, judges should not intervene in an intrusive manner but leave broader questions of structural reform to these other institutions. Of course, the longer legal violations are going on without democratic branches or others satisfactorily addressing them, the less acceptable deference will become, and thus, the no-more-democratic-means-test is something we will have to keep in mind as we think about which cases warrant judicial interventions in the service of pursuing structural reform. Asking about alternatives requires saying more about the kind of cases and contexts where courts might undertake structural reform, and thus about proportionality.

5.4 Proportionality or: Conceptualizing Institutional Failure in Structural Reform Cases

When it comes to proportionality, I argued above that we should consider three central criteria: functionality, necessity and costs. But what does this mean exactly?

Functionality is often a significant hurdle when it comes to structural reform litigation. Existing studies demonstrate that courts in reality have

[22] T. Khaitan, 'Guarantor (or "Fourth Branch") Institutions', in J. King and R. Bellamy (eds.), *Cambridge Handbook of Constitutional Theory* (Cambridge University Press); M. Tushnet, *The New Fourth Branch: Institutions for Protecting Constitutional Democracy* (Cambridge University Press, 2021).

very limited ability to change entrenched behaviours or overcome resistance.[23] Reforming state institutions often not just involves significant expertise in fields other than law, making judges suboptimal problem-solvers, but also requires multiple institutions to work together, including both state and private actors. Not least, it frequently involves polycentric questions that can be hard to address within the traditional formats of the judicial trial.[24] At the same time, we also know that courts have achieved important successes in some cases, such as the Indian Right to Food litigation as well as the Colombian Court's intervention for internally displaced persons, discussed above, albeit some caveats apply even here.[25] Unfortunately, we do not have a clear template or checklist that would allow us to assess under what conditions courts may successfully intervene and in which cases judicial intervention is likely to fail. This is all the more true if we consider potential longer-term risks and indirect costs, such as the risks of eroding trust in public institutions or budgetary implications, in addition to the question whether intervention will help resolve the particular issue at stake.

However, while there is no clear empirical framework to help us, judges will usually have some indication of the kind of issues involved in individual cases and their chances of success, which will depend at least inter alia on the existence of an engaged civil society.[26] Courts are typically not able to initiate large-scale reforms on their own, without civil society support, and they will have a very hard time unless there is at least some recognition of the problem within the failing institutions

23 V. Gauri and D. M. Brinks, *Courting Social Justice: Judicial Enforcement of Social and Economic Rights in the Developing World* (Cambridge University Press, 2008); see also the contributions in A. E. Yamin and S. Gloppen (eds.), *Litigating Health Rights: Can Courts Bring More Justice to Health?* (Harvard University Press, 2011).

24 L. L. Fuller and K. I. Winston, 'The Forms and Limits of Adjudication' (1978) 92:2 *Harvard Law Review* 353, but see J. King for a convincing reply: id., *Judging Social Rights* (Cambridge University Press, 2012).

25 Decision T-760/08 (Colombian Constitutional Court). On the reasons for the varying success see D. Landau, 'The Reality of Social Rights Enforcement' (2012) 53:1 *Harvard International Law* 190. On the Indian right to food campaign see P. Chitalkar and V. Gauri, 'India: Compliance with Orders on the Right to Food', in M. Langford, C. Rodríguez-Garavito and J. Rossi (eds.), *Social Rights Judgments and the Politics of Compliance: Making It Stick* (Cambridge University Press, 2017), p. 288 as well as other contributions in this volume.

26 On the role of a support structure for court-driven institutional reform see, e.g., Ch. Epp, *The Rights Revolution: Lawyers, Activists, and Supreme Courts in Comparative Perspective* (Chicago University Press, 1998) and id., *Making Rights Real: Activists, Bureaucrats, and the Creation of the Legalistic State* (Chicago University Press, 2009).

themselves.[27] This is also the place where the democratic experimentalism literature provides helpful guidance, suggesting ways in which judges might open up processes and bring in interested persons, stakeholders and members of civil society, as well as independent experts, to develop plans for structural reform that remain subject to judicial control, as well as ensuring regular scrutiny and opportunity for revision, if needed.

Yet, even where structural interventions will be arguably necessary to bring about change, the costs associated with intervening may be too great to do so. Considering necessity requires saying more about the kind of rights violations whose persistence gives rise to accusation of failure in the first place. In other words, it involves assessing what kind of problem we are dealing with. Drawing on the development of the mandate of rights review in the United Nations, as discussed in Chapter 3, I argue that four central questions should guide our analysis in these cases, in addition to the broader themes discussed above. They are:

1. Are we dealing with a large number of rights violations?
2. What is our time frame? Are rights violations occurring repeatedly over some time?
3. What kind of rights and rights violations are we dealing with?
4. Is there any evidence of governmental intent or planning?

These four questions build on the existing literature on responsive review and the idea that courts have a role to play in addressing political malfunction, as well as on Cecilia Medina's work on the Inter-American system.[28] Thus, in the typical case, a great quantity of rights violations recurring over longer time periods will be a strong indication of institutional failure. But how many people must be concerned and how long precisely this must have been going on for a court to take extraordinary steps and get involved is not a question we can answer in the abstract, independent of case and context. Quality and intent will matter, too, albeit in different and somewhat more complicated ways.[29]

[27] Ibid., *Making Rights Real*, chapter 2, who emphasizes that the best results were often achieved in cases where administrators, activists and judges collaborated.

[28] C. Medina Quiroga, *The Battle of Human Rights: Gross, Systematic Violations and the Inter-American System* (Springer Netherlands, 1988); for more, see Chapter 3.

[29] While the first elements are fairly self-explanatory in this regard, it is less clear how to assess the quality of rights violations. Medina (*The Battle of Human Rights*) argues for an integrated approach that would consider the quality of the right or prohibition in question, the kind of violation and the status of the victim. Regarding the quality of the

Not least, there are some cases, as we will see, where all indicators point towards institutional failure, but it may not on close inspection actually be a case of institutional failure because we are dealing with a rare case of reasonable disagreement.

In what follows, I explain the role these factors might play in determining when courts may invoke failure as a reason to intervene in unconventional forms, drawing on examples in the jurisprudence of different courts including the *Floyd* case with which we started this chapter.[30] Thinking through these elements and questions will necessarily also involve some reflection on the considerations of functionality, costs and necessity and what they can tell us about the need for distrust and intervention in individual cases.

5.4.1 *Quantity and Time*

5.4.1.1 Relevance

The standard case for distrust is one where a great number of similar rights violations occur repeatedly, but prompt no or no adequate response from state institutions. Both quantity and time, that is recurrence over time, are hence necessary conditions for courts to intervene in a structural manner. Without the passing of time, officials may still be busy attempting to respond to rights violations, which of course happen even in the best of all possible democracies. Both factors are also part of the few explicit frameworks employed to delineate cases that require a structural approach, such as in the Colombian unconstitutional state of affairs doctrine[31] or in Rule 61 of the European Court of Human Rights, which reads: 'The Court may initiate a pilot-judgment procedure and adopt a pilot judgment where the facts of an application reveal in the Contracting State concerned the existence of a structural or systemic problem or other similar dysfunction which has given rise or may give

right in question, she refers to the category of ius cogens offenses, the categorization as international crimes, or the fact that some rights tend to be non-derogable in human rights treaties while others are. The fourth and final element of planning is unfortunately not fleshed out much by Medina, who argues that violations cannot be committed 'at random' but typically serve a specific goal and are thus part of a broader plan or policy (pp. 15 ff.). This understanding, as we will see later, would make it very hard to capture socio-economic rights violations, today a major area of expansive action by domestic courts.

30 *Floyd et al. v. City of New York et al.*, 959 F. Supp. 2d 540 (S.D.N.Y. 2013).

31 See Chapter 4.

rise to similar applications.'[32] That said, efforts to define systemic and structural problems in the literature have to date not been entirely successful.[33] The best way of approaching this matter may well be through the lens of trust/distrust rather than by setting out an abstract definition that can ultimately not capture the range of different cases and constellations. Thus, judges have no reason to distrust the government and intervene in more expansive ways, where different rights violations are not sufficiently connected in the sense of stemming from the same or similar source/dysfunction.

Framing this as a matter of trust is also helpful to distinguish cases of institutional failure from more standard cases of constitutional review, where, for example, a law of general application affects a great number of people and triggers a high quantity of rights violations. On its own, the latter should not be considered a case of institutional failure and a sufficient basis for distrust, because there is only *one action at one point in time* (the passing of an unconstitutional law), which does not constitute institutional failure even though the rights of multiple persons are violated. Thus, not only the quantity of the rights violations in question but also of the actions leading to those rights violations matter. In cases of omission in contrast, we will refer to the quantity of rights violations rather than state actions involved. Here the time element is particularly important: At the heart of the matter is the fact that considerable time has passed without the government taking action.

Finally, my arguments so far rely on the existence of an underlying condition, namely that the government is *aware* of what is happening. This underlying condition is not usually built into existing jurisprudence as a requirement simply because we can generally assume awareness. This is obvious in cases where the issue has been previously litigated and adjudicated, and thus, government will have been formally put on notice. But even where no prior judgments on the issue exist, this is not necessarily a reason to rule out awareness. In the standard case where rights violations are sufficiently clear, we can reasonably expect that

[32] European Court of Human Rights, Rules of Court, Mar. 28, 2024, available at https://www.echr.coe.int/documents/rules_court_eng.pdf.

[33] See, e.g., for a discussion and different proposals Mart Susi, 'The Definition of a Structural Problem in the Case-Law of the European Court of Human Rights Since 2010' (2012) 55 *German Yearbook of International Law* 385 at 399; Jakub Czepek, 'The Application of the Pilot Judgment Procedure and Other Forms of Handling Large-Scale Dysfunctions in the Case Law of the European Court of Human Rights' (2018) 20 *International Community Law Review* 347.

institutions are aware of them. Only in very rare cases where for legal or factual reasons it is not clear that rights violations have occurred, will this default assumption break down.

Return to *Floyd* for a concrete example: Both the quantity and the consistency/time element are clearly present here and mark it as a case of institutional failure. The analysis of police reports in the trial (in 2013) goes back to 2004, thus covering multiple years of police conduct. And though the judgment does not provide a concrete number of unconstitutional stops during that time period, it includes an estimate that the number is higher than the 'unnecessarily conservative' one of 200 000 suggested by the expert witness.[34] *Floyd* also involved a 'consistent pattern' of rights violations, building on a previous racial profiling case, *Daniels, et al. v. City of New York*, which was filed in 1999 after an unarmed African immigrant, Amadou Diallo, had been shot by the NYPD Street Crime Unit.[35] That case had ended with a settlement that required the NYPD to provide the plaintiff, the Center for Constitutional Rights, with stop-and-frisk data from 2003 to 2007. This data not only demonstrated an increase in the overall number of stops conducted by the NYPD, but also confirmed suspicions that black or hispanic citizens were targeted in the overwhelming majority of cases (over 80%).[36] Finally, awareness is not an issue in this case either given that the NYPD's practice of stop-and-frisk had repeatedly been criticized on legal grounds, including by New York's Attorney General, without triggering any response by the police over a period of several years.

5.4.1.2 Relationship with Other Factors

How do quantity and time relate to our other two factors, quality and intent?

Quality and intent matter too, but in different ways, as we will see below. Neither quality nor intent should be considered essential attributes for structural remedies, which are often deployed in cases where enduring rights violations result from both incompetence and incapacity. Nevertheless, I include them in my normative framework because they are central to the question when and how courts should intervene. We may wonder, in particular, if quality and intent can compensate for quantity or time. Consider cases where we encounter a particularly grave

[34] *Floyd et al. v. City of New York et al.*, 959 F. Supp. 2d 540 (S.D.N.Y. 2013) at 8.

[35] *Daniels v. City of New York*, 138 F. Supp. 2d 562 (S.D.N.Y. 2001).

[36] *Floyd et al. v. City of New York et al.*, 959 F. Supp. 2d 540 (S.D.N.Y. 2013).

violation of human rights, say police torture of a suspect. The answer is that quality and intent can compensate for quantity to some degree, but not entirely. The more obvious (and less new) our rights violation is, for example, the more important the right involved and the graver the violation, the less we will expect there to be a large quantity of rights violations to justify structural intervention. But this applies only to a point. If we are dealing with one case involving one rights violation only, even where a particularly important right is concerned and the violation is severe, this will not be enough to draw conclusions with regard to institutional failure. This is because there can always be one isolated case, one outlier, where something has clearly gone badly wrong. In order to decide whether to take on a structural problem, judges don't just have to determine whether the institution involved has acted illegally but must also assess whether other oversight institutions will respond in a way that addresses the problem. If so, this will typically provide a more appropriate means and thus constitute a reason for judicial deference. However, the greater the number of individual rights violations involved, and the more time has passed, the less trust in other actors will seem appropriate. (In some cases, governance failures may thus be indicative of broader democratic failures.) Even in cases of grave rights violations, then, quantity is not just relevant, but a *necessary* condition for judges to get involved in addressing the broader problem, even though we will require a smaller number of cases where the violations in question are sufficiently serious.

The same applies with regard to intent. Where there is evidence that the government has intentionally violated rights, we will require less in terms of quantity. If rights violations are deliberate – whether the government is deliberately ignoring or causing them – this means that judges have less reason to trust that a declaratory judgment on its own will lead to efforts to address the underlying problem. In turn, where there is no evidence for intent, we will require a greater quantity of rights violations before we will accept courts intervening in a structural manner. Again, however, the broader institutional context will matter. Though governments should as a matter of the rule of law certainly stop or endeavour to stop rights violations, governing is a complex enterprise. There may be a host of reasons why issues are not addressed appropriately. One important reason why governments may deliberately ignore even a series of rights violations may be burdens of inertia, where governments have previously declared certain policy priorities and seek to make good on those or avoid certain issues to keep fragile political coalitions together.[37] Yet, as Dixon argues, burdens of inertia do not necessarily justify intervention in strong forms.[38] The more cases and rights violations arise, however, the less defensible governmental inaction will become.

Something similar applies to our time factor. Time will matter less where there is evidence for governmental intent or even planning *and* the rights violations in question are of a certain quality. Where public institutions are deliberately violating important rights of many people, courts can typically place less trust in the government to address the issue. But exceptions apply and context matters. When dealing with cases arising as a result of an individual governmental agency going rogue within an otherwise well-functioning democratic system, the no-more-democratic-means-test suggests that courts should wait longer before taking drastic steps in order to give existing mechanisms a chance to resolve the issue. As previously discussed, we might think of administrative or, for that matter, federal oversight in such cases. The longer the rights violations drag on, of course, the less plausible it will be that other institutions will indeed take up the issue. At a certain point, there is no longer a need to wait and see if other more democratic mechanisms will fix things, but judges will justifiably step in.

5.4.1.3 Judicial Responses

The existence of a great quantity of cases of a similar kind typically poses challenges of an administrative and technical nature for courts that suddenly have their dockets swamped by new applications. In many cases, therefore, quantity itself drives major innovations, independently of whether we are actually dealing with a case of institutional failure. This at least is the story of the development of the pilot procedure in the European Court of Human Rights, which saw itself confronted with a significant rise of new cases in the late 1990s and early 2000s.[39] The pilot procedure allowed the court to take one of a set of similar cases and order governments to adopt a general remedy within a year to address not just the case at hand but also other similar cases on the Court's docket.

[37] Dixon, 'The Core Case'.

[38] Ibid.

[39] L. Wildhaber, 'Pilot Judgments in Cases of Structural or Systemic Problems on the National Level', in U. Deutsch and R. Wolfrum (eds.), *The European Court of Human Rights Overwhelmed by Applications: Problems and Possible Solutions* (Springer, 2009), p. 69.

Another way of handling a large quantity of cases is to allow for class actions, as already discussed. Perhaps the most straightforward and common technique is, however, to bundle similar cases, as is done in a wide range of jurisdictions. However, where courts adjudicate the claims of multiple persons at a time, this will often necessitate changes to existing procedures in the interest of efficiency. As there are now many plaintiffs rather than just one, it also means less attention to individual cases. Thus, courts may decide to make changes to existing standards for admissibility and evidence as well as potentially introduce new methods of evidence-gathering. In some cases, it will not be possible to conduct a full inquiry into each individual rights' violation. In practice, courts may often turn to other forms of fact-finding, more familiar from legislative or administrative practices. This might involve holding hearings with the stakeholders involved, or commissioning reports from other bodies, ideally bodies with significant independence of their own, such as ombudspersons, auditors, independent commissions and the like. They may also involve scientific experts, civil society organizations or governmental institutions themselves and sometimes create new commissions or committees tasked with evidence-gathering. Which of those mechanisms is most appropriate will depend on the concrete case and problem at hand as well the broader legal context in which they operate. In some cases, such efforts at fact-finding may blur into solution-finding.

Courts will also often seek structural remedies when they need to address a large quantity of rights claims – whether by selecting one case for a pilot judgment or by bundling cases or allowing for a class action – and when those rights violations have been going on for a long time. Considerations of efficiency and distrust come together in such cases. The fact that the rights violations have been going on for some time suggests that trust in existing mechanisms to address the issue is no longer warranted. And the multitude of rights violations suggests the need for a structural approach that goes to the roots of the problem concerned.

5.4.2 *Quality*

5.4.2.1 Relevance

We have already seen above that quality, too, has a role to play in assessing institutional failure. Quality should be considered a necessary criterion for a diagnosis of failure insofar as we must be dealing with rights that are either constitutional or human rights, or – in systems without constitutional rights – rights with a quasi-/small-c-constitutional status.[40] For if the rights at stake are ordinary statutory rights, this should not be considered a sufficient basis for expansive structural intervention. Statutory rights have been granted by the legislature in the first place. Where failure refers to a violation of statutory rights, it is therefore ultimately about holding legislators to their own word. Judges may of course intervene to declare that such rights have been violated. However, insofar as they seek to exercise more expansive powers that run counter to their established role, the lack of legislative consistency, demonstrated by a pattern of violations of statutory rights, is not a sufficient basis insofar as it may simply indicate changing opinions within the legislature. Structural intervention in such cases may also create problematic incentives for governments to outsource administrative control and oversight to courts, following the pattern that US structural reform litigation has often taken, with the enforcement of (sometimes unrealistic) federal mandates by federal courts.[41] This is different when constitutional, human rights or statutory rights that enjoy a higher, quasi-constitutional status of some kind are involved. Governments are bound to protect such rights, and parliaments cannot decide within the ordinary process to abolish them.

Apart from this qualifier, however, quality – in terms of rights or rights violations – should not per se be understood as a *necessary condition* for diagnosis of failure, while nevertheless being relevant to choosing how to respond. In brief, quality matters particularly where the quantity and time element themselves do not provide sufficient reason for distrust. For even if rights violations may be considered as relatively minor, the fact that there is a great number of them and significant time has passed where nothing has been done to respond suggests a governmental failure, and so courts should be allowed to address it by initiating structural reform, at least where such an intervention comes with a chance of success. However, the more we are dealing with minor violations, the longer judges will wait to intervene in a broad structural manner – and thus, quality matters. This raises the question what quality refers to and thus what counts as 'minor' and 'major'.

[40] E.g., Adam Chilton and Mila Versteeg, 'Small-c Constitutional Rights' (2022) 20:1 *International Journal of Constitutional Law*, Volume 141.

[41] Ross Sandler and David Schoenbrod, *Democracy by Decree: What Happens When Courts Run Government* (Yale University Press, 2003), pp. 17 ff.

5.4.2.2 Unpacking and Identifying Quality

Medina argues that quality is determined by three factors: the type of right, the character of the violation and the status of the victims in question.[42] I agree with Medina, but add a fourth factor: newness.

Start with the quality of the right in question. What we mean by quality here is of course the importance of the right, which can often be difficult to determine at the outset.

Among constitutional or human rights, some will be weightier than others. The paradigmatic example is the right to life. Life is generally understood to be one of the most important rights, if not *the* most important, and the jurisprudence of constitutional and human rights courts generally underlines that. That said, in not a few cases, it will be more uncertain how important a given right is. Given that few systems rank rights in any straightforward manner, the importance of a given right may be contested. Judges may need to draw on arguments from sources like constitutional theory to resolve the issue: for example, to articulate the importance of free speech to democracy. In some systems, certain rights may also be more important than others given their respective constitutional histories, and this is something courts may take into account. Judges may also consider arguments from international law to assist in determining the quality of right. Thus, Medina notes that in international debates, the question whether something gives rise to *erga omnes* obligations is considered part of *ius cogens* or is part of a human rights treaty from which no derogation is possible is relevant to this kind of analysis,[43] and at least in cases of doubt, such distinctions may help inform decisions in domestic courts as well.

The character of the rights *violation* seems somewhat more straightforward to assess at first glance. But in practice, this, too, may be difficult and tied in with our third factor, the status of the victim. The gravity of the rights violation can often be hard to assess in the abstract. But there is no way around such an abstract assessment where courts are not dealing with one individual case but instead face a great quantity of rights violations and thus have to rely on generalizations that may ignore that different plaintiffs may experience the violation of their rights differently. One attempt to accommodate some differences in this regard is to pay attention to the social status of the victim and his or her need for

[42] Quiroga, *The Battle of Human Rights*, p. 13.
[43] Ibid., p. 14.

protection, cashed out sometimes in international and less often in constitutional law in terms of vulnerability.[44] In other words, it matters who the victims are and what their means of redress are, that is whether they will likely have a hard time responding if a government inadequately responds to judgments finding their rights violated.

Finally, we should consider a fourth important factor, namely the newness of the rights' claim in question. The concept of newness as an argument for assessing the justiciability of claims has been developed in more detail by James Fowkes. The basic idea is that the newer a given legal claim, the more assistance judges will need to enforce it or the more they will themselves have to try and do.[45] That may imply the need to proceed more carefully. There are some overlaps with Jeff King's arguments for incrementalism in socio-economic rights adjudication,[46] but I use the term newness here in the most straightforward sense, as applied relative to the existing case law and doctrine on a given issue.

Why should newness matter to our assessment of institutional failure? Where our understanding of what qualifies as a right is new – such as rights to same-sex marriage or environmental rights – or enforcing such rights requires thoroughly new mechanisms, it may take longer for institutions to respond to a pattern of such 'new' rights violations. That may be so even once it has been judicially established in previous judgments that we are in fact dealing with rights violations in these cases. The reason for that is that newer rights claims can require more extensive changes to existing laws or practices or may encounter significant social resistance.[47] Delays may therefore be more understandable and provide less of a reason for distrust, even though this will change over time. Thus, the lagging enforcement of *Brown v. Board of Education* in the United States was initially viewed by the judges with some understanding. That started to wane as resistance increased and no progress was made, which

[44] On vulnerability in the ECtHR's jurisprudence see, e.g., Corina Heri, *Responsive Human Rights: Vulnerability, Ill-Treatment and the ECtHR* (Hart Publishing, 2021); Alexandra Timmer, 'A Quiet Revolution: Vulnerability in the European Court of Human Rights' in M.A. Fineman and A. Grear (eds.), *Vulnerability* (Routledge, 2016), p. 147.

[45] J. Fowkes, *Building the Constitution: The Practice of Constitutional Interpretation in Post-Apartheid South Africa* (Cambridge University Press, 2016), pp. 235–6. See also J. Fowkes, 'Normal Rights, Just New: Understanding the Judicial Enforcement of Socioeconomic Rights' (2020) 68:4 *The American Journal of Comparative Law* 734. Fowkes' use of newness is slightly different from my own here, however.

[46] Jeff King, *Judging Social Rights* (Cambridge, 2012), pp. 287 et. seq., to whom Fowkes, 'Normal Rights', refers as well, pp. 726–7, 743.

[47] For a broader discussion Fowkes, 'Normal Rights'.

ultimately led to the development of structural remedies like busing.[48] Newness also matters when it comes to tailoring judicial responses insofar as courts themselves may also find it hard to set out upfront what needs to be done and thus may need to preserve room for flexibility.[49]

Return once again to *Floyd*. Looking only at the violation, we might be tempted to dismiss the quality aspect. A stop-and-frisk overall represents a fairly short and minor incursion of privacy and equality, as compared to the taking of a life. However, the quality of the right involved matters, too, as does the status of the victims. *Floyd* is a case dealing with structural racism against a classical minority that has long faced hostile prejudice and oppression. And while *Floyd* involves doing substantially new things, Judge Scheindlin emphasizes that the rights violated were 'sacred'[50] and long-established rights.

5.4.3 *Intent*

5.4.3.1 Relevance

Intent should not be considered a necessary condition for structural intervention, but is nevertheless relevant to the question when and how to intervene.

In Quiroga's understanding of the concept of gross human rights violations in the international sphere, this fourth element is labelled, not intent, but planning. She quotes the Austrian scholar Ermacora, who argued that the violations 'must form an integral part of a political system where effective remedies do not exist and where the authorities tolerate or even ordered their perpetration'.[51] However, while this requirement may have had its place in the development of international mechanisms of human rights review,[52] it should not be considered a necessity in a domestic context.

[48] M. J. Klarmann, 'Brown V. Board of Education and the Civil Rights Movement' (Oxford University Press, 2007), chapters 4 and 5.

[49] Fowkes, 'Normal Rights'.

[50] *Floyd et al. v. City of New York et al.*, 959 F. Supp. 2d 540 (S.D.N.Y. 2013), Remedies Opinion at 3.

[51] Quiroga, *The Battle of Human Rights*, p. 15 with reference to F. Ermacora, 'Procedures to Deal with Human Rights Violations: A Hopeful Start in the United Nations?' (1974) 7 *Human Rights Journal* 670.

[52] That said, Quiroga acknowledged that the government did not necessarily have to be the perpetrator of the human rights violations in question if it did not put a stop to violations by others by providing protection and/or remedies to address the situation, ibid., p 16.

Many cases in domestic structural reform litigation, involve situations where there is no such deliberate planning at all, but instead (relative) incapacity.[53] Incapacity arises where rights violations continue not because of deliberate intent or indifference by the government, but because governmental institutions cannot put a stop to them within the existing institutional infrastructure, budgetary and legal framework, and fail to address the issue adequately for this reason. That said, as I have argued previously, incapacity and resistance are often combined in cases of structural reform litigation, even though some scholars consider the difference between them to be central.[54] If a situation were entirely beyond repair, there would be no need to involve courts. We will expect institutions thus make serious efforts to resolve the problem, potentially working with other state institutions and other actors, including, if necessary, making major changes. Where they fail to do so, there will at the very least be an element of negligence, and thus unwillingness.

And both in cases involving incapacity and involving resistance, a declaratory judgment is unlikely to put a stop to other identical rights violations. This is straightforward in cases of intransigence where governments tolerate or intentionally commit repeated violations of law, in particular, where previous judgments have not brought about needed change. But even in cases of incapacity and incompetence, judicial intervention beyond the ordinary may be required given that it seems unlikely that another declaratory judgment will trigger major changes if existing institutions have previously demonstrated incompetence in addressing the problem.

Existing scholarship suggests that courts should defer more in cases of incapacity and adopt more robust responses in cases of intransigence.[55] This is correct, with one important exception for cases of disagreement, to which I return below. Where there is evidence for governmental planning or deliberate indifference to ongoing rights violations, courts should be more sceptical towards adopting dialogic approaches that hand an issue back to the parties for consensual problem-solving. They should be more inclined to issue firmer directions and potentially increase judicial oversight. The more institutions exhibit explicit resistance and

[53] Incapacity should be understood in relative terms insofar, not in absolute terms as the absolute inability to remedy legal violations, for there to be an institutional failure.

[54] K. Roach and G. Budlender, 'Mandatory Relief and Supervisory Jurisdiction: When Is it Appropriate, Just and Equitable?' (2005) 122:2 *South African Law Journal* 325.

[55] Ibid.

bad faith, the less there is a basis for trust. The absence or presence of intent is thus relevant to assessing quantity and time, such as how long judges should wait to get involved in a more expansive way. In cases of incapacity, this waiting period is more important than in cases of intransigence and resistance. At the same time, cases involving significant intent may often be hard for courts to tackle successfully, as there is likely to be resistance that needs to be overcome and this may imply the need for some creativity.

5.4.3.2 Identifying Intent

Intent can often be hard for courts to assess. There are two approaches towards identifying intent in constitutional jurisprudence. One is the indirect route, which often plays a role in anti-discrimination law. Thus, where courts can find no rational basis for a particular law or where the aim pursued by the government might be achieved equally effectively in another less rights-restrictive manner, courts may assume discriminatory intent.[56] More recently, some courts have also adopted more explicit procedural forms of scrutiny,[57] sometimes in the form of so-called semi-procedural review.[58] This, too, opens up avenues to inquire into governmental intent (inter alia). For example, US courts have in the past few years increasingly relied on what US commentators describe as small-p process arguments, drawing on the procedural faults or simply deviations from ordinary procedures as an argument for heightened judicial scrutiny.[59] Such arguments have played a role in

[56] See, e.g., on this N. Petersen, 'Legislative Inconsistency and the "Smoking Out" of Illicit Motives' (2016) 64:1 *The American Journal of Comparative Law* 121.

[57] Consider, e.g., the jurisprudence of the ECtHR, *Animal Defenders International v. United Kingdom*, No. 48876/08 (GC) [2013] (ECHR). O. Mjöll Arnardóttir, '*Res Interpretata, Erga Omnes* Effect and the Role of the Margin of Appreciation in Giving Domestic Effect to the Judgments of the European Court of Human Rights' (2017) 28:3 *European Journal of International Law* 819; T. Kleinlein, 'Consensus and Contestability: The ECtHR and the Combined Potential of European Consensus and Procedural Rationality Control' (2017) 28:3 *European Journal of International Law* 871; id. 'The Procedural Approach of the European Court of Human Rights: Between Subsidiarity and Dynamic Evolution' (2019) 68:1 *International & Comparative Law Quarterly* 91.

[58] Semi-procedural review is semi-procedural because the aim remains to establish violations of substantive rights; see I. Bar-Simon-Tov, 'Semiprocedural Judicial Review' (2012) 6:3 *Legisprudence* 271.

[59] J. Landau, 'Process Scrutiny: Motivational Inquiry and Constitutional Rights' (2019) 119:8 *Columbia Law Review* 2147; see also N. W. Eggleston and A. Elbogen, 'The Trump Administration and the Breakdown of Intra-Executive Legal Process' (2018) 127 *The Yale Law Journal Forum*, 16 February 2018, https://tinyurl.com/zcvubkde.

scholarly debates on the Trump travel-bans, though the Supreme Court itself did not want to inquire into the motivations for introducing the bans.[60] In Britain, the Court assessed the legality of the prorogation of the British Parliament through an inquiry into the governmental process leading up to the advice given by the government to the Queen to prorogue Parliament.[61] Scrutinizing procedure may therefore enable courts to identify hidden agendas and motivations. However, this is not a failsafe approach. Some procedural flaws will merely signal that there is something wrong, for example that there was no good faith effort to address certain issues and problems or indeed sloppiness, rather than intent to cause them in the first place. Nevertheless, such investigations into governmental processes can also serve the additional purpose of providing information about how the institutional failure came about and/or of the government's response to it. This in turn may enable courts to tailor their own response in a way that is both minimally invasive and efficient.

Return once more to *Floyd*. Though it would go too far to say that the rights violations in that case were intentional, it clearly mattered in the case that the NYPD had long disregarded questions of constitutional rights, focusing instead narrowly on considerations of efficiency in evaluating staff performance, even after it had been put in notice by the previous litigation in *Daniels*. Overall, the NYPD emerges from this litigation as an institution that not only practised an unconstitutional policy for a long time but also showed little willingness to change that fact even after several judicial and other interventions, the last one in the trial at hand. This is expressed in Judge Scheindlin's assessment and is ultimately an important reason for the adoption of particularly expansive remedies in the case. Unlike in many other similar US cases, *Floyd* did not involve a consent decree: The remedy was not negotiated by the parties and then 'accepted' into law by the court, because the city and the NYPD refused to agree to it.

5.5 Disagreements

We now have a rough picture of what the inquiry in standard cases of institutional failure might look like. However, things don't always map

[60] *Trump v. Hawaii*, No. 17-965, 585 U.S. 667 (2018).

[61] *R (Miller) v. The Prime Minister* and *Cherry v. Advocate General for Scotland* [2019] UKSC 41.

quite as neatly onto our framework as they do in *Floyd*. The most obvious and important exception are cases of disagreement.

Disagreements over the right interpretation of existing law, and rights in particular, pose a challenge to arguments for expansive judicial action in cases of institutional failure. If institutions deliberately engage in actions that courts consider rights violations, this is prima facie a case of resistance – and thus within our existing framework legitimizes expansive judicial intervention. But what about disagreements where institutions and officials act according to their own best understanding of their role and legal duties?

The correct answer to that question is – as so often in law – 'it depends'. First, it seems important to note that we are not discussing whether governments are obliged to follow judicial orders. As a matter of law, they clearly are. However, it is a separate question what precisely courts may do and how far they may go, if other state institutions refuse to implement judicial orders or governments otherwise show resistance. The latter question, which is our question here, is not one to which positive law holds an answer. Instead, it calls for a broader discussion of the role of courts in a democratic society.

Disagreements about law and rights are real. Some authors, such as Jeremy Waldron, have suggested that parliaments are better suited than courts to deal with disagreements about rights in particular.[62] Parliaments are directly elected by the citizens, and they can address issues in a more comprehensive manner than courts that operate in the language of law. This language may be an obstacle to addressing issues adequately, because it forces us to frame the discussion in particular ways, in terms of applying previous precedents or the original meaning of constitutional framers long since dead.[63] In some countries, parliaments therefore retain the legal right not to act on judicial findings – as in the United Kingdom – or to pass laws notwithstanding their incompatibility with certain rights – as is permitted under the Canadian Charter. Such mechanisms have been described as part of a 'dialogic' or 'weak form' model of rights review, though that idea is not exclusively confined to formal frameworks of legislative override.[64] As Mark Tushnet

[62] J. Waldron, 'The Core of the Case Against Judicial Review' (2006) 115:6 *The Yale Law Journal* 1346.

[63] Ibid, at 1383.

[64] R. Dixon, 'The Forms, Functions, and Varieties of Weak(ened) Judicial Review' (2019) 17:3 *International Journal of Constitutional Law* 904.

explains, weak form review seeks to reconcile the idea of democracy and self-governance with the idea that there are some limits to self-governance, as expressed by judicial review.[65] Formal provisions for legislative override are comparatively rare. Somewhat more common are softer forms of weak review, where courts retain the last word but exercise their authority in a way that typically provides legislators with the means to pursue their chosen policies in some other way rather than obstructing specific policies wholesale.[66]

These considerations are useful in our context here as well. Insofar as courts adopt structural remedies, they intervene more directly in legislative and/or administrative processes and thus leave less room for disagreement and dialogue among the different branches. If governments deliberately do not implement judgments, there is – under a traditional conception of the separation of powers and the judicial role – often little courts can do, apart from holding officials in contempt and or taking other similar measures to sanction the non-compliance. Yet, whether this is a problem and gap in the system that needs addressing – for example by means of structural reform litigation – or whether it should be considered as part of the original design that preserves spaces for institutional disagreement is not a straightforward question. It depends on the scope and precise meaning of judicial supremacy and the judicial role in individual systems.

One way of dealing with disagreements in the context of accusations of institutional failure might be to approach this solely as a matter of selecting the right remedies. We might then, for example, argue that while cases of resistance qualify as institutional failure, courts should respond flexibly to them, for example by initiating a process of shared problem-solving among stakeholders rather than decreeing policy from the bench. However, not only is it problematic to qualify rights disagreements as failures as a matter of ordinary language, but it also doesn't solve the problem, given that existing scholarship routinely calls for more robust intervention in cases of resistance.[67] Thus, we still need to distinguish cases of illegitimate resistance from cases of legitimate disagreement along the lines sketched out by Jeremy Waldron.[68]

65 M. Tushnet, *Weak Courts, Strong Rights: Judicial Review and Social Welfare Rights in Comparative Constitutional Law* (Princeton University Press, 2009), p. 23.
66 Dixon, 'The Core Case'.
67 Roach and Budlender, 'Mandatory Relief'.
68 Waldron, 'The Core of the Case'.

To do that, I propose four criteria to consider in order to decide if we are dealing with a legitimate disagreement – and note again that this is relevant here only to the question how to intervene, not whether to intervene at all:

1. First, the institution that disagrees must be a legislature.
2. Second, the disagreement must be publicly aired and serious, that is, there must have been a genuine public debate that did not exclude key voices or stakeholders.
3. Third, the legal system overall must be a well-functioning democracy.
4. Fourth, the right in question or its application to the case(s) in question should typically not be part of long-established judicial precedents or doctrine.

Why these criteria and where are they coming from? The first criterion is ultimately a reference to Waldron as well as existing mechanisms of override, which presuppose a *parliamentary* decision. This may seem unnecessarily narrow, in particular where we are dealing with presidential systems. Should we not instead consider opposition by any directly elected officials, including, for example, presidents?[69] I would argue though that we shouldn't because we need to construct our exception narrowly. We need to know if we are dealing with a serious and well-considered disagreement, and thus, it is vital that there be a debate and that the body that represents the people is involved and at the very least backs a government that wants to disagree. This means that while we may not need an explicit parliamentary statement or decision as we have in more dialogic systems, such as the United Kingdom or Canada, we do need some parliamentary accountability. Merely presidential opposition does not qualify therefore, even where the president in question has been directly elected. This is because one person is not representative in the same way as a parliament is, and if we are considering when disagreements with judicial decisions are legitimate, this should matter.

The second criterion links to these considerations and concerns the necessity of an inclusive and serious public debate. The rationale for this criterion is again to enlarge the democratic legitimation by ensuring that

[69] In this direction US theories and claims of departmentalism, as discussed in K. E. Whittington, *Political Foundations of Judicial Supremacy: The Presidency, the Supreme Court, and Constitutional Leadership in U.S. History* (Princeton University Press, 2007).

key voices have a say and can be heard. A public debate also forces the government to stand up for the issue and argue its case. This makes it more unlikely that it will adopt self-serving positions or positions that seek to indirectly discriminate against parts of society and which it will therefore not want to defend publicly. Similarly, scholars such as Matthias Kumm have argued in the context of proportionality analysis that courts should take into account whether parliament has previously debated an issue in a serious and respectful manner and tailor the degree of judicial scrutiny accordingly.[70] This criterion links to our previous discussion about identifying intent and the possibilities of procedural review.

The third requirement is closely connected to the other two. The democratic legitimacy of a parliament depends on whether it operates in a fully democratic system. It will be lacking this legitimacy where there are significant electoral flaws and/or significant parts of the population are in principle or in practice disenfranchised. Thus, the resistance of Southern institutions in the United States to federally mandated school desegregation would not constitute a legitimate disagreement, given that black citizens were in practice disenfranchised in large parts of the South at the time. This also ties back in with other broader arguments about more robust judicial review in cases of democratic dysfunction.[71]

Finally, resistance to a judgment will be more likely to be legitimate where it involves an element of precedential or doctrinal newness, whether it is the right in question that is new or its interpretation by the court.[72] I have mentioned newness already in the context of discussing the quality of rights violations, but it should also play a role in the context of assessing the legitimacy of disagreement. Where courts interpret rights in a new way or create new rights, we should be more open to the existence of a legitimate disagreement. In contrast, where we are dealing with a disagreement with respect to long-settled understandings of law, this should typically not be considered legitimate – and we should scrutinize the quality and inclusiveness of public debates particularly carefully.

[70] M. Kumm, 'Institutionalising Socratic Contestation: The Rationalist Human Rights Paradigm, Legitimate Authority and the Point of Judicial Review' (2008) 1 *European Journal of Legal Studies* 153.

[71] E.g. Landau, 'Political Institutions'.

[72] Fowkes, 'Normal Rights'.

5.6 Conclusion

In this chapter, I have situated structural intervention by judges as a way of responding to governmental failure within our broader normative framework. Drawing on existing theories of judicial review, and in particular the work of John Hart Ely and, more recently, the writing on comparative representation reinforcement by scholars such as Rosalind Dixon, I argue that those theories and, in particular, the idea of malfunction suggest that courts may address dysfunction through structural remedies and in other unconventional ways.

That said, I have argued that malfunction in our context here needs to be defined narrowly and targeted towards combatting enduring rights violations rather than broader democratic dysfunction. To this end, I have proposed a set of questions in the second part of this chapter to help judges determine whether they are dealing with a case of institutional failure that requires judicial responses that go beyond the ordinary role of judges: to declare what the law is in individual cases, and typically retrospectively. These questions pertain to the quantity, consistency and quality of rights violations and the intent of those responsible for the situation not having been remedied.

This framework is hardly revolutionary. Judges already ask many of these questions, and elements of the framework are familiar from the existing judicial repertoire. This is a good thing, I believe, because it shows that the task is manageable. Nevertheless, what I propose here goes beyond the existing literature by offering a path for structural intervention under a set of narrowly defined conditions where courts cannot trust other institutions to fulfil their role. It, thus, attempts to chart a middle path between the traditional position still held in many jurisdictions of the world, where courts would never intervene in a structural manner, and the growing expectation in other parts of the world that courts are there to fix all manner of problems and make up for broader democratic dysfunction. In this context, it is important to recall that structural intervention will not always or necessarily serve those who are weak or vulnerable but may be a tool for very different interests.

6

Failure and Legal Innovation

Arguments from Failure as Judicial Trumps

6.1 Introduction

Arguments from failure not only play a role in courts when it comes to structural reform litigation. Start by considering two examples from my home jurisdiction – Germany.

Germany has a comparatively well-developed public health system. Within this system, private companies provide both private and public healthcare services and medication according to guidelines developed by the Joint Federal Committee (G-BA). The G-BA consists of representatives of public health providers and German hospital associations. Individual doctors can prescribe for patients within the public system treatments and medication that fall within these guidelines, but not those outside of it. However, in a famous line of jurisprudence, the German Federal Social Court has granted individual patients a right to certain treatments or medications outside of these schedules in exceptional situations: specifically, where there were signs of *a systemic deficiency or systemic failure* on the part of the G-BA.[1] Such systemic deficiencies are understood to exist, for example, if new treatments, in particular treatments or medications accepted in other states, have not been assessed within a reasonable time for the purposes of adding them to the German catalogue. System failure (*Systemversagen*) is thus a doctrinal concept in German social law, providing a basis for courts to step in where they would ordinarily defer to other institutions.[2]

[1] Bundessozialgericht, B 1 KR 12/05 R, 4 April 2006, para. 28 (Federal Social Court, Germany).

[2] For a short (German) overview of the concept, see H. Lang, '§ 27 Krankenbehandlung', in U. Becker and T. Kingreen (eds.), *SGB V, Gesetzliche Krankenversicherung* (C.H. Beck, 2022), para. 69 with further references to case law; see also for a short discussion C. Burgardt, 'Das Systemversagen in der GKV' (2014) 5 *Medizinprodukterecht* 145.

Compare this to the famous *Soraya* judgment of the German Constitutional Court.[3] The case dealt with a decision by German civil courts to accord personal injury compensation (*Schmerzensgeld*) to the second wife of the Iranian Shah because the German newspaper *Die Welt* had published an entirely fictive interview with her. The case was a hard case not because of the facts involved, but because there existed no explicit textual basis for this kind of compensation in German law at the time. The respective courts decided, however, to create a right to such a compensation by adopting a very broad purposive approach to the existing statutory rules. In response, *Die Welt* filed a constitutional complaint against the judgment, claiming that by granting personal injury compensation the civil courts had overstepped their role as judges and turned into lawmakers, violating the principle of the separation of powers and *Die Welt*'s constitutional rights. Analyzing the law in question, the German Constitutional Court agreed with the previous courts that there had indeed been a gap in the law because existing rules did not provide for personal injury compensation in such cases. The Constitutional Court then proceeded to ask whether courts should close this gap with their own means (i.e. by building analogies) or whether in a case like this they had to wait for the legislature to act. Most scholars, the Court noted, supported the former. It then went on to make an argument that is worth quoting directly:

> The alternative, to wait for the legislature to address the issue, is in light of all circumstances not considered constitutionally required. For while the government attempted twice to find a statutory solution for the problem of the protection of the right to privacy with regard to third parties, its draft bills from 1959 and 1967 were abandoned in the early stages of the drafting process – without this suggesting that the legislature had actually wanted to leave matters as they were. The judge confronted with the issue can therefore not be blamed if he decides that he cannot observe the (merely) formal legal rules in anticipation for an entirely uncertain legislative intervention in the future at the price of a very unjust result in the individual case at hand.[4]

With this argument, the Court tied together ideas of injustice with an assessment of legislative performance, ultimately justifying judicial innovation. Though few German judgments discuss the role of courts as explicitly as the German Constitutional Court in *Soraya*, assessments

[3] BVerfGE 34, 269 – *Soraya* (German Constitutional Court).

[4] BVerfGE 34, 269 para. 45 (translation by this author).

of governmental performance are central to any form of public law litigation. Yet, sometimes such assessments of failure become central to justifying particularly innovative judicial action, not merely when it comes to remedies or judicial procedure, but to legal interpretation more broadly. Both two judgments rely on arguments from failure to overcome a previous practice of judicial deference to other institutions, using them as a sort of judicial trump card. But the two cases are also different. In the first type of case, courts step in where an administrative body has failed to act. In the second, we are confronted with a presumed legislative failure, leading to more permanent legal innovations which raise questions about the role of failure in justifying judicial 'law-making' more broadly.

In what follows, I begin by considering the relationship between arguments from failure and deference in judicial interpretation and their normative stakes as arguments for interpretive innovation. I then turn to the question if and when courts can justifiably rely on arguments from failure, given that failure in both cases serves as a basis for finding a rights violation in the first place, rather than a tool to justify unconventional remedies by identifying specific kinds of rights violations. This matters because it complicates our twin tasks of treating arguments from failure as a legal rather than political concept and of distinguishing failures from disagreements. Finally, in the last part of this chapter (Section 6.4.), I consider some examples from the field of climate change litigation to explore the connection between newness, innovation and failure in these and other cases.

6.2 Deference and Failure

If we are to understand how arguments from failure operate to override more standard arguments for judicial deference, it makes sense to begin by briefly recalling why and when courts exercise deference in the first place.

6.2.1 Theories of Deference

Courts defer to other institutions for many reasons and in different ways. If previously courts tended to pursue bright-line distinctions between legal and political questions, as famously set out by the US Supreme Court in *Baker v. Carr*,[5] more recently political question doctrines have

[5] *Baker v. Carr*, 369 US 186 (1962).

become unfashionable.[6] Of course, this doesn't mean that courts no longer exercise deference. Rather, what we see in many courts today is a more nuanced, contextualized – some would say arbitrary – approach to deference where courts do not declare certain questions to be political per se, but instead tailor their scrutiny to the particular issue and context in question.[7]

Existing scholarship distinguishes mainly between epistemic and constitutional reasons for judicial deference.[8] Epistemic reasons concern the limited capacity of courts to deal with certain questions because they may be polycentric and thus not ideal for judicial resolution in a trial between two parties only, or because they require non-legal expertise to resolve, which judges do not typically possess.[9] Constitutional deference, in contrast, implies that certain kinds of issues or questions should ideally be reserved for parliaments or other institutions. Thus, foreign policy questions have often been considered a matter of governmental prerogative, and issues that involve significant budgetary commitments in turn have been considered a parliamentary matter.[10] Some courts will also consider how and to what degree an issue has been extensively deliberated in other institutions as a reason for exercising more, or less, restraint.[11] Existing scholarship also often treats the question how clear a legal text is and how settled an issue is as a matter of existing legal doctrine as relevant to the degree of scrutiny judges should exercise.[12]

6 R. E. Barkow, 'More Supreme Than Court: The Fall of the Political Question Doctrine and the Rise of Judicial Supremacy' (2002) 102 *Columbia Law Review* 237.

7 See, e.g., for a South African discussion M. Mhango, 'Is It Time for a Coherent Political Question Doctrine in South Africa? Lessons from the United States' (2014) 7:4 *African Journal of Legal Studies* 457. Similarly, the German Constitutional Court has never adopted an explicit political question doctrine; see, e.g., M. Hailbronner, *Traditions and Transformations: The Rise of German Constitutionalism* (Oxford University Press, 2015), pp. 125 ff. For international courts, see J. Odermatt, 'Patterns of Avoidance: Political Questions Before International Courts' (2018) 14:2 *International Journal of Law in Context* 221.

8 E.g., J. H. Fahner, *Judicial Deference in International Adjudication: A Comparative Analysis* (Bloomsbury Publishing, 2020), pp. 149 ff. See also on good and bad reasons for judicial deference, albeit in the context of social rights, Jeff King, *Judging Social Rights* (Cambridge, 2012), Part II.

9 Fahner, *Judicial Deference*, p. 151.

10 Fahner, *Judicial Deference*, p. 154.

11 See, e.g., the ECHR in *Animal Defenders International v. United Kingdom* [GC], 22 April 2013, No. 48876/08 (ECHR).

12 J. Fowkes, 'Normal Rights, Just New: Understanding the Judicial Enforcement of Socioeconomic Rights' (2020) 68:4 *The American Journal of Comparative Law* 734.

In *Baker v. Carr*, the US Supreme Court declared as non-justiciable political questions those questions for which there existed no justiciable standards by which to resolve them. Similar qualifiers can be found in many theories of review that are designed to provide a template for dealing with those questions on which there is 'no clear law' as with John Hart Ely's theory of representation reinforcing review, a consideration also taken up in Rosalind Dixon's responsive theory of review.[13]

6.2.2 *Judicial Law-Making*

The existence of clear legal standards is, however, not only a relevant criterion for assessing constitutional deference. It lies at the heart of the familiar distinction between law-making and legal interpretation. Though that distinction is – as existing scholarship shows[14] – not tenable as a distinction between courts and other institutions such as parliaments (because all of them 'make' law), courts typically do so differently, and not least in a much more 'piecemeal and incremental' fashion.[15] Accordingly, we tend to think that judges should not usually adopt interpretations that significantly diverge from previous precedents and/or the consensus existing in their respective community of interpreters.[16]

That courts engage in innovation is not a secret, of course. It is to some degree accepted as a part of routine judicial activity, sometimes explicitly so in theories of interpretation, such as living constitutionalism or dynamic interpretation. On this view, courts may modify and adapt existing arguments to fit new challenges. Over time therefore, the law evolves. But sometimes courts introduce more radical changes. Such more abrupt and obvious changes typically pose challenges for courts since law reform on a more substantial scale is generally considered a matter for legislatures rather than judges. Major innovations are

13 R. Dixon, *Responsive Judicial Review: Democracy and Dysfunction in the Modern Age* (Oxford University Press, 2023), chapter 2; J. H. Ely, *Democracy and Distrust: A Theory of Judicial Review* (Harvard University Press, 1980), p. 13.

14 E.g. C. Möllers, *The Three Branches: A Comparative Model of Separation of Powers* (Oxford University Press, 2013), p. 82 f.; A. Kavanagh, 'The Constitutional Separation of Powers', in D. Dyzenhaus and M. Thorburn (eds.), *Philosophical Foundations of Constitutional Law* (Oxford University Press, 2016), p. 221 at 232.

15 Kavanagh, 'Separation of Powers', p. 232; see also J. King, *Judging Social Rights* (Cambridge University Press, 2012).

16 On communities of interpretation, see S. Fish, *Is There a Text in This Class? The Authority of Interpretive Communities* (Harvard University Press, 1980).

therefore almost certain to trigger critical questions. They may be seen to compromise the court's authority as the reliable and final interpreter of law, endangering the principles of legal certainty and fairness as consistency. It is thus important for judges to marshal good arguments to justify more dramatic changes in their interpretive practices.

This is where institutional failure arguments often come in – as a tool to justify intervention when there are otherwise good epistemic or constitutional reasons to exercise restraint. Arguments from failure may provide a trump card in such cases, setting aside arguments for non-intervention. Sometimes, they help judges overcome deference in light of administrative malfunctioning; in other cases, such as *Soraya*, they may also furnish an argument for courts to get involved in the context of legislative inertia.

As I have argued previously, however, it matters which institutions are involved. Where courts step in to address legislative failure, they take prospective decisions not confined to individual cases. They are thus stepping much further outside the traditional judicial role than if they substitute for an administrative failure in a concrete case. At the same time, it is important to recall that the difference compared to the more ordinary case of incremental adaptation and updating the law is one of degrees; unsurprisingly therefore, the line between the two will often be blurry, as we will see later in the climate change decisions.

6.3 Evaluating Arguments from Failure

Can we justify judicial innovation in these cases? Overall, I argue here that the framework developed in this book still applies to such cases. The broader legal and political context and the existing regulatory framework, as well as the question what other institutions might step in, remain relevant here. The same is largely true with regard to considerations of functionality and cost, as I argue below. Yet, there are also some new problems, because we often can no longer presuppose a rights violation in such cases. Rather, the presumed failure is a necessary condition for identifying a rights violation in the first place and for assessing the necessity of intervening.

6.3.1 Functionality and Costs

Start with the more familiar questions about the functionality and costs of judicial intervention. Especially where arguments from failure are employed to overcome *epistemic* deference, functionality can become a problem. Given the reasons for epistemic deference in the first place, it may seem doubtful whether courts will have a realistic chance to address the problem, for example because the problem will be polycentric or because they lack the necessary expertise to address the issue.[17] Ultimately, their chances of success will depend both on existing procedural rules and judicial willingness to adjust and develop those rules to deal with cases of institutional failure. If the problem consists of a lack of expertise, courts can bring in external experts, but the rules for doing so matter. Thus, in some systems, like the United States, it is usually the parties who bring in their own experts to make the case for their own side. In other systems, such as Germany, the process is judge-managed rather than party-driven. Courts have a list of external experts they might draw on for specific issues, who are not associated with either of the parties.[18] The challenge of polycentricity may be harder to overcome, but here too we have seen in previous chapters how courts transform judicial trials in some cases and bring in other stakeholders rather than relying only on the parties involved in the original case.

Costs to consider may be short-term or longer-term, with the latter harder to assess. Short-term costs may involve political backlash, but also the risk that courts may get things wrong and make the situation worse rather than better. This goes back to the problems of functionality discussed above: courts may not have been able to make up for their own lack of expertise in other ways and therefore intervene in a manner that ends up being counterproductive to the aims pursued. There may also be shorter- or longer-term consequences for related issues and persons who are not parties to the case at hand if the case involves polycentric questions. For example, courts deciding on what medications and treatments will be funded may – if this happens sufficiently frequently – decrease the share of the health budget available to others, in particular those with less ability to access courts. This is not only a theoretical possibility as studies on Brazilian health care litigation show, where this is precisely what happened.[19] Other longer-

[17] See, e.g., for a discussion of such epistemic challenges (with regard to social rights adjudication) King, *Judging Social Rights*, chapters 7 and 8.

[18] J. Fowkes, 'Civil Procedure in Public Interest Litigation: Tradition, Collaboration and the Managerial Judge' (2012) 1:3 *Cambridge Journal of International and Comparative Law* 235.

[19] O. L. M. Ferraz, *Health as a Human Right: The Politics and Judicialisation of Health in Brazil* (Cambridge University Press, 2020), chapter 8, noting that complying with health litigation now accounts for 3% of the total health budget of the country.

term consequences may be that judicial intervention may actually discourage responsible politics. In such cases, we may encounter what Mark Tushnet calls 'democratic debilitation' – which may occur because legislators know that the court will take care of things.[20]

6.3.2 Necessity and Breach of Law

If functionality and costs are familiar concerns, things become more complicated when it comes to assessing the necessity of judicial interventions. As I argued in Part I, if we want to minimize the risk of failure arguments becoming politically instrumentalized and abused, we need to identify some breach of law as a threshold requirement. Yet, this can no longer be taken for granted here. A breach of law, or violation of rights, is no longer something we can presuppose, but rather the thing we are trying to establish in the first place. Recall our two examples: Failure was a prerequisite in the healthcare case to give plaintiffs an enforceable right to a specific medication or treatment, and in the *Soraya* judgment, the (presumed) legislative failure provided an argument for granting individual plaintiffs new unwritten rights to compensation, which they did not have before. Can we still therefore rely on failure arguments in this context?

6.3.2.1 Administrative Failure

Begin with our German example from above. Why and when should we assume that there is a case of *Systemversagen* (system failure)? The Joint Federal Committee has not usually violated any specific laws in cases of *Systemversagen*. The only thing we can say is that it has not acted in accordance with its function or role, as expressed in its statutory mandate. However, as lawyers know, such general mandates often are very vague. Nor are there typically hard benchmarks as to what constitutes adequate performance, though there are exceptions. Reasonable people will therefore often disagree as to what constitutes adequate institutional performance. How then do German courts reason in such cases? Broadly speaking, they ask if the institutions responsible for amending these schedules have failed to initiate the relevant procedure assessing the need for inclusion, either completely or in a timely manner, or have failed to

[20] M. Tushnet, 'Policy Distortion and Democratic Debilitation: Comparative Illumination of the Countermajoritarian Difficulty' (1995) 94:2 *Michigan Law Review* 247.

conduct them in accordance with existing rules.[21] Overall, German courts have been fairly cautious in assuming failure. The mere registration of a treatment in other countries, for example, does not automatically imply that not including the same treatment in German catalogues constitutes a failure, according to the German Federal Social Court.[22] Rather, the courts will assess the internal procedures in detail, taking into account the different opinions of medical experts, the time needed to conduct an analysis and other actions of the different participants involved in the process.[23] Only where these different factors taken together suggest that there were no good reasons for non-inclusion in the case at hand are we confronted with *Systemversagen*.

This is a start, but it is not a comprehensive answer. The easiest scenario is clearly one where we can identify some breach of law: for example, when the institution in question has not properly followed procedural rules and/or its institutional mandate. Not every violation of procedural rules, however, should be considered a failure that warrants judicial intervention where deference is otherwise more appropriate. The rules in question may sometimes only be in the organization's own rules or in administrative guidelines, instead of being a matter of statutory rules. In other cases, there may be no written standards at all, but merely a set of 'best practices' usually followed by the institution in question. Given the risks of abuse, it seems clear that the less we have clear statutory rules, and the more courts need to rely on broad institutional mandates or best practices, the more they should exercise caution when it comes to diagnosing institutional failure. But this still leaves many questions open.

6.3.2.2 Legislative Failure

Difficulties are compounded where courts confront straightforward legislative failure. Unlike administrative agencies, legislatures have no specific mandate in the sense of being charged with one particular task. There are of course constitutional constraints and duties and in some systems directive principles, but such provisions nevertheless typically leave legislatures large discretion, as we should expect it in a democracy. Where legislatures do not act on a particular issue therefore, this is not

21 Lang, '§ 27 Krankenbehandlung'; Burgardt, 'Das Systemversagen' 145 at 147.
22 Bundessozialgericht, B 1 KR 12/05 R.
23 Ibid.

necessarily problematic, let alone constitutes a failure. Legislators may have other priorities or indeed believe that there is no need to do something.

There are only two ways in which we might be able to get a handle on the idea of legislative failure. One is substantive, as a matter of the legislature failing to protect and guarantee existing (quasi-)constitutional or human rights. The second is procedural, that is where the processes in question may in some ways be considered deficient.

6.3.2.2.1 Procedural Approaches Procedural standards are partly tied to specific substantive human or constitutional rights, but they can also represent independent procedural rights. Such rules are sometimes part not of constitutional or human rights law but of administrative law. This includes, for example, principles such as transparency and participation requirements, reason-giving and the possibility of review.[24] Such violations of procedure in turn might indicate that we are dealing with a case of capture of the political process by special interests[25] or indeed legislative inertia triggered by coalition-building problems or legislative blindspots.[26] Yet, absent a specific constitutional duty to act such cases will typically be hard for judges to identify.

Moreover, judges will need to be very careful to distinguish between cases of failure and cases of reasonable disagreement, in particular where the situation is one of legislative inaction. Because the failure in question is not tied to established rights violations, this is a harder challenge than when it comes to structural reform litigation. Several factors are relevant in this regard. First, we cannot assume failure where inaction is a deliberate choice reached after a full and inclusive debate on the issue. Deliberation particularly matters in cases where the failure in question appears as a failure to follow through on previous commitments. Again, however, we need to be careful to distinguish failure from the deliberate change of a political position. Not every inconsistency will indicate governmental failure, but it may express simply a legitimate change of

[24] B. Kingsbury and M. Donaldson, 'Global Administrative Law', in A. Peters and R. Wolfrum (eds.), *Max Planck Encyclopedia of Public International Law* (Oxford University Press, 2011).

[25] N. Petersen, *Proportionality and Judicial Activism: Fundamental Rights Adjudication in Canada, Germany and South Africa* (Cambridge University Press, 2017), pp. 27 ff. and throughout.

[26] R. Dixon, 'The Core Case for Weak-Form Judicial Review' (2016) 38:6 *Cardozo Law Review* 2193.

opinion. To determine if this is the case, courts will have to know more about the reason for the shifting positions – and potentially look to governmental records as well as procedures to find out more. Such an analysis, however, should not be undertaken lightly. As commentators of this kind of procedural scrutiny have pointed out, there is a risk of treating legislatures and governments like administrative offices.[27] Doing so may ignore the nature of democratic decision-making which will often be subject to the need for political compromises and thus cannot follow the standards of consistency we expect of administrative actions. In a multiparty democracy, and in particular when governments are formed as coalitions between several parties, political deals and compromises may be necessary to enable effective government. In scrutinizing consistency, courts must thus be sure not to adopt a purely administrative perspective and be wary of holding democratic processes to unrealistic ideals.[28]

6.3.2.2.2 Substantive Standards In theory, things are easier if the legislature's inaction violates certain constitutional duties or positive rights. For we do, of course, have a range of criteria to assess governmental performance when it comes to adjudicating violations of positive rights, dependent on case and jurisdiction. The ECtHR, for example, requires states to fulfil their protective duties to provide an adequate regulatory framework to prevent rights violations and to establish corresponding institutional rules and safeguards and measures to implement the said framework, as well as procedures to investigate and sanction violations ex post.[29] The German Constitutional Court has emphasized in its jurisprudence the need for consistency within regulatory frameworks.[30] Perhaps the most interesting and internationally influential approach has been that of the South African Constitutional Court.

[27] P. Dann, 'Verfassungsgerichtliche Kontrolle gesetzgeberischer Rationalität' (2010) 49:4 *Der Staat* 630 at 640; C. Möllers, 'Legalität, Legitimität und Legitimation', in M. Jestaedt et al. (eds.), *Das entgrenzte Gericht*, 3rd edn (Suhrkamp, 2019), p. 383; see also O. Lepsius, 'Die maßstabsetzende Gewalt', in ibid. (eds.), *Das entgrenzte Gericht*, 3rd edn (Suhrkamp, 2019), pp. 229–30; see also for a persuasive general critique M. Payandeh, 'Das Gebot der Folgerichtigkeit: Rationalitätsgewinn oder Irrweg der Grundrechtsdogmatik?' (2011) 136 *Archiv des öffentlichen Rechts* 578.

[28] Dann, 'Verfassungsgerichtliche Kontrolle' 630 at 640.

[29] See, e.g., M. Klatt, 'Positive Obligations Under the European Convention on Human Rights' (2011) 71 *Zeitschrift für ausländisches öffentliches Recht und Völkerrecht* 691.

[30] See, e.g., BVerfGE 125, 175 – Hartz IV and BVerfGE 132, 134 – Asylbewerberleistungsgesetz (German Constitutional Court).

Rather than following the International Committee on Economic, Social and Cultural Rights' suggested minimum core approach,[31] the South African Constitutional Court in the *Grootboom* case famously adopted a reasonableness standard for the right to housing under the South African Constitution.[32] Assessed in those terms, the judges considered the failure to develop a policy dealing with short-term housing needs and thus provide 'relief for those in desperate need' to be unreasonable – and thus to violate the South African Constitution. Thus, reasonableness essentially provides a measure for what we may expect of the government in a particular context, which is why the Constitutional Court has used it generally to assess positive rights obligations.[33] And so on.

These standards are, however, part of the ordinary arsenal of constitutional and human rights review – and this begs the question what, if any, role they might play in our context here as a tool to justify judicial innovation.[34] The answer to that question must be that failure only really comes into the picture in these cases if we are dealing with a rights claim that involves significant newness – and thus where the court is going beyond established precedent, in a way that requires special justification because it involves more than incremental legal change. If so, however, the standards we find in the broader jurisprudence for assessing violations of positive rights are the best yardstick for assessing the existence

[31] ICESCR, General Comment No. 3: The Nature of States Parties' Obligations (Art. 2, para. 1 of the Covenant), Fifth Session (1990).

[32] *Government of the Republic of South Africa and Others v. Grootboom and Others* 2001 (1) SA 46 (CC) (S.Afr.); see also on reasonableness, e.g., K. Young, 'The Canons of Social and Economic Rights' (2021) 553:1 *Boston College Law School Legal Studies Research Paper* 1.

[33] J. Fowkes, 'Normal Rights, Just New: Understanding the Judicial Enforcement of Socioeconomic Rights' (2020) 68:4 *The American Journal of Comparative Law* 722 at 734; J. Fowkes, *Building the Constitution: The Practice of Constitutional Interpretation in Post-Apartheid South Africa* (Cambridge University Press, 2016), pp. 235–6. For more on reasonableness, see, e.g., L. Chenwi, 'Unpacking "Progressive Realization", Its Relation to Resources, Minimum Core and Reasonableness, and Some Methodological Considerations for Assessing Compliance' (2013) 46:3 *De Jure* 742; G. Quinot and S. Liebenberg, 'Narrowing the Band: Reasonableness Review in Administrative Justice and Socio-Economic Rights Jurisprudence in South Africa' (2011) 22 *Stellenbosch Law Review* 639.

[34] It is not accidental, of course, that the jurisprudence on positive rights operates with indicators we might draw on to assess failure. Given that the justiciability of positive rights has long been contested, the judicial enforcement of such rights has long involved arguments about malperformance and failure. But as the justiciability of such rights has been accepted in the past few decades, what started out as arguments from failure have turned into broader arguments about governmental performance on which the existence of a rights violation is seen to depend.

of failure in other contexts, where judicial intervention is not usually accepted.

6.3.2.2.3 *Soraya* Revisited Let's return for a moment to the *Soraya* case. The German Constitutional Court in that case provided no real reasoning or justification as to why we might be dealing with a case of failure. To start with, the Court did not argue in terms of a constitutional obligation to protect constitutional rights, such as a right to privacy in that case. We merely learnt that several attempts had been made to change the law in question and that they had faltered, but it was not clear that legislators had actually changed their minds on the issue. The only way of treating this as a failure would presumably have been to show that the legislators' inaction in this case was not due to disagreement or something like that, but instead indicative of dysfunctionalities within the democratic process. Again, however, this was not clear from the German Court's reasoning. In order to know therefore whether we were indeed dealing with a case of failure, we would simply need to know a lot more. Without such information, the argument for judicial intervention in this case of legislative inertia remains unconvincing.

6.4 Climate Change Litigation

To better understand the way arguments from failure work and should work in the context of courts developing the law in bold ways, consider recent litigation on climate change. Climate change litigation is of course a broad field and no longer an entirely new phenomenon. Nevertheless, it remains contested if and to what extent the struggle to respond to and contain climate change should involve courts.

Though courts can certainly assess the state of the scientific consensus, this in itself is generally not sufficient to create legal obligations to act. Responding to the threat climate change poses requires policy changes that come with trade-offs and costs, in particular with regard to economic development. Balancing the competing imperatives and interests requires making choices that democratically elected leaders supported by institutions with significant expertise in the area are generally better suited to make than judges.

Nevertheless, in recent years climate change has increasingly been framed as a human or constitutional rights issue. From a legal perspective, such approaches face a number of challenges. To start with, climate change emission targets are typically not laid down in a way that grants individuals justiciable rights to hold governments to those targets. To frame the issue in terms of human rights hence involves not just judicial creativity, using existing rights as a basis for creating new obligations in changing circumstances, but also poses several legal and strategic challenges. It is often difficult to establish causal links between specific acts or omissions and harm to individual rights, in particular where such harm is only likely to materialize much later.[35] These problems are exacerbated by the fact that we are dealing with a situation where the resulting harm may often be transboundary, thus raising questions as to the extra-territorial effect of human rights obligations.[36] Besides these more straightforward legal challenges, there are functional ones that may also be framed in terms of the separation of powers and the judicial role. Climate change represents a paradigmatically complex and polycentric problem, requiring specific scientific and other expertise to address it. All of this makes courts less than ideal fora and opens them up to broader criticisms of judicial overreach if they decide to intervene.[37]

Nevertheless, courts have increasingly begun to engage climate change in their jurisprudence. Much of this jurisprudence has been framed – by judges themselves or by scholars writing on climate change – as a response to the failure of other institutions to do enough to tackle the issue. Early litigation in particular has often been understood as an attempt to fill a 'governance gap', resulting from the unwillingness of governments to agree on binding international standards or put forward credible domestic legislation.[38] Yet, existing accounts have shown that the governance gap explanation is not entirely accurate as a descriptive matter. We frequently see more litigation and judicial action in those countries where significant legislation already exists, as opposed to those where it is largely absent.[39] Other commentators have defended judicial action in these cases more broadly on the basis of an Elyian argument for

[35] J. Setzer and L. C. Vanhala, 'Climate Change Litigation: A Review of Research on Courts and Litigants in Climate Governance' (2019) 10:3 *Wiley Interdisciplinary Reviews: Climate Change* 580.

[36] Setzer and Vanhala, 'Climate Change Litigation'.

[37] E.g., B. Wegener, 'Urgenda – Weltrettung per Gerichtsbeschluss' (2019) *Zeitschrift für Umweltrecht* 3.

[38] *Ashgar Leghari v. Federation of Pakistan*, W.P. No. 25501/2015 (Lahore High Court, Pakistan).

[39] See, e.g., Setzer and Vanhala, 'Climate Change Litigation', comparing Canada with the UK.

the need to protect future generations not represented in the political process. It thus responds to a standard deficit, or indeed 'failure', of democratic processes.[40] But there are also strategic reasons for drawing on the language of failure in these cases. Given the lack of legally binding emission reduction rates in the Paris Agreements, which some have argued sets up governments for failure, '[o]ther than public shaming, [litigation is] the only way to hold nations accountable'.[41] Thus, courts have increasingly started to hold governments to their public commitments and sought to secure compliance with international agreements, such as the Paris Agreement, with its deliberate integration of legally binding and non-legally binding elements.[42]

Governmental failure has certainly been one important driver for judicial intervention, including structural remedies. An example is the now famous decision of a Pakistani court in response to a public interest petition in *Leghari v. Federation of Pakistan*. The judgment framed climate change justice as a matter of constitutional rights, putting forward a range of expansive orders which included the establishment of new bodies to tackle the issue: 'In the present case, the delay and lethargy of the State in implementing the [previously developed] Framework offends the fundamental rights of the citizens which need to be safeguarded', the Court argued.[43] Though in *Leghari*, governmental failures are not used to justify the existence of a rights violation in the first place – because the Court rather skates over the legal issues at stake – they play a role in justifying the need for more robust judicial intervention.[44]

The Dutch *Urgenda* decisions offer a more standard example of the role of failure arguments in climate change litigation, and it is to them that I now turn. As we will see, some of the analysis conducted by Dutch courts essentially represents an assessment of the performance of the

40 K. Fischer Kuh, 'The Legitimacy of Judicial Climate Engagement' (2019) 46:3 *Ecology Law Quarterly* 731.

41 S. Stefanini, 'Next Stop for Paris Climate Deal: The Courts; First Came the Agreement. Now Comes the Litigation', *Politico* 11 January 2016, www.politico.eu/article/paris-climate-urgenda-courts-lawsuits-cop21/.

42 L. Bergkamp and S. Stone, 'The Trojan Horse of the Paris Agreement on Climate Change: How Multi-level, Non-hierarchical Governance Poses a Threat to Constitutional Government' (2015) 4 *Environmental Liability* 119.

43 *Ashgar Leghari v. Federation of Pakistan*, W.P. No. 25501/2015 (Lahore High Court, Pakistan).

44 In the terms of the framework proposed here, the structural intervention in Leghari would be hard to justify, given that the court develops the law and adopts structural remedies at the same time.

Dutch government, which overlaps with an argument from failure, albeit not being explicitly cast in those terms.

6.4.1 *The Urgenda Decisions*

Urgenda is a Dutch environmental NGO. It decided to bring a case against the Dutch government with the aim of legally obliging it to reduce, by the end of 2020, greenhouse gas emissions by at least 25% as compared to the levels in 1990. A Dutch District Court, a Court of Appeals and, finally, the Dutch Supreme Court (the Hoge Raad) agreed, with the Court of Appeals and the Supreme Court relying on a human rights framework, in particular Arts. 2 (right to life) and 8 (right to privacy, family life) of the European Convention on Human Rights, with some references by the Supreme Court also to Art. 13 (right to remedies).[45] While acknowledging the need to combat climate change, the Dutch government opposed the decisions. In the Supreme Court, state representatives argued in particular that the earlier decision of the Court of Appeals should be overturned because of the absence of legally binding international obligations (3.4.) and given that states enjoy a margin of appreciation in fulfilling their positive obligations under the ECHR (3.2.). Moreover, courts – whose role in the Netherlands has traditionally been restrained – were not allowed under Dutch law to issue orders to create legislation, as they had essentially done here (3.5).

What are the key steps in the Dutch Supreme Court's reasoning? I leave aside some of the more technical details, such as the question of Urgenda's standing, and focus instead on the arguments with respect to Arts. 2 and 8 ECHR. First, the Dutch Supreme Court confirmed that Arts. 2 and 8 ECHR generally applied to climate change and obliged the Netherlands to do its part to counter the dangers resulting from it (para. 5.2.). It seems hard to fault this reasoning in general. The real challenge came in the next step as the Court asked what followed from this conclusion, and in particular what concrete obligations the Netherlands had. It noted that as a matter of international law, there were no binding obligations to reduce emissions to a certain level. The Dutch Supreme Court first gestured to the role of the Dutch government and legislature in deciding how to fulfil its obligations and concluded that '[i]t is clear, for example [. . .] that the State cannot at any rate do nothing

[45] *State of the Netherlands v. Stichting Urgenda*, 20 December 2019 ECLI:NL:HR:2019:2007 (Supreme Court of the Netherlands). English translation: https://tinyurl.com/yc7kytja.

at all and that the courts can rule that the State is in breach of its obligation [. . .] if it does nothing' (para. 6.3.). The Court next set out to determine what the 'minimum obligations' of the Dutch government were with respect to climate change. The judges first pointed to the international developments with regard to combating climate change, drawing in particular on international declarations and soft law, arguing that there was indeed a consensus that emissions needed to be reduced by 25–40% by 2020. This – perhaps the key step in the Court's argument – also applied to the Netherlands, notwithstanding the fact that the existing reduction rate of 20% complied with the Netherlands' obligations under EU law. According to the Court, that did not mean that the Netherlands had no further-reaching obligations under human rights law, however. Not only had the Netherlands long been on the list of countries with the highest emissions per capita, but several other EU Member States had also adopted higher targets than the 20% reduction rate, and the European Union overall envisaged cuts of 26–27% by 2020. Finally, the Court added that a higher rate also corresponded to the previous policy of the Dutch government itself, which had originally planned for a reduction of 30% by 2020 (para 7.4.1.). It only deviated from this policy later, but without giving any reasons as to why it did so, and in spite of the fact that it was uncontested that emission reductions would become more costly the longer they were delayed (para 7.4.6.).

Unsurprisingly, the *Urgenda* decisions prompted an extensive debate in the legal community, about deriving concrete obligations in terms of percentages for emission reductions from the European Convention, and about what the role of courts with regard to climate change should more generally be.[46] Some Dutch critics have argued that the *Urgenda* line of reasoning might justify expansive judicial interventions in a wide range of other policy areas, which would be contrary to both existing Dutch law

[46] See, e.g., (sceptical of the reasoning, but applauding the result) C. Backes and G. van der Veen, 'Urgenda: The Final Judgment of the Dutch Supreme Court' (2020) 17:3 *Journal for European Environmental & Planning Law* 307; M. Wewerinke-Singh and A. McCoach, 'The State of the Netherlands v Urgenda Foundation: Distilling Best Practice and Lessons Learnt for Future Rights-Based Climate Litigation' (2021) 30:2 *Review of European, Comparative & International Environmental Law* 275 (with approval); L. Bergkamp, 'The Dutch Supreme Court's Climate Judgment: Its Consequences and Implications for Business – Revolution Through Litigation' (2020) 29: 3 *European Energy and Environmental Law Review* 89; B. Mayer, 'The Contribution of Urgenda to the Mitigation of Climate Change' (2022) 35:2 *Journal of Environmental Law* 167 (sceptical of its impact).

and the separation of powers. A standard comparison seems to be making the wearing of bike helmets obligatory.[47]

The key question, of course, is if the critics are right. The answer is both yes and no. It is yes insofar as the Supreme Court's analysis is worrying with regard to the separation of powers in a scenario where the Court uses soft law standards to give content to binding human rights obligations. Given that states routinely choose to rely on soft law when they want to avoid creating legally binding obligations, this move is problematic at least from the perspective of a more traditional consent-based understanding of international law. The Dutch Supreme Court's analysis skates over this problem very quickly and without sufficiently engaging with the question whether we can use human rights as a back-door to hold states to commitments that were not meant to be legally binding in the first place.

The answer is no, insofar as there are other more convincing arguments in the *Urgenda* decisions, both in the Appeals Court and in the Supreme Court, which frame the question in terms of the comparative performance of the Dutch government – and, I would argue, at least implicitly in terms of institutional failure.

First, in analyzing the content of its obligation with regard to reducing emissions, the Supreme Court pointed out that the Netherlands had long been on the list of high per capita emitters. The details are, however, only spelled out in the decision of the Court of Appeals, which noted that the Netherlands at the time ranked '34th of 208 countries. Of the 33 countries with even higher emissions, only nine have a higher per capita emission, and not a single one is an EU Member State.'[48] More particularly, the Court subsequently argued, the Netherlands' reduction efforts were lagging far behind states such as Germany, the United Kingdom, Denmark, Sweden and France (para. 56). Second, and more importantly still, both courts emphasized the lack of convincing reasons for the lowering of the previous 30% reduction rate to 20%. The Court of Appeals noted that

> 'a substantiation based on climate science was never given, while it is an established fact that postponing (higher) interim reductions will cause

[47] I. Leijten, 'Human Rights v. Insufficient Climate Action: The Urgenda Case' (2019) 37:2 *Netherlands Quarterly of Human Rights* 112 with reference to C. Backes and G. van der Veen, *Administratiefrechtelijke Beslissingen* 2018/417.

[48] *Netherlands v. Urgenda Foundation*, 9 October 2018, ECLI:NL:GHDHA:2018:2610, para 26 (The Hague Court of Appeal). English translation quoted from Columbia Law Blog https://tinyurl.com/2tscepcu.

> continued emissions of CO_2, which in turn contributes to further global warming. More specifically, the State failed to give reasons why a reduction of only 20% by 2020 (at the EU level) should currently be regarded as credible, for instance by presenting a scenario which proves how – in concert with the efforts of other countries – the currently proposed postponed reduction could still lead to achieving the 2° C target.'

In the proceedings itself, the government subsequently argued that it preferred to adopt higher reduction rates after 2020, but the Supreme Court dismissed that argument. Given that it could not be ascertained that a delay would achieve the same effects, it emphasized again the lack of convincing reasons for adopting only a 20% target:

> 'The State has not provided any insight into which measures it intends to take in the coming years, let alone why these measures, in spite of the above, would be both practically feasible and sufficient to contribute to the prevention of dangerous climate change to a sufficient extent in line with the Netherlands' share. The State has confined itself to asserting that there "are certainly possibilities" in this context'.[49]

These arguments provide a comparative institutional perspective. First, they compare Dutch efforts with those of other similar countries, and find them insufficient. Second, they assess the institutional performance through the lens of procedure, here the requirement of reason-giving familiar from administrative law. This kind of perspective is also precisely what we would expect when we are addressing the question whether to intervene in response to legislative failure. The comparison with other states and indeed with the government's own previous policy provides a particularly important – and I believe necessary – counterweight in this case to the move from soft-law standards and scientific expertise to legal obligations, which some have viewed as the weak point in the Court's reasoning.[50] By drawing on a procedural argument – here the lack of reasons for switching from a 30% to a 20% reduction target in 2020 – the Supreme Court and Appeals Court recognize the need to accord the government discretion with regard to the details of its environmental policy. However, this discretion is not unlimited. By insisting that the government provide convincing reasons for abandoning its previous policy, courts exercise some scrutiny.

49 *Urgenda*, 20 December 2019, para 7.4.6.
50 Backes and van der Veen, 'Urgenda'.

6.4.2 Comparison and Analysis

Yet, not every court arguing in terms of governmental performance or even applying a standard of consistency is putting forward an argument from failure. This is true even when it comes to an issue like climate change, though it can sometimes be hard to identify the core of the argument.

Compare *Urgenda* to the German Constitutional Court's climate change decision as a case in point. In its decision, the German court argued that the Basic Law's Art. 20a on the duty to protect the environment required the government to lower emissions, without, however, granting individuals a right to enforce this provision (Art. 20a) directly. At the same time, the Court argued that since the German government had chosen to pursue the goal of limiting temperature increases to well below 2°C and preferably to 1.5°C above pre-industrial levels in line with Art. 20a, it had to do so in a proportional manner, requiring that the 'reduction burdens are not unevenly distributed over time and between generations to the detriment of the future'.[51] Setting out clear emission reduction rates only up to 2030 but not beyond, however, did not ensure a fair distribution of such burdens. It placed an excessive share of the burden on younger people. Invoking ideas of intergenerational consistency and ultimately fairness, the Court argued that this violated the plaintiffs' constitutional rights.

The difference between these two cases is instructive of what it means to present an argument from failure to justify judicial intervention. At first glance, the reasoning is quite similar in both cases. Like the Dutch courts, the German Constitutional Court seeks to measure governmental performance. Its focus in doing so is different, however. Rather than focusing on what the government has done wrong – as the Dutch court does – the German Constitutional Court places the emphasis on elaborating what the government's duties are in this case, in order to then conclude that it did not live up to them. Though this difference may appear insignificant at first, it matters in practice. The Dutch court's approach is ultimately more deferential, essentially grounding its analysis in an institutional comparison of the Netherlands with other states, thus taking state practice more clearly into account rather than developing its own standard for good performance. The German Constitutional Court, by contrast, focuses on

[51] BVerfGE 157, 30 – *Klimaschutz*, para. 192 (German Constitutional Court).

developing the government's duties in constitutional terms and ultimately in terms of independently developed standards of good governance, albeit standards derived inter alia from existing German legislation. As a result, there is no argument from failure here in a meaningful sense. The German decision needs to be evaluated on its own terms, as a matter of its doctrinal persuasiveness and without recourse to governmental failure.

If we compare the three cases mentioned – *Leghari*, *Urgenda* and the German case – we see that they are on a continuum when it comes to evaluating performance and diagnosing failure. In *Leghari*, the court diagnoses a complete failure to deal with the issue and accordingly intervenes in robust ways, albeit that the combination of developing the law and adopting structural remedies is hard to justify. In *Urgenda*, the court finds a comparative failure to take the issue sufficiently seriously, drawing on state practice elsewhere and the government's insufficiently explained change of policy. In the German case, the court essentially finds the government's policy insufficient for distributing higher burdens on the younger generation, but there is no longer a diagnosis of failure. This is a more conventionally 'legal' analysis. This is not surprising, insofar as the development of rights and aspects of rights has long been a feature of the German Constitutional Court's jurisprudence, in contrast to the Netherlands, where only review with regard to the compatibility with international law is allowed and usually practised relatively cautiously.[52] Accordingly, the need for a failure argument was more pressing in this context.[53] Framing an issue in terms of failure is thus also an indication as to how revolutionary courts believe themselves to be, and a rhetorical device to overcome resistance to judicial involvement.

As more and more courts have begun to treat climate change as a fundamental or human rights issue, we have also begun to consider it more normal for courts to deal with the issue. As Fowkes points out, this is because the essential question for judges to decide whether to intervene or not depends not so much on the polycentricity or complexity of an issue but its newness: Courts, he argues, tackle plenty of highly complex

[52] G. van der Schyff, 'The Prohibition on Constitutional Review by the Judiciary in the Netherlands in Critical Perspective: The Case and Roadmap for Reform' (2020) 21:5 *German Law Journal* 884.

[53] See, e.g., the helpful analysis of several of the cases re. justiciable standards for reasonable governmental efforts towards combatting climate change by L. Maxwell, S. Mead, and D. van Berkel, 'Standards for adjudicating the next generation of Urgenda-style climate cases' (2022) 13:1 *Journal of Human Rights and the Environment* 35.

questions, but they typically do so in a context where there already exist institutional or legislative frameworks that they may seek to improve or other actors who expect judicial interventions and can adjust to them.[54] Thus, being less of a new issue, there will also necessarily be more space for judicial intervention in climate change cases. This may appear ironic, given that governments now are mostly doing something with regard to the issue, and thus, judicial intervention may seem less necessary than it was a few years ago. Yet, it speaks to the role of courts as institutions making law incrementally only. It also means that we are less likely to encounter arguments from failure in the future, as the barriers for judicial intervention have – with good reasons – been lowered. On a normative level, therefore, the role of failure arguments in climate change litigation not only depends on the existing legal resources and the newness of the issue but also on other existing reasons for intervention and the judicial role within a given system. The better our general reasons for intervention, the less need there is for an argument from failure.

6.5 Conclusion

Failure drives innovation – and as this chapter shows, not just in the realm of structural remedies but when it comes to legal interpretation more broadly. Courts may decide to intervene in cases of administrative failure and sometimes even in cases of legislative failure in cases where they would ordinarily exercise restraint and defer to other institutions. And while judicial law-making is in many ways a routine and standard matter, sometimes, courts make law in bolder and less incremental ways than we would expect. If and when they do so, arguments from failure provide a way of justifying their interventions.

[54] Fowkes, 'Normal Rights'.

III

International and European Perspectives

7

Arguments from Failure in International Law

7.1 Introduction

Korea had only barely emerged from Japanese occupation during the Second World War when tensions between the newly independent Northern and Southern states began to rise. In 1950, Northern military forces crossed into the Southern area. Notified of the invasion, the UN Security Council acted promptly, quickly passing several resolutions that called on Member States to assist the (Southern) Republic of Korea to resist the invasion and establish a unified command under US leadership.[1] This decisive action was possible only because Russia had been boycotting the Security Council to protest the representation of China in the United Nations by the previous and now deposed Chinese Republican leaders. Jacov Malik, Russia's representative, nevertheless, quickly realized the mistake of the boycott and returned to the Council, subsequently vetoing further actions. In this context, representatives of key powers, such as US Secretary of State Dean Acheson, sought to circumvent the Security Council by going through the General Assembly instead.

The result was the famous Uniting for Peace Resolution, adopted 52–5 on 3 November 1950. The Resolution represented not the first,[2] but the most explicit, invocation of a reserve competence by the Assembly. After affirming the Security Council's primary responsibility to deal with issues

1 UNSC Res. 82 (1950) UN Doc. S/RES/82; UNSC Res. 83 (1950) UN Doc. S/RES/83; UNSC Res. 84 (1950) UN Doc. S/RES/84; UNSC Res. 85 (1950) UN Doc. S/RES/85. Whether the Security Council could actually legally pass these Resolutions given the absence of a permanent member is debatable and has been challenged given Art. 27(3) UN Charter, see C. Tomuschat, '"Uniting for Peace" – ein Rückblick nach 50 Jahren' (2001) 76:2/3 *Die Friedens-Warte* 289 at 290.

2 Thus, UNSCOB (the UN Special Commission on the Balkans) was a precedent to Uniting for Peace, deployed in 1947 under the authority of the General Assembly, not the Security Council; see T. M. Franck, 'U.S. Foreign Policy and the U.N.' (1986) 14 *Denver Journal of International Law & Policy* 159.

of international peace and security, it set out an argument for why the General Assembly might address with issues ordinarily reserved to the Security Council in cases where the Security Council failed to fulfil its responsibility under the Charter due to a lack of unanimity.[3] Notably, the Assembly claimed for itself the authority to recommend measures to Member States, which would – unlike a Security Council Resolution – not be legally binding on them, but merely support and encourage intervention in line with the purpose laid out.

In doing so, the General Assembly in essence put forward an argument from failure – which was, however, blurred with emergency arguments as well as arguments about implied powers. Thus, the Peruvian representative in the Assembly debate argued in terms of emergency powers: 'The Assembly's jurisdiction is thus clearly defined; it constitutes what may be called the legal foundation for any proposal for convening the Assembly in case of *emergency* to deal with the exigencies of peace when the Council is paralysed.'[4] These early emergency arguments were often couched in moral terms, with failure resulting from an 'abuse' of the right of veto,[5] as the Brazilian delegate De Freitas Valle phrased it, involving ultimately a question of 'light or darkness'.[6] Such moralistic arguments were, however, backed up by what were understood to be more 'legal' constitutionalist arguments, both in the debate itself and in the later scholarly literature. The then-US ambassador to the United Nations, Cohen, invoked domestic law analogies to argue for a competence of the General Assembly, drawing in particular on the doctrine of 'implied powers', as elaborated in the canonical US Supreme Court decision in *McCulloch v. Maryland*.[7] Notably, all this happened in a context where previous efforts to get rid of the veto power of permanent members had failed, though the practice of not treating abstentions as a veto had already been established.[8] The Resolution was thus part of

[3] UNGA Res. 377 V (1950) UN Doc. A/377V.

[4] Official records of the UNGA Fifth Session, 279th Plenary Meeting, 20 September 1950, para. 156.

[5] See ibid. the Brazilian representative ambassador De Freitas Valle, para. 4.

[6] Ibid.

[7] *McCulloch v. Maryland*, 17 US 316 (1819).

[8] T. M. Franck, *Recourse to Force: State Action Against Threats and Armed Attacks* (Cambridge University Press, 2002), p. 33, with reference to B. V. Cohen, *The United Nations, Constitutional Developments, Growths, and Possibilities* (Harvard University Press, 1961), pp. 18–9.

broader efforts by the UN General Assembly to take on a more active role in light of the Security Council's failure to do so.[9]

7.2 Failure in International Law

The Uniting for Peace Resolution provides a straightforward example of an argument from failure in international law. But this is not the only international setting where we encounter arguments from failure, often combined with emergency arguments or arguments about implied powers and effective realization.

This is not surprising. Authority in international law, Nico Krisch argues, is best understood as a 'liquid' concept. International relations are shaped by a range of more informal institutions and soft law, leading to a range of different sites of governance and, frequently, a high degree of legal fragmentation.[10] Building on the deference model developed by international relations scholars, according to which authority constitutes 'the ability to induce deference in others',[11] Krisch explains that the key feature of liquid authority is its dynamic character: 'The more liquid an authority structure is, the more its elements are in motion and the more difficult it is to pinpoint a site of authoritative decision making.'[12]

This environment is unsurprisingly receptive to arguments from failure, which should in turn be understood as one important rhetorical mechanism and legal concept for shifting authority.

Add to this that the origins and legitimacy of many international institutions can be traced to their ability to fulfil certain tasks that states cannot realistically perform on their own. By shifting authority to the international level, Member States seek to coordinate their behaviour – and potentially that of other actors – to (better) achieve certain goals, including the avoidance and resolution of conflicts.[13] Even more than at

[9] G. F. Sinclair, *To Reform the World* (Oxford University Press, 2017), p. 131–32.

[10] N. Krisch, 'Liquid Authority in Global Governance' (2017) 9:2 *International Theory* 237.

[11] D. D. Avant, M. Finnemore, and S. Sell, 'Who Governs the Globe?', in id. (eds.), *Who Governs the Globe?* (Cambridge University Press, 2010), pp. 1, 9. I owe the reference to this useful definition to Krisch.

[12] Krisch, 'Liquid Authority'.

[13] A. Buchanan and R. O. Keohane, 'The Legitimacy of Global Governance Institutions', in J. Babic and P. Bojanic (eds.), *World Governance: Do We Need It, Is It Possible, What Could It (All) Mean?* (Cambridge Scholar Publishing, 2010), pp. 214, 216. This is not to say that international law will always improve outputs and can never improve input. There may be cases when actions of one state affect people(s) outside of its national territory and who can therefore not participate in the decisions in question, but which

the national level, effectiveness arguments are therefore hardwired into the DNA of international law. Indeed, the expansion of the powers of international organizations underwrote in many ways the 'forming and reforming of modern states' as 'rational' and efficient instruments of territorial governance.[14] This project of reforming domestic states with the help of international organizations could tap into a discourse of efficiency and rationalist reform particularly prevalent in the years after the First World War among American progressives, but also in many European circles.[15] To justify the necessary expansion of international organizations' authority, a host of legal arguments were deployed. These included arguments about the need for flexible and purposive interpretation of relevant treaties, often rooted in a constitutionalist language, more specific arguments about implied powers, arguments about the need to contain crises and emergencies and, not least, arguments from failure.[16]

7.2.1 Arguments from State Failure

One of the most famous examples for the role of failure as a trope in international relations is the discourse on 'state failure'. This began with a now-famous article by Helman and Ratner in *Foreign Policy* in the Winter issue of 1992–1993, though it was based on much earlier practices and ideas. Helman and Ratner wrote: 'From Haiti in the Western Hemisphere to the remnants of Yugoslavia in Europe, from Somalia, Sudan, and Liberia in Africa to Cambodia in Southeast Asia, a disturbing new phenomenon is emerging: the failed nation-state, utterly incapable of sustaining itself as a member of the international community.'[17]

Originally a category of political science and political economy rather than law, state failure – and the related concept of an 'unwilling or unable state'[18] – was never fully recognized as a legal concept in mainstream

may participate in those decisions, albeit mediated through governments or organizations, if they are taken on an international level. But whether such arguments are convincing or not, they constitute at best a secondary and supplementary source of the legitimacy of international law. For a critical discussion, see, e.g., A. Somek, *The Cosmopolitan Constitution* (Oxford University Press, 2014), part III.

[14] Sinclair, *To Reform the World*, Introduction (and throughout).

[15] Ibid., pp. 55 ff.

[16] Ibid., see especially chapter 4, pp. 160 ff. On emergency arguments, see especially C. Kreuder-Sonnen, *Emergency Powers of International Organizations: Between Normalization and Containment* (Oxford University Press, 2019), chapters 4–6 (part II).

[17] G. B. Helman and S. R. Ratner, 'Saving Failed States' (1992–1993) 89 *Foreign Policy* 3.

[18] P. Starski, 'The "Unwilling or Unable" State as a Challenge to International Law', Habilitation Thesis, Bucerius Law School (2020).

international law. Yet, it played an important role both in political and legal practice as a rhetorical device to strengthen the powers of international organizations as well as empower other states to act in ways otherwise not considered legal. No discussion of failure in international law would be complete without mentioning this line of argument. But what was meant by a 'failed state'? Jones argues that 'a "failed state" is one which is unable to perform a set of functions taken to be characteristic and definitive of what constitutes a properly functioning state: to maintain secure boundaries, ensure the protection and security of all of the population, provide public goods and effective governance, maintain law and order throughout the territory'.[19]

Earlier uses of the idea of state failure in international law primarily occurred in the context of expanding the mandate of the United Nations to act. The concept also played an important role in granting the Security Council the authority to take actions under Chapter VII with regard to internal situations in the 1990s.[20] Intervention in such internal affairs had originally been considered outside the scope of the UN's authority. Art. 39 of the UN Charter contemplates action only in cases of a 'threat to the peace, breach of the peace, or act of aggression', thus apparently envisaging situations involving at least two states. In a series of resolutions dealing with Somalia, Rwanda and, not least, Yugoslavia, the Security Council began to expand its authority to intervene. The first step in this regard addressed situations that, while internal, had effects on other states, such as refugee flows.[21] In later Resolutions, such as when dealing with the Somalian Civil War and ensuing mass starvation,[22] internal situations increasingly came to be accepted as a basis for intervention under certain circumstances.[23] Thus, in Resolution 794 (1992) dealing with Somalia, which was considered the paradigm for a failed state in the literature,[24] the Security Council spoke of 'the unique

[19] B. Gruffydd Jones, 'The Global Political Economy of Social Crisis: Towards a Critique of the "Failed State" Ideology' (2008) 15:2 *Review of International Political Economy* 180 at 180.

[20] D. Thürer, 'The "Failed State" and International Law' (1999) 81:836 *International Review of the Red Cross* 731, at 738 ff.

[21] Gruffydd Jones, 'The Global Political Economy'.

[22] UNSC Res. 794 (1992) UN Doc. S/RES/794.

[23] See also UNSC Res. 918 (1994) UN Doc. S/RES/918 and UNSC Res. 929 (1994) UN Doc. S/RES/929; UNSC Res. 940 (1994) UN Doc. S/RES/940; UNSC Res. 1132 (1997) UN Doc. S/RES/1132 with the resolutions against Haiti and Sierra Leone dealing with military coups.

[24] E.g. Helman and Ratner, 'Saving Failed States'.

character of the present situation in Somalia'. Being 'mindful of its deteriorating, complex and extraordinary nature, requiring an immediate and exceptional response', it argued that 'the magnitude of the human tragedy caused by the conflict in Somalia, further exacerbated by the obstacles being created to the distribution of humanitarian assistance' amounted to a threat to international peace and security and thus, according to the Security Council, justified Chapter VII measures. In the context of the law on the use of force, ideas of state failure thus served to justify interventions where explicit state consent was lacking or considered irrelevant since the government had essentially become one of many parties to an ongoing civil war and no longer exercised meaningful authority over its territory. The precise requirements for when such interventions would legally be justified remained, however, contested, as did the concept of state failure or failed states itself.[25]

The most problematic use of the concept of state failure occurred in the context of the so-called unwilling or unable doctrine under Art. 51 of the UN Charter. It concerns the right of states to defend themselves against external aggression,[26] arising in response to the attacks of 11 September 2001.[27] The attacks had been planned by Al Qaeda, who were private actors on Afghan territory, without a legally relevant involvement of the Afghan government. The United States therefore found it hard to justify military intervention in Afghanistan on the basis of a right to self-defence under Art. 51 of the UN Charter as a matter of existing international law. US representatives argued that this situation was not acceptable and that a right of self-defence existed if 'the government of the State where the threat is located is unwilling or unable to prevent the use of its territory for such attacks'.[28] State failure based on unwillingness or inability would thus trigger a right to self-defence. This

[25] E.g. Thürer, 'The "Failed State" and International Law'; id., 'Failing States' *Max Planck Encyclopedias of International Law [MPIL]* (online source); R. Geiss, '*Failed States*': *Die normative Erfassung gescheiterter Staaten* (Duncker & Humblot, 2005); C. T. Call, 'The Fallacy of the "Failed State"' (2008) 29:8 *Third World Quarterly* 1491.

[26] See more in Starski, 'The "Unwilling or Unable" State'. See also N. Tzouvala, *Capitalism as Civilisation: A History of International Law* (Cambridge University Press, 2020) and N. Tzouvala, 'TWAIL and the "Unwilling or Unable" Doctrine: Continuities and Ruptures' (2015) 109 *American Journal of International Law* 266.

[27] Call, 'The Fallacy' at 1493 ff.

[28] Letter dated 23 September 2014 from the Permanent Representative of the United States of America to the United Nations, UN Doc S/2014/695, cited acc to Starski, 'The "Unwilling or Unable" State', p. 1.

claim has been severely contested in the legal literature,[29] but the Security Council in Resolutions 1368 and 1373 reaffirmed the existence of the right to self-defence in the context of terrorist attacks shortly after the attacks, providing in the latter Resolution for a broad, if vague, mandate to 'take steps' in response.[30] In the subsequent 'war on terror', state failure became a standard reference point for US foreign policy, as failed states were seen as safe havens for terrorist organizations.[31]

Finally, arguments about state failure and dysfunctionality also played a role outside of the law on the use of force, in particular in the domain of development economics. The turn from modernization theory to a governance framework in the World Bank emerged partly amidst a widespread perception of governance failures in the late 1980s and 1990s, in the context of fragile or failed states.[32] Thus, 'internal deficits' such as corruption or inefficient domestic administrations were seen as obstacles that needed to be addressed in order for financial support to be provided.[33] So-called structural adjustment programmes, often pursuing neo-liberal policies, were meant to help with this task. This drove an expansion of the World Bank's mandate beyond monetary politics to questions of the rule of law and related issues.[34]

'A root cause of weak economic performance in the past has been the failure of public institutions. Private sector initiative and market mechanisms are important, but they must go hand-in-hand with good governance – a public service that is efficient, a judicial system that is reliable, and an administration that is accountable to its public', a World

[29] E.g., D. Murray, 'Flawed and Unnecessary: The "Unwilling or Unable" Doctrine Pertaining to States' Use of Force in Self-Defence against Non-State Actors' (2017) 30 *Hague Yearbook of International Law* 59; I. Couzigou, 'The Right to Self-Defence against Non-State Actors: Criteria of the "Unwilling or Unable" Test' (2017) 77 *Heidelberg Journal of International Law* 53.

[30] UNSC Res. 1373 (2001) UN Doc S/RES/1373.

[31] Call, 'The Fallacy'.

[32] Sinclair, *To Reform the World*, part III. For a thorough discussion of the different intellectual paradigms, see P. Dann, *The Law of Development Cooperation: A Comparative Analysis of the World Bank, the EU and Germany* (Cambridge University Press, 2013), chapter 2.

[33] Dann, ibid., chapter 2, pp. 90 ff.

[34] Sinclair, *To Reform the World*, pp. 251 ff.; Dann, *The Law of Development Cooperation*, pp. 260 ff. Both Sinclair and Dann stress, however, that there was not a straightforward neo-liberal paradigm at work, but that the real story of these developments is more complex, with different motivations involved.

Bank Report argued, mainly with respect to African states.[35] As Sinclair shows, Ibrahim Shihata, the Bank's vice president, and top lawyers assumed a key role in this regard. It is also in this context that we see a more constitutionalist framing of the argument emerging. It included references to the doctrine of implied powers and a broad purposive approach to the Bank's mandate, according to which the expansion of the Bank's role constituted a natural response to the frequent dysfunction, emergencies and, ultimately, failures of state institutions.[36] Dealing with questions of international development assistance, the idea of fragile statehood emerged as a new category, sometimes substituting for state failure. It still plays an important role today in grouping together certain states or situations for international policy-making in the interest of increasing efficiency.[37]

7.2.2 Failure, Crisis and International Authority

This broader language of failure was part of a functionalist understanding of law within the United Nations, as sketched out in the academic literature by Sinclair, Orford and others. Anne Orford in particular has argued that we should understand the expansion of the powers of the United Nations in terms of its function to guarantee freedom and security, thus continuing the intellectual tradition associated with Hobbes and others.[38] International organizations, Orford argues, step into the shoes of nation states, and we should therefore understand the modern concept of the Responsibility to Protect not as a new thing, but rather as a ratification of existing UN practices as they emerged after the Second World War.[39]

Orford's emphasis on security as key to understanding the legitimacy of both modern nation states and the United Nations connects to Saptarishi Bandopadhyay's recent work on the importance of disaster

[35] B. B. Conable, 'Foreword', in World Bank (ed.), *Sub-Saharan Africa: From Crisis to Sustainable Growth* (World Bank, 1989), p. xi.

[36] Sinclair, *To Reform the World*, pp. 260, 279.

[37] M. von Engelhardt, 'Dealing with Fragile States: The Law and Practice of International Development Organizations', PhD Dissertation, Humboldt University, Berlin (2015), p. 25.

[38] A. Orford, *International Authority and the Responsibility to Protect* (Cambridge University Press, 2011), Introduction (and throughout).

[39] Ibid.

management to the formation of modern states.[40] As Orford and Sinclair show, modern nation states were not unique in building their legitimacy on their ability to grapple with disasters and emergencies. A similar story can be told in the international realm about institutions such as the United Nations or the World Bank. Arguments about protection – sometimes framed in terms of arguments from failure – were part of broader efforts of these institutions to frame their own authority in constitutional terms. This authority in turn was entangled with their efforts to define and assist the creation of modern, efficient states. Not accidentally, modernization theory and later theories of governance would play an important part in framing proposals for an expanded role for the United Nations and its different bodies. In many cases, this kind of expansion was justified in relatively traditional legal categories, in particular on the basis of a broadly purposive interpretive approach to the United Nations' powers, often coupled with constitutionalist imagery.[41] In other cases, actors invoked the more dramatic language of exception and of emergencies.[42] Thus, the General Assembly's creation of UNEF in the Suez crisis, building on the Uniting for Peace rationale, was seen as an extreme and thus exceptional situation by Secretary General Dag Hammerskjold.[43] When the United Nations intervened in Congo, emergency rhetoric again surfaced, for example when Hammerskjold suggested to Cordier (…) that 'At any time, you may face the situation of complex disintegration of authority that would put you in a situation of emergency which in my view would entitle you to greater freedom of action in protection of law and order. The degree of disintegration thus widening your rights is a question of judgment.'[44]

Critical legal scholars have pointed to the neo-colonial language and ambitions of those wielding the language of state failure. Indeed, a contemporary reading of Helman and Ratner's *Foreign Policy* essay, with its uncritical take on the post-war UN trusteeship system, combined with

40 S. Bandopadhyay, *All Is Well: Catastrophe and the Making of the Normal State* (Oxford University Press, 2022), p. 173.

41 See Sinclair, *To Reform the World*, pp. 176–81.

42 See also Kreuder-Sonnen, *Emergency Powers*, chapter 4.

43 D. Hammarskjöld, 'Do We Need the United Nations?', Address Before the Students Association, 2 May 1959, 4 *Public Papers of the Secretaries-General of The United Nations 1958-1960* at 368.

44 B. Urquhart, *Hammarskjold* (Knopf, 1972), p. 444. I am referred here by Sinclair.

its call for more involvement in Africa by the great powers, will see it tapping into a now familiar broader discourse of efficiency and modernization with distinctly neo-colonial undertones. The very idea of a failed state is clearly modelled on a Western-centric concept of statehood that treats Western European states as paradigm cases for successful statehood, leaving relatively little room for different conceptions and forms of organizing public authority.[45] Moreover, critical scholars argue that even where the idea of state failure arguably corresponds to the facts on the ground, as in Somalia in the 1990s, the concept holds limited explanatory power and distracts from understanding the context and origins of that 'failure' rooted in colonial and neo-colonial policies.[46]

7.3 Evaluating Arguments from Failure in International Law

What then should we make of arguments from failure in the international realm?

Our examples here speak again to the close relationship of failure arguments to emergency arguments, on the one hand, and to arguments about implied powers and efficiency, on the other. They demonstrate how the different concepts are tied together via the shared underlying logic of output-legitimacy, so prevalent in international law. And the more the exceptional character of the problem is emphasized, the less there is a need for implied powers arguments. The same applies in reverse: The stronger the argument for a broad reading of the rights or competences in question, the less there is a need to invoke an emergency/exception template. As we see here, arguments from failure incorporate elements of both. On the one hand, they are concerned with inter-institutional relationships and thus build on collaborative ideas of working together to achieve a shared purpose. On the other, they operate with a norm/exception distinction. All of this suggests that the framework developed in Part I remains relevant here, too. That said, in the international setting, arguments from failure encounter some specific challenges.

45 Gruffydd Jones, 'The Global Political Economy'; P. Bilgin and A. D. Morton, 'Historicising Representations of "Failed States": Beyond the Cold-War Annexation of the Social Sciences?' (2002) 23:1 *Third World Quarterly* 55; also S. Sundstøl Eriksen, '"State Failure" in Theory and Practice: The Idea of the State and the Contradictions of State Formation' (2011) 37:1 *Review of International Studies* 229.

46 Gruffydd Jones, 'The Global Political Economy', at 197.

7.3.1 Separation of Powers

Because international organizations are not constitutional democracies, central elements of constitutional democracy, such as the separation of powers, have no clear equivalent here. This raises the question what happens when we encounter shifts of authority between different organs of one institution or among several institutions. Broadly speaking, the consensus is that the concept of separation of powers does not fit international relations or indeed even more constitutionalized international and regional organizations without significant adaptations.[47] Though international organizations may have courts, access is often not straightforward. Most importantly, there are no global legislatures comparable to national ones. The UN General Assembly is the closest analogue in this regard, but its powers, nevertheless, differ significantly from those of national parliaments. This also means that it is much more questionable whether the expectations and principles of mutual support and collaboration that we usually encounter in domestic constitutions exist here.

Yet, this is not to say that international law is free of conceptions of functional differentiation and mutual checks. Drawing on Christoph Möllers' work,[48] Joana Mendes and Ingo Venzke have put forward a concept of relative authority to address legitimacy questions in international relations. Mendes and Venzke argue in essence that different actors and institutions can claim different forms of authority that need to be understood and conceptualized in relationship to each other, similar to the separation of powers in domestic states:

> Different actors make different legitimacy claims with which they justify their authority. Authority is relative in this sense even on any single level of governance. In basic terms, the ideal type of judicial adjudication gains its legitimacy from the law that it applies, from party consent, independence, and impartiality. Its legitimacy bases are different from those assets that underlie the idea of legislation (representativeness, inclusion) or the idea of administration(competence, expertise). Specific actors feed different legitimacy assets into global governance.[49]

47 I. Venzke and J. Mendes, 'The Idea of Relative Authority in European and International Law' (2018) 16:1 *International Journal of Constitutional Law* 75 at 95-6.

48 C. Möllers, *The Three Branches: A Comparative Model of Separation of Powers* (Oxford University Press, 2013), chapter 4.

49 Venzke and Mendes, 'The Idea of Relative Authority' at 90.

Without fully importing the idea of the separation of powers, Mendes and Venzke suggest that three key forms of legitimacy are particularly important as a basis for allocating authority: the actor's inclusiveness, its functional specialization and its capacity to protect rights.[50] The challenge, as Mendes and Venzke formulate it, is to determine which mix of these three sources of legitimacy is normatively required in any given instance of exercising public authority.

All of this suggests, on the one hand, that the normative stakes of arguments from failure may be somewhat lower in the international context, absent a clear expectation that particular institutions fulfil one particular function. But it shows also that considerations of legitimacy along the lines sketched above must play a central role. This suggests that our framework developed in Chapter 2 can still provide useful assistance in dealing with such arguments, though more needs to be said about its applicability, as I argue below.

7.3.2 Quasi-Constitutional Framework

More precisely, arguments from failure can only be deployed in a context where expectations of collaboration and mutual support and control have a place, similar to domestic constitutional systems. For shorthand, I call this a quasi-constitutional framework, but I am not tied to the term 'constitutional' as such.[51] What I mean is that the organization in question must be able to lay a credible claim to regulating a broader area of international law in a broadly comprehensive manner. It must, for that purpose, be equipped with institutions that are expected to work together towards their shared goal, albeit that they may each fulfil separate functions. In other words: There needs to be a sense of joint responsibility for a broader political project. Where such a framework is lacking, not only is standing in for others hard to justify, but it also increases risks of abuse when arguments from failure are deployed without being controlled by other institutional checks or by the expectation of longer-term collaboration. The central example of an international organization that fits such an understanding is, of course, the United Nations, given its scope and self-understanding as the core international forum, independently of whether it makes sense to understand the Charter as such as a

[50] Ibid. at 80.

[51] In other words: I do not want to open the debate here if constitutionalism is a concept that can be applied outside a nation state context.

world constitution.[52] For other international organizations, however, this will often be harder to argue.

How much and what do we really need in terms of a shared framework? In particular, we may wonder if we should assume there to be room for arguments from failure whenever the failure in question is closely tied to an international organization's core mission. However, not just any functional orientation should be considered sufficient to generate mutual responsibilities for a shared political project. Absent a broader legal framework in terms of which it makes sense to assume that a range of different actors are ultimately pursuing a broader shared project, we should not assume that there is room for arguments from failure. Actors are not necessarily left without resources in this situation; in particular, they may draw implied powers doctrines if there are clear functional imperatives.

It follows that where states invoke arguments from failure to expand their powers as against other states, such as the 'unwilling or unable' doctrine employed in the so-called war on terror or in the context of humanitarian interventions without UN approval, this cannot be justified in terms of our framework.[53] There simply is no shared institutional framework in this case, in which we may identify gaps, in terms of which states may justify expanding their powers in the light of certain failures of others.

In addition, there are high risks of abuse if we allow interventions outside such a framework, as Paulina Starski shows by pointing to continuities with colonial legal arguments that establish hierarchies between states on the basis of functionalist considerations.[54] Ntina Tzouvala pushes this line of argument further, describing the 'unwilling or unable' doctrine as rooted in a broader international law discourse on the 'standard of civilisation'.[55] This discourse, Tzouvala argues, oscillates

[52] B. Fassbender, 'The United Nations Charter as Constitution of the International Community' (1998) 36 *Columbia Journal of Transnational Law* 529; N. D. White, 'The United Nations System: Conference, Contract or Constitutional Order' (2000) 4 *Singapore Journal of International & Comparative Law* 281; P. Dupuy, 'The Constitutional Dimension of the Charter of the United Nations Revisited' (1997) 25:1 *Max Planck Yearbook of United Nations Law Online* 89; for a critique, see, e.g., G. Teubner, 'Constitutionalising Polycontexturality' (2011) 20 *Social and Legal Studies* 210, focusing on the embeddedness of constitutionalism in a nation state context, which is not central to my understanding here.

[53] See also Starski, 'The "Unwilling or Unable" State', pp. 640 ff.

[54] Ibid., pp. 644 ff.

[55] Tzouvala, *Capitalism*, chapter 1 (and throughout).

between an ultimately racist 'logic of biology', which denies equality to some actors with a 'logic of improvement' towards an ultimately pro-capitalist/(neo)liberal state.[56] Whether we share Tzouvala's critical approach or not, her analysis and that of Starski certainly speak to the risks of employing arguments from failure in a political and historical context where entrenched hegemonic structures shape the discourse. Insofar as arguments for intervention are put forward here, they therefore have to be justified in terms of the international law on self-defence, but without drawing on the unwilling or unable doctrine. Similar arguments apply with regard to humanitarian interventions by individual states or groups of states. In particular, the fact that a state may have signed a human rights treaty and is nevertheless violating human rights on a massive scale, potentially in the context of a civil war, does not provide enough of a shared institutional framework for individual states to justify intervening militarily.

Even where we do encounter a broader constitutional framework in the international realm, we also need to consider which entities are putting forward an argument from failure – a state or a body within another organization – in order to determine if they can indeed legitimately act for others in our broader analysis. To a degree, we might find horizontal power shifts on the international level to be less normatively problematic insofar as they do not conflict with a strict conception of functional integrity of the different branches as they might in the national realm. At the same time, they still raise the kind of issues that Mendes and Venzke draw attention to, prompting some modifications to our framework. As international bodies are, for example, typically not directly democratically legitimated, inclusiveness – understood in a broad way to encourage both broad representation and participation rights for stakeholders and civil society organizations – will have to serve as a proxy.

It is less clear whether and how this applies if arguments from failure are invoked in a vertical context. While laying out a more comprehensive framework for arguments from failure, Chapter 2 operated mostly on the basis of theories and examples developed for horizontal power shifts. In the international realm, however, such arguments are often deployed vertically, as we will also see in Chapter 8, dealing with the European Union.

At the bottom line, this also means, however, that where the hurdle of a 'constitutional' context can be overcome, the situation at the

[56] Ibid.; for a summary, see pp. 210–1.

international level is not fundamentally different to domestic constellations. Though the normative stakes shift somewhat, our framework in Part I can still usefully inform our discussions.

7.3.3 The Uniting for Peace Resolution Revisited

With the above qualifications, let's return to the Uniting for Peace Resolution and its argument for a subsidiary competence of the General Assembly. Its legality and scope remain contested today. While it has been invoked in a number of Security Council Resolutions[57] and General Assembly Resolutions,[58] and played a role in other contexts, scholars differ on whether it actually formed the legal basis for any concrete actions.[59] Though the better arguments suggest that the Resolution was legally important, at least for the establishment of the UNEF peace mission in the wake of the Suez crisis in 1956,[60] it only ever served as a basis for recommending military action in the Korean case.[61] At the same time, it has been cited to justify other actions by the General Assembly.

Towards the end of the Cold War, the Security Council was for a while back in the driver's seat again, decreasing the need for General Assembly intervention, until the newfound consensus began again to falter. Since then, the Uniting for Peace Resolution has made a partial comeback.[62] More recently, it has been invoked to defend a bigger role for the General Assembly to combat grave human rights abuses in Syria.[63] It has also been referred to in calls on Russia to cease its unlawful aggression against Ukraine, which cite the Resolution and the fact that 'the lack of

57 See, e.g., UN Security Council Resolutions 119 (1956), 120 (1956), 129 (1958), 157 (1960), 303 (1971), 462 (1980), 500 (1982).

58 E.g., UNGA Resolutions USSR (A/6717), Senegal (A/ES-7/1), Zimbabwe (A/ES-8/1), Qatar (A/ES/10/1).

59 C. Binder, 'Uniting for Peace Resolution (1950)', in A. Peters and R. Wolfrum (eds.), *Max Planck Encyclopedia of Public International Law* (Oxford University Press, 2017), p. 10.

60 UNGA Res. 1000 (ES-I) (1956) UN Doc. A/3354.

61 A. J. Carswell, 'Unblocking the UN Security Council: The Uniting for Peace Resolution' (2013) 18:3 *Journal of Conflict and Security Law* 453 at 459.

62 On this, arguing for the continuing utility of the Resolution M. Ramsden, 'Uniting for Peace and Humanitarian Intervention: The Authorising Function of the U.N. General Assembly' (2016) 25:2 *Washington International Law Journal* 267.

63 G. Melling and A Dennett, 'The Security Council veto and Syria: responding to mass atrocities through the "Uniting for Peace" resolution' (2017) 57 *Indian Journal of International Law* 285.

unanimity of the permanent members of the Security Council at its 8979th meeting has prevented it from exercising its primary responsibility for the maintenance of international peace and security'.[64] And unsurprisingly, some commentators have suggested that the General Assembly should rely on the Resolution to justify some form of intervention in Gaza, given the blockage of Security Council action by the United States.[65]

In the original debate about the Resolution, two questions were central: first, whether the competence of the Security Council to take 'action' in cases of a breach of peace was exclusive; and second, what the Security Council's precise obligations were and thus what might constitute failure in terms of the Resolution, focusing primarily on Arts. 10, 11, 12, 14 and 24 as well as 41 and 42 of the UN Charter.[66] The debate was thus framed mainly in terms of implied powers. Nevertheless, it frequently verged into broader arguments about necessity and ultimately proportionality, thus reflecting in many respects the framework developed in this book.

The text of the Charter makes clear that the Security Council indeed has primary responsibility to discuss disputes or functions assigned to it (Arts. 24 and 12 of the UN Charter), and this suggests that the General Assembly may at least have a subsidiary or secondary competence,[67] as the International Court of Justice also explicitly accepted in its *Certain Expenses* Advisory Opinion.[68] This argument seems largely accepted today, but it is less clear what precisely this entails and when the Assembly's secondary competence is activated.

As many diplomats and lawyers have pointed out, the Security Council is tasked to 'ensure prompt and effective action by the United Nations' and to 'act in accordance with the Purposes and Principles of the United Nations' according to Art. 24. If the Security Council thus fails to act, this arguably contravenes the purpose of the United Nations and triggers the subsidiary competence of the General Assembly, or so some argue.[69] This

64 UNSC Res. 2623 (2022) UN Doc. S/RES/2623.

65 E.g., Maziar Motamedi, 'What's UN Resolution 377A, Can It Help in Efforts to Stop Israel-Gaza War?', *Al Jazeera*, 11 Dec. 2023, https://tinyurl.com/3chch8ww.

66 J. Andrassy, 'Uniting for Peace' (1956) 50:3 *The American Journal of International Law* 563. See also for a discussion of its later uses H. Reicher, 'The Uniting for Peace Resolution on the Thirtieth Anniversary of its Passage' (1981) 20:1 *Columbia Journal of Transnational Law* 1 at 10; more sceptical Tomuschat, 'Uniting for Peace', 296.

67 Andrassy, 'Uniting for Peace', 564.

68 *Certain Expenses*, ICJ Rep. (1962), p. 151.

69 Ibid. at 565.

entails a more straightforward argument from failure. Yet, the questions what constitutes failure and who gets to decide it loom large, given that the exercise of veto powers is explicitly envisaged by the Charter and does not, as such, constitute an abuse of powers. Moreover, some interventions may cause further harm rather than help. We might also ask whether only complete inaction constitutes a failure or whether failure is possible if the Council merely doesn't do enough.[70] The wording of Arts. 41 and 42 suggests that the Security Council has discretion ('may decide. . .', 'may take such action. . .') how to respond once it has established the existence of any threat to the peace, breach of the peace or act of aggression (Art. 39). Some scholars have suggested that one should therefore require a referral by the Security Council itself, which counts as a procedural decision and so is not subject to the veto.[71]

Finally, there is the question of what exactly the General Assembly might do. May it recommend (in a non-binding manner) military action that would otherwise violate Art. 2 (4) of the UN Charter? Can it make binding recommendations to Member States in that regard? Do either or both of these suggestions go too far? Here, too, scholars disagree, but it bears noting that the practice of the General Assembly has been very restrained in this regard in the past.

Treating the Uniting for Peace Resolution as a justification for the General Assembly to expand its power to deal with the fallout from Security Council vetoes, and thus as an argument from failure, would not fundamentally change the terms of the discussion. However, it might help to sharpen and emphasize some points. It would mainly highlight that the situation envisaged by the Resolution is not an everyday or routine case, and thus that the expansion of powers entails a divergence from standard practice and the rules rather than simply serving to increase the effectiveness of the United Nations. Clearly, the existing frameworks are not comprehensive in the sense that the General Assembly may never take action when it comes to Chapter VII of the Charter. It would also highlight a few additional aspects that play no, or a more marginal, role in current discussions. For example, it matters that the General Assembly is the closest analogue to a parliament we have on the international level. It can boast an inclusivity not shared by the Security Council, whose composition and processes are still shaped by the political constellations relevant in the mid-twentieth century and

[70] Reicher, 'The Uniting for Peace Resolution', 10.

[71] Art. 27 (2) UN Charter. See Carswell, 'Unblocking the UN Security Council', 466.

whose legitimacy is more shaky accordingly. That said, this argument is predicated on the idea that a large majority of states in the General Assembly are democratic states rather than authoritarian regimes.

Nevertheless, understanding the Security Council's inaction in terms of a breach of law remains challenging, given the wide discretion it enjoys when it comes to acting under its framework. To put forward an argument from failure, we thus need something more concrete. Art. 39 of the UN Charter provides an entry point to such arguments, albeit letting the Security Council itself determine the existence of any threat to the peace, breach of the peace or act of aggression. Yet, the terms in question are legal terms, and while the Security Council has adopted an increasingly broad reading of Art. 39 since the end of the Cold War, this does not mean that it has no legal content. Scholars have moreover drawn on the emerging responsibility-to-protect (R2P) doctrine,[72] the better to come to grips with the Security Council's obligations. This might be complemented by the Code of Conduct for the Security Council,[73] as Rebecca Barber has suggested.[74] R2P stipulates several conditions for triggering the UN's responsibility, including just cause (in the form of serious and massive human rights violations, i.e. quality and quantity), reasonable prospects of improving the situation (capacity/functionality), last resort and proportionality. These closely overlap with the kind of arguments we would be interested in under a proportionality framework as applied to arguments from failure.

Would this be sufficient to differentiate cases of failure from mere disagreement? An explicit referral by the Security Council to the General Assembly would certainly bolster arguments that we are dealing not with a disagreement but a breach of obligations and ultimately failure. To draw this distinction, we might also consider the majorities in the Security Council. If action is blocked on the basis of just one permanent member's veto, the case for treating this as a failure is stronger than if the

[72] UNGA Res. 60/1 (2005) UN Doc. A/RES/60/1; see also General Assembly Fifty-Ninth Session: Report of the Secretary-General, 21 March 2005 at 135.

[73] Code of Conduct Regarding Security Council Action Against Genocide, Crimes Against Humanity or War Crimes, Annex I to the letter dated 14 December 2015 from the Permanent Representative of Liechtenstein to the United Nations addressed to the Secretary-General, UN Doc. A/70-621-S/2015/978 (14 December 2015).

[74] R. Barber, 'Accountability for Crimes Against the Rohingya: Possibilities for the General Assembly Where the Security Council Fails' (2019) 17:3 *Journal of International Criminal Justice* 557.

issue is a truly contested one in the Security Council. Scholarly opinions might also help to clarify the issue since scholarly commentary is today much more readily and often immediately available on blogs and other fora, albeit we would have to consider a strong Global North bias in that context. Not least, we might also consider the majorities within the General Assembly itself.

All things considered then, there are good a priori reasons to assume that credible arguments from failure can be put forward in some cases to justify the General Assembly stepping in. However, the key question still remains as to what this implies in the next step and what and how much the General Assembly might do. And this is where an argument from failure would open the doors more widely than if we are relying on an implied powers justification. If we indeed encounter, for example, a situation involving massive violations of *ius cogens* norms and where there is no credible argument for non-intervention, as demonstrated by a referral and strong majorities in the Security Council and General Assembly, etc., and intervention would likely seem to be the only way to put an end to such a situation, under our framework the General Assembly would be able to exercise fairly robust powers, including recommending military action.

The real question in such cases is, of course, a political one. Where any of the major powers with a veto in the Security Council are themselves involved in breaches of international law, whether directly, as in the case of Russia's war on Ukraine, or in a supporting role, as in the United States, when it comes to Gaza, the reason for eschewing stronger forms of international intervention is not legal but political.

From a normative perspective, however, it bears emphasizing that the alternatives to General Assembly intervention are hardly more appealing. We have seen military alliances such as NATO acting without a UN mandate but relying on the concept of humanitarian intervention.[75] And both in this context and in others, arguments from failure have regularly surfaced in cases where the Security Council is seen to be failing, as, for example, in the Syrian civil war.[76] Yet, while the General Assembly has repeatedly criticized the Security Council's 'failure' to take action on

[75] On the latter, see Starski, 'The "Unwilling or Unable" State', pp. 264 ff.

[76] Y. Nahlawi, 'Overcoming Russian and Chinese Vetoes on Syria Through Uniting for Peace' (2019) 24:1 *Journal of Conflict and Security Law* 111; see also Carswell, 'Unblocking the UN Security Council'.

Syria,[77] it ultimately did not rely on the Uniting for Peace Resolution mechanism in doing so.[78] However, from a normative perspective, intervention sanctioned by the United Nations and ideally within a UN framework is clearly preferable to individual powerful states acting in such cases. That said, it bears emphasizing that in an African context, intervention through the African Union, as provided for by Art. 4 (h) of its Constitutive Act, may provide a more appropriate alternative.[79]

7.4 Conclusion

The liquid character of many authority structures in international law and their output orientation make failure arguments a recurring feature of public international law, often embedded in broader theories of modernization and sometimes with neo-colonial undertones. Yet, arguments from failure are problematic here, because the idea of taking over for others (while expanding one's own powers) implies a context where expectations of cooperation and support are legally entrenched. This condition is not always met at the international level, particularly in inter-state relationships. And even where it is, the stakes of arguments from failure in international law can be very high and the discussion around them strongly ideologically shaped, as the various discourses of state failure demonstrate. One important conclusion to draw from this is thus that it matters who puts forward an argument from failure, as a matter of the power relationships involved. Given just how broad and hard to define arguments from failure are, we should be more careful and restrained with such arguments the more their proponents are speaking from a position of power. If those who dominate the discourse about expectations are the same as those who draw on failure to claim new rights, risks of abuse run particularly high.

[77] UNGA Res. 66/253B (2012) UN Doc. A/RES/66/253B Preamble; UNGA Res. 68/182 (2014) UN Doc. A/RES/68/182 para. 12; see also UNGA Res. 71/130 (2016) UN Doc. A/RES/71/130 Preamble.

[78] See Nahlawi, 'Overcoming Russian and Chinese Vetoes' for a detailed discussion.

[79] D. Kuwali, 'The End of Humanitarian Intervention: Evaluation of the African Union's Right of Intervention' (2009) 9 *African Journal on Conflict Resolution* 41.

8

Efficiency and Failure in the European Union

8.1 Introduction

Efforts to capture what the European Union is about can be akin to the story of the blind men drawing an elephant. If the standard political narrative is a success story, with European integration bringing peace and wealth to Europe after centuries of war, another way of looking at the Union is through the lens of crisis. In this second reading, efforts at European integration have failed and failed again, been challenged, rejected and challenged some more, with its nature and future contested until today – from the abandonment of the European Political Community and the European Defense Community in 1954 to the lingering crisis of the 1960s with its empty chair, the economic challenges in the 1970s and the failed referenda for a constitutional treaty in the early 2000s and then, in short order, the financial crisis, the migration crisis and, not least, the rule of law crisis. Yet, as professional optimists in politics and European lawyers will point out, European integration has not just continued but been deepened through these challenges: per aspera ad astra!

Indeed, the crises of the past were not simply obstacles to European integration but often enabled it. 'Men take great decisions only when crisis stares them in the face',[1] said Jean Monnet, one of the European Union's founding fathers who revelled in his ability to work through a good crisis.[2] European Union law – as well as, occasionally, domestic constitutional law geared towards accommodating the EU – reflects this crisis-driven history in its particular flexibility. It has sometimes provided the arguments for further integration based on a teleological reading of

[1] J. Monnet, *Memoirs*, R. Mayne (trans.) (Third Millennium Publishing, 2015), chapter 16, p. 268 (pdf).

[2] B. Szele, '"Crises are Opportunities": Jean Monnet and the First Steps Towards Europe' (2003) 2:2 *European Integration Studies* 5.

the treaties and secondary Union law (the law of the EU institutions), and sometimes by not standing in the way of political action outside its framework.[3] And perhaps unsurprisingly, the flexibility that appears to some as an admirable exercise in dialogue and legal pluralism[4] suggests to others a return to the 'law of the jungle',[5] where not law but power ultimately prevails.

In this chapter, the story I want to tell is only partly about arguments from failure, though we will find some such arguments in this context, too. Mainly, I want to draw attention to a particular style of flexible legal argument when it comes to allocating and shifting responsibility and competences in a multilevel system, such as the European Union. The language of failure is bound up here with the theme of mutual trust as a constitutional principle of EU law. Tracing such arguments reveals a lot about the different political landscapes of different eras of European law. More importantly, it sketches the best picture we have as to what a more flexible approach to legal interpretation might look like on a grander scale. Arguments from failure are part of this approach, but they are not the whole or indeed even the most important element of it. Rather, the lesson of this chapter is a broader one about the need to draw more careful legal distinctions and take law as a constraint more seriously in the Union.

In the following, I start with an overview of the kind of flexible legal argument prevalent in European Union law, in particular, the so-called *effet utile*, that is the idea of interpreting the European treaties in a purposive manner with the aim of realizing the internal market.[6] After this, I turn to consider some more specific concepts and doctrines in European law, namely the concept of systemic deficiencies and the *Solange*-jurisprudence, as arguments from failure or variations thereof. Finally, I discuss the normative stakes of such arguments, against the backdrop of the EU's broader functionalist approach.

[3] Case C-370/12, *Thomas Pringle v. Government of Ireland and Others* [2012]; see also J. White, *Politics of Last Resort: Governing by Emergency in the European Union* (Oxford University Press, 2019), p. 151. See more below.

[4] M. Kumm, 'The Jurisprudence of Constitutional Conflict: Constitutional Supremacy in Europe before and after the Constitutional Treaty' (2005) 11:3 *European Law Journal* 262.

[5] A. Somek, *The Cosmopolitan Constitution* (Oxford University Press, 2014), p. 198.

[6] The literature on the *effet utile* encompasses library shelves by now. For a useful contemporary analysis of the *effet utile*'s relevance in European law, including from an empirical perspective, see U. Sadl, 'The Role of *Effet Utile* in Preserving the Continuity and Authority of European Union Law: Evidence from the Citation Web of the Pre-accession Case Law of the Court of Justice of the EU' (2015) 8:1 *European Journal of Legal Studies* 18.

8.2 Flexibility and *Effet Utile* in European Law

Arguments about failure, relative capacities and effectiveness have long functioned as an important driver for European integration. As in the case of the United Nations, in the EU, a sense of crisis and the language of efficiency have been closely entwined with a constitutionalist understanding of the then-European Communities, today the European Union. Thus, the neo-functionalist school of thought on the EU has long emphasized the importance of output legitimacy over input legitimacy.[7] It builds on early descriptions of the European communities as a purposive association for functional integration ('Zweckverband'), highlighting its limited, utilitarian scope compared to sovereign states.[8] But if this functional delimitation is what distinguishes the EU from its Member States, it is the breadth and depth of its powers that distinguishes it from other international organizations and that ultimately constitutes a political community, even absent a European demos.[9] This ambivalence is captured particularly well by Turkuler Isiksel's theory of the European Union. On the one hand, Isiksel accepts the constitutional character of the European Union, on the other hand she stresses, that the Union is nevertheless functionally limited and that its legitimacy depends on realizing its overarching goal of economic union.[10] This functionalist orientation has shaped European law and enabled a particularly flexible approach to legal interpretation.[11]

[7] F. W. Scharpf, *Governing in Europe: Effective and Democratic?* (Oxford University Press, 1999), p. 6. See also for a discussion of these concepts in the EU J.H.H. Weiler, 'In the Face of Crisis: Input Legitimacy, Output Legitimacy and the Political Messianism of European Integration' (2012) 34:7 *Journal of European Integration* 825.

[8] H. P. Ipsen, *Verfassungsperspektiven der Europäischen Gemeinschaften* (Walter de Gruyter & Co, 1970), p. 8; H. P. Ipsen, *Europäisches Gemeinschaftsrecht* (J. C. B. Mohr, 1972), p. 198.

[9] T. Isiksel, *Europe's Functional Constitution: A Theory of Constitutionalism Beyond the State* (Oxford University Press, 2016), p. 78. This understanding of what constitutes a constitution thus does not involve popular sovereignty and/or democracy as a necessary element, but builds on earlier work by scholars such as Teubner; see G. Teubner, *Constitutional Fragments: Societal Constitutionalism and Globalization* (Oxford University Press, 2012), p. 18.

[10] Ibid., p. 78.

[11] The term 'functionalism' has assumed a variety of different meanings in international law. My own use of the term is drawing in particular on Turkuler Isiksel's work (ibid.), which uses it somewhat differently than other international law scholars, in particular J. Klabbers, 'The EJIL Foreword: The Transformation of International Organizations Law' (2015) 26:1 *European Journal of International Law* 9–82, who adopts a narrower understanding of the concept.

8.2.1 Early Landmarks

Start by considering the early jurisprudence of the European Court of Justice. Its early landmark cases, *Van Gend en Loos* and *Costa v. ENEL*, ushered in the two central innovations of European law as compared to other bodies of international law. In these two cases, the CJEU famously developed the then-revolutionary doctrines of the direct effect and supremacy of Union law. Together, these doctrines guaranteed not only that individual citizens could rely on treaty provisions directly in domestic courts (under certain broadly defined conditions), but also that domestic laws conflicting with treaty provisions would have to give way. In its reasoning, the Court famously distinguished the European Communities from other international organizations. Adopting a constitutionalist language, the judges in *Van Gend en Loos* argued that the Communities constituted 'a new legal order of international law for the benefit of which the states have limited their sovereign rights (...) and the subjects of which comprise not only the member states but also their nationals'.[12] Restricting the enforcement of the treaty to the Commission and other Member States would be 'ineffective', the judges argued, 'if it were to occur after the implementation of a national decision taken contrary to the provisions of the treaty'.[13] The Court continued this line of reasoning in its subsequent *Costa v. ENEL* judgment, where the judges reasoned that Union law would lack effectiveness 'if a state could unilaterally nullify its (the treaty's) effects by means of a legislative measure which could prevail over community law'.[14] Once again, this was bound up in a broader argument about the special character of the European Treaties.

This revolutionary jurisprudence did not emerge out of nowhere, but was a result of lobbying by pro-European groups as well as the Commission's legal service.[15] When the Court finally adopted their suggestions, the judges were responding to the lingering political crisis of the new European Communities. At that time, joint decision-making and the project of a positive harmonization of Member State laws had stalled because of disagreements among the governments involved.[16] This

[12] Case 26/62, *Van Gend & Loos v. Nederlandse Administratie der Belastingen* [1963] ECR 1.

[13] Ibid.

[14] Case 6/64, *Flaminio Costa* v. *E.N.E.L.* [1964] ECR 585.

[15] M. Rasmussen, 'Establishing a Constitutional Practice of European Law: The History of the Legal Service of the European Executive' (2012) 21:3 *Contemporary European History* 375.

[16] In this direction already J. H. H. Weiler, 'The Transformation of Europe' (1991) 100:8 *The Yale Law Journal* 2403 at 2428–29.

situation was seen as 'disappointing' by many, including Robert Lecourt, then-judge of the European Court.[17] Various attempts to revitalize the project of political integration had failed, and as scholars have noted, it seemed unrealistic then to place trust in the Commission or the Parliament to change this state of affairs.[18] This backdrop of political crisis and failure of the Communities' political institutions has been described as a 'critical pre-condition' for the Court's early landmarks.[19] In other words: Here, too, a sense of failure was driving judicial innovations, as discussed in Chapter 6. As Justice Lecourt put it: 'It may seem excessive to present Law as a particularly efficient tool to unify Europe. It is, however, worth the demonstration. It may indeed offer the chance to acknowledge – and, who knows?, to adopt – this new path, protected from the great controversies, in order to achieve the goal the Six Member States have established'.[20]

This protection 'from the great controversies' of course brought with it a degree of depoliticization, which recent scholars have not unreasonably identified as the early seeds of the democratic deficit of European integration.[21] We see a similar logic in the second landmark case of *Costa v. ENEL*, setting out the supremacy of Community law over domestic laws. For if the force of community law varied across different Member States, the objectives of the treaty would be put at risk – and hence, European law needed to prevail over national law. As the crisis intensified and cooperation between Member States in the community institutions reached a new low with France's empty-chair approach in 1965, the Court and the Commission's legal service became central to making political progress.

8.2.2 Consolidation

Van Gend and *Costa* marked only the beginning, albeit an auspicious one. The argument about the need for effectively realizing the treaties' goals – the so-called *effet utile* – came to play a key role in driving legal

[17] A. Vauchez, '"Integration Through Law": Contribution to a Socio-history of EU Political Commonsense' (2008) 10 *EUI Working Papers*, p. 7.

[18] Ibid., with further references.

[19] Ibid., without relying on a monocausal explanation, pp. 7–8.

[20] R. Lecourt, 'Le rôle du droit dans l'unification européenne' (1964) 17–8 *Bulletin de l'Association des juristes européens* 5; I am referred here by Vauchez, '"Integration Through Law"'.

[21] M. A. Wilkinson, *Authoritarian Liberalism and the Transformation of Modern Europe* (Oxford University Press, 2021), p. 112; see also Weiler, 'The Transformation', 2403 at 2428–29."

innovation and political and economic integration in the European Union. Famous examples are the creation of state liability for breaches of EU law in *Francovich*[22] and *Brasserie du Pechêur*,[23] the direct effect of EU directives[24] and the doctrine of implied powers expanding the authority of European institutions vis-à-vis the Member States,[25] among many others. Insofar as the CJEU referred more explicitly to state failures in these cases, however, this was not where its emphasis lay. In the Court's language, failure often simply indicated a breach of EU law. That then required effective remedies and thus drove legal innovation, but without making the latter too explicit. Only in the liability decisions in *Brasserie du Pechêur/Factortame* did the Court put forward a more specific concept of a breach of law that we might label failure, in the sense that individuals seeking to hold a state liable for damages suffered as a result of a violation of EU law had to show that the breach was sufficiently serious.[26] The broader rationale of efficient ordering also came to play a role in the CJEU's doctrine of implied powers, later adopted in the Lisbon Treaty, but developed in the context of foreign relations in the early 1970s. Thus, in its 1971 *ERTA* judgment, the Court reasoned that where the Community had powers to regulate certain matters internally, 'the full effect of this provision would be jeopardized if the powers which it confers (. . .) did not extend to the conclusion of agreements with third countries'.[27]

Once the initial crises had been overcome, the Court's early precedents were on the books and the CJEU's broader teleological approach to the

[22] Joined Cases C-6/90 and C-9/90, *Andrea Francovich and Others v. Italian Republic* [1991] ECR I-5357.

[23] Joined Cases C-46/93 and C-48/93, *Brasserie du Pêcheur SA v. Federal Republic of Germany and Others* [1996] ECR I-1029.

[24] Case 41/74, *Yvonne van Duyn v. Home Office* [1974] ECR 1337.

[25] Case 8/55, *Fédération Charbonnière de Belgique* v. *High Authority of the European Coal and Steel Community* [1956] ECR 245.

[26] Joined Cases C-46/93 and C-48/93, *Brasserie du Pêcheur SA v. Federal Republic of Germany and Others* [1996] ECR I-1029, para. 56: 'The factors which the competent court may take into consideration include the clarity and precision of the rule breached, the measure of discretion left by that rule to the national or Community authorities, whether the infringement and the damage caused was intentional or involuntary, whether any error of law was excusable or inexcusable, the fact that the position taken by a Community institution may have contributed towards the omission, and the adoption or retention of national measures or practices contrary to Community law'.

[27] For an overview, see M. Chamon, 'Implied Exclusive Powers in the CJEU's Post-Lisbon Jurisprudence: The Continued Development of the ERTA Doctrine' (2018) 55:4 *Common Market Law Review* 1101.

interpretation of the Treaties had become entrenched. Thus, functionalism continued to play an important role in the Court's jurisprudence even when European politics subsequently changed, as a result of the introduction of majority voting, which furnished the means to overcome blockages by individual members. The Court's expansive approach increasingly prompted scholarly and political criticism from the late 1990s onwards.[28] The more formal response came, inter alia, in the form of a treaty amendment, the subsidiarity clause, which many Member States hoped would provide a mechanism to constrain the exercise of Union powers in the future.[29] Yet, the clause did not fulfil that purpose, at least not in the first two decades after its introduction. Instead, it constitutionalized in many ways the CJEU's outcome-oriented approach to EU competences. Today, encapsulated in Art. 5(3) TEU, the subsidiarity principle provides that

> Under the principle of subsidiarity, in areas which do not fall within its exclusive competence, the Union shall act only if and in so far as the objectives of the proposed action cannot be sufficiently achieved by the Member States, either at central level or at regional and local level, but can rather, by reason of the scale or effects of the proposed action, be better achieved at Union level.

While the subsidiarity principle resembles other rules for dividing federal and state competences on the basis of concepts such as implied powers and necessity, its framing makes clear that (non-exclusive) competences in the EU are a priori understood not as fixed allocations of authority but rather as instruments to increase regulatory output.[30] As such, it

[28] This is particularly, but not only, true for German law scholars; see K. Hailbronner, 'Die Unionsbürgerschaft und das Ende rationaler Jurisprudenz durch den EuGH?' (2004) 57:31 *Neue Juristische Wochenschrift* 2185; R. Herzog and L. Gerken, 'Stoppt den Europäischen Gerichtshof', *Frankfurter Allgemeine Zeitung*, 08 September 2008, p. 8.

[29] K. van Kersbergen and B. Verbeek, 'The Politics of Subsidiarity in the European Union' (1994) 32 *Journal of Common Market Studies* 215, who also point out though that the first ideas of subsidiarity in the EU context was introduced to empower the Commission, rather than constrain its powers.

[30] Though such an understanding of the (federal) separation of powers seems likely to lead to instability and permanent contestation, this risk of instability did not realize in the European Union as the CJEU has proved unwilling to use subsidiarity as a real constraint on Union competences, granting wide discretion to Community institutions to make their own assessment in this regard; see Case 58/08, *Vodafone Ltd. and Others v. Secretary of State for Business, Enterprise and Regulatory Reform* [2010] ECR 4999, paras. 52 and 68. In light of the CJEU's unwillingness to use subsidiarity as a sharper sword, Member States have subsequently introduced further mechanisms to raise subsidiarity concerns, in

contributed to further entrenching the EU's legitimacy in functional terms – that is, in terms of enabling effective governance – rather than in terms of increasing democratic legitimacy.

8.3 Fundamental Rights Protection in a Multilevel System: Mutual Trust and Its Limitations

Arguments about relative capacities and effectiveness not only played a role in the realm of European economic law, however. Through the concept of systemic deficiencies and the Solange-jurisprudence they also appear in the very different realm of fundamental rights protection, where they provide a basis for intervention in cases of failure and for restraint, where trust in other bodies is appropriate. While such arguments play a different role in these cases than in the economic realm, their attractiveness in such different contexts speaks to their importance for negotiating responsibilities within multilevel legal systems.

8.3.1 Systemic Deficiencies and Mutual Trust

8.3.1.1 The *N.S.* Case

Start with a well-known decision of the CJEU on migration law. In the *N.S.* case, Belgian and UK courts had asked the CJEU whether their respective governments were still allowed to transfer asylum seekers back to the country through which they entered the European Union. This standard rule constituted an important element of the 'Dublin system',[31] given that reports had emerged showing that both the housing conditions as well as the legal procedures in place in Greece at the time were dreadful and violated asylum-seekers' fundamental rights.[32] In other words, they asked if Belgium and the United Kingdom could really send people back to such conditions.

particular the so-called early warning mechanism, which gives national parliaments an option to force the Commission to reconsider legislative proposals and under certain conditions to force the Council and Parliament to take a stance on the issue.

[31] The term refers to a set of EU law instruments regulating the common policies of the Union with regard to the processing of asylum claims. The *N.S.* case mainly dealt with Regulation No 343/2003 of the European Union (Dublin II-Regulation), which has since been replaced by Regulation No 604/2013 (Dublin III).

[32] Case C-411/10, *N.S. v. Secretary of State for the Home Department and Others* [2011] ECR I-13905.

Drawing on an ECtHR judgment, in which the ECtHR had identified structural problems in Greece's system for housing and processing asylum-seekers,[33] the CJEU answered the question negatively. In doing so, it developed the concept of systemic deficiencies, but coupled this with an individual assessment. Where systemic deficiencies provided sufficient grounds for believing that asylum seekers 'face(d) a real risk of being subjected to inhuman or degrading treatment', they could no longer be transferred back to their port of entry within the Dublin system. With this, the CJEU distinguished systemic deficiencies from 'minor infringements' of the existing European provisions. The latter would not trigger a deviation from the ordinary rules allocating responsibilities under the Dublin framework. However, where systemic deficiencies existed, they would shift responsibility for the asylum-seekers among the Member States, contrary to the existing rules which provided that the countries through which asylum-seekers entered the Union were responsible for dealing with their claims.

The *N.S.* judgment was a momentous decision because it involved a significant departure from the Court's previous jurisprudence. The judges had always emphasized the principle of mutual trust, which echoes this theme in John Hart Ely's theory of judicial review.[34] In the European Union, however, the principle of mutual trust had assumed a specific meaning in the context of creating the common market. Establishing such a truly integrated common market where products, capital and people can freely travel was and is no mean feat. It requires Europeans to recognize as valid in their own state acts of other Member States, from product safety standards and academic degrees to something as simple as driving licenses.[35] In a canonical case of the European Court of Justice, *Cassis de Dijon*, the Court had understood this principle to imply that Germans could not prohibit or hinder the marketing of a French liqueur, Cassis de Dijon, because its alcohol content was lower than the percentage required for beverages to be sold as liqueur in

[33] *M.S.S. v. Belgium and Greece* [GC], 21 January 2011, No. 30696/09 (ECHR). Note, however, that the ECHR did not issue a pilot judgment in this case.

[34] J. H. Ely, *Democracy and Distrust: A Theory of Judicial Review* (Harvard University Press, 1980); see also discussion in Chapter 5.

[35] See, e.g., for an overview T. Wischmeyer, 'Generating Trust Through Law? Judicial Cooperation in the European Union and the "Principle of Mutual Trust"' (2016) 17:3 *German Law Journal* 339.

Germany.[36] Instead, German authorities had to recognize the French standards, according to which the liqueur had been produced, instead of imposing their own, thus admitting products of other Member States into their own internal markets. Because only some areas and some rules are truly standardized across the Union and because even where they are standardized, these standards are implemented by domestic administrators, the principle of mutual recognition became enormously important. The CJEU supplemented the principle of mutual recognition with the parallel principle of mutual trust.[37] Because Member States could trust each other to comply with European law, the standard argument went, they had to recognize each other's actions and procedures as presumptively legal. This also applied when the EU later assumed competences in the realm of judicial and police cooperation, with regard to criminal law and asylum law.[38]

The concept of 'systemic deficiencies' was thus developed by the Court to carve out an exception to the rule of mutual trust. In specific cases, Member States were not just allowed but legally required to set aside the fiction of trust and cease sending asylum-seekers back to their port of entry. In Elyian terms, we might also label this a malfunction in the integration process, which then triggers intervention, albeit in a specific supranational context.

8.3.1.2 The Rule of Law Crisis

Following the *N.S.* judgment, the term 'systemic deficiencies' quickly became familiar in European Union law. It was invoked in a host of European and domestic European judgments in the field of migration and adopted in subsequent legislation (Art. 3(2) of EU Regulation 604/2013). The concept migrated to questions of extradition, where it became

[36] Case 120/78, *Rewe-Zentral AG v. B undesmonopolverwaltung für Branntwein* [1979] ECR 649.

[37] Iris Canor points to the first use in Opinion 1/75, Opinion of the Court given pursuant to Art. 228 (1) of the EEC Treaty – Arrangement OCDE – Norme pour les dépenses locales [1975] ECR 1355; see, I. Canor, 'Suspending Horizontal Solange: A Decentralized Instrument for Protecting Mutual Trust and the European Rule of Law', in A. von Bogdandy et al. (eds.), *Defending Checks and Balances in EU Member States* (Springer Verlag, 2021), p. 183.

[38] Case C-420/07, *Meletis Apostolides v. David Charles Orams and Others* [2009] ECR I-3571, para. 73.

relevant in the context of the rule of law crisis.[39] In the case of *Aranyosi and Caldaru* (2016), the question arose if Germany could extradite two criminal suspects to Hungary and Romania on the basis of a European Arrest Warrant given the broader rule of law problems in the two countries and the questionable status of judicial independence there. Once again drawing on previous jurisprudence of the ECtHR,[40] the CJEU argued that cooperation between states under the European Arrest Warrant mechanism could be suspended only 'in the event of serious and persistent breach by one of the Member States of the principles referred to in Article 2 TEU, and in accordance with the procedure provided for in Article 7 TEU'.[41] Thus, only once the Council had taken a decision according to Art. 7 TEU, Member States would have to suspend cooperation under the respective framework automatically.[42] Absent such a Council decision, judicial authorities would only be able to refuse extradition requests in certain exceptional cases where there was no longer a basis for mutual recognition and trust. In the case at hand, the Court concluded that it needed to investigate further and request information before extraditing persons in cases where

> objective, reliable, specific and properly updated evidence (. . .) demonstrates that there are deficiencies, which may be systemic or generalised, or which may affect certain groups of people, or which may affect certain places of detention, the executing judicial authority must determine, specifically and precisely, whether there are substantial grounds to believe that the individual concerned by a European arrest warrant (. . .) will be exposed, because of the conditions for his detention in the issuing Member State, to a real risk of inhuman or degrading treatment, within the meaning of Article 4 of the Charter, in the event of his surrender to that Member State.[43]

With this, it largely followed the advisory opinion of Advocate General Bot, who had pointed out that the situation resulted from 'a damaging

[39] Case C-578/16 PPU, *C. K. and Others v. Republika Slovenija* [2017]; C-220/18 PPU, *ML v. Generalstaatsanwaltschaft Bremen* [2018]; Joined Cases C297/17 and C318/17, and C438/17, *Bashar Ibrahim and Others v. Bundesrepublik Deutschland and Others* [2019].

[40] *M.S.S. v. Belgium and Greece* [GC], 21 January 2011, No. 30696/09 (ECHR).

[41] Joined Cases C-404/15 and C-659/15 PPU, *Pál Aranyosi* and *Robert Căldăraru v. Gene ralstaatsanwaltschaft Bremen* [2016].

[42] Ibid. See also more explicitly, e.g., Case C-216/18 PPU, *The Minister for Justice and Equality v. LM* [2018], para. 72.

[43] Joined Cases C-404/15 and C-659/15 PPU, *Pál Aranyosi and Robert Căldăraru v. Generalstaatsanwaltschaft Bremen* [2016].

failure to act, on the part both of the Member States and of the Union institutions'.[44] Once again, then, the argument about systemic deficiencies served to disapply the existing regulatory framework and shift responsibilities among Member States.

The CJEU has since reaffirmed its approach in the widely discussed *Celmer* case,[45] which dealt with a reference by an Irish Court that had questioned an extradition request to Poland given the ongoing rule of law proceedings against the Polish government's attempt to capture the judiciary.[46] The CJEU, however, made it even clearer in *Celmer* that systemic deficiencies on their own did not suffice to deny extradition but rather that there had to be an assessment of the specific risk to the concerned person in each individual case. What exactly the double-conditionality of systemic flaws and individual risk really requires is nevertheless somewhat unclear in the Court's jurisprudence and subject of scholarly critiques.[47]

Not least, the concept of systemic deficits subsequently also appeared in the context of the 2020 Rule of Law Conditionality Framework. This allows the European Commission to withhold certain funds from Member States inter alia in case of systemic deficits that 'directly affect or seriously risk affecting the sound financial management of the Union budget or of the financial interests of the Union in a sufficiently direct way'.[48] It thus enabled the Commission to expand its powers (of withholding funds) in order to better respond to structural problems in Member States.

8.3.2 *Solange and Reverse-Solange*

8.3.2.1 The *Solange*-Jurisprudence

Though the concept of systemic deficiencies constituted a new doctrine in European law, it shared an underlying rationale with a much earlier

[44] Opinion of AG Bot in Joined Cases C-404/15 and C-659/15 PPU, *Pál Aranyosi* and *Robert Căldăraru v. Generalstaatsanwaltschaft Bremen* [2016], para. 176.

[45] Case C-216/18 PPU, *The Minister for Justice and Equality v. LM* [2018].

[46] Ibid.

[47] E.g. P. Bárd and W. van Ballegooij, 'Judicial Independence as a Precondition for Mutual Trust? The CJEU in Minister for Justice and Equality v. LM' (2020) 9:3 *New Journal of European Criminal Law* 353–365.

[48] Regulation (EU, Euratom) 2020/2092 of the European Parliament and of the Council of 16 December 2020 on a general regime of conditionality for the protection of the Union budget, OJ 2020 L 433I, p. 1 and corrigendum OJ 2021 L 373, p. 94.

line of jurisprudence, recognizing the need for effective rights protection in a multilevel system and for a certain degree of flexibility accordingly.

Indeed, the protection of constitutional and human rights by the CJEU itself constituted a response to a push-back by some constitutional courts, in particular the German. European law did not at that point include a catalogue of fundamental rights as opposed to a set of economic fundamental freedoms. This was particularly problematic because European law had been declared to be supreme in conflicts with domestic law. Such supremacy, as the CJEU had explained early on, applied not just to ordinary statutory domestic law but also to domestic constitutional law.[49] However, since the European Treaties themselves did not contain any human or fundamental rights norms in the traditional sense – the so-called economic freedoms were just that and not more – this meant that European law de facto operated without any human or fundamental rights safeguards. This, the German Constitutional Court decided in 1974, was not acceptable. It thus claimed for itself the competence to scrutinize European law with regard to its compatibility with German fundamental rights, limiting the supremacy of EU law with respect to the Basic Law '[A]s long as the integration process has not progressed so far that Community law receives a catalogue of fundamental rights decided on by a parliament and of settled validity, which is adequate in comparison with the catalogue of fundamental rights contained in the Basic Law'.

This line of reasoning, however, posed a threat to the CJEU, which was just starting to develop its own fundamental rights jurisprudence. As the CJEU's willingness to develop and engage with fundamental rights picked up speed and somewhat more credibility, the German Constitutional Court subsequently relinquished its jurisdiction over European law in *Solange II*: '[A]s long as the European Communities, in particular European Court case law, generally ensure effective protection of fundamental rights as against the sovereign powers of the Communities which is to be regarded as substantially similar to the protection of fundamental rights required unconditionally by the Constitution, and in so far as they generally safeguard the essential content of fundamental rights.'[50]

[49] Case 11/70, *Internationale Handelsgesellschaft mbH v Einfuhr- und Vorratsstelle für Getreide und Futtermittel* [1970], ECR 1120.

[50] BVerfGE 73, 339 – *Solange II* (German Constitutional Court).

This later *'solange' (so long as)* argument thus entails a variation on the theme of assuming power on the basis of failure. It goes like this: As long as another institution/system offers an adequate system of rights protection, the court/institution in question will not exercise its own jurisdiction in this regard. This is different to the first *Solange*-decision, which involved an argument from failure, albeit with one twist: *Here*, the German court claimed jurisdiction as long as the European system was failing to provide adequate rights protection. That decision was thus concerned not with a typical institutional failure in the sense of malperformance, but rather responded to a design or adaptation failure in the broader legal system of EC law. This design failure had led to a gap in fundamental rights protection, which the German Court initially sought to fill by exercising jurisdiction over EC law, contrary to the CJEU's postulate of EU law supremacy. Once the gap had been closed – albeit not quite in the way initially envisaged by the German Court – there was no further need to exercise jurisdiction. That said, recourse to failure arguments remains a latent possibility should the EU fall significantly below its current standard of fundamental rights protection.

This concept has also surfaced in other decisions,[51] including in the European Court of Human Rights in the *Bosphorus*-decision (in modified form[52]). And it featured in an advisory opinion of Advocate General Maduro[53] in a CJEU case, arguing for European rights review in dealing

[51] See, e.g., Final Judgment *HM Treasury v. Mohammed Jabar Ahmed and Others* [2010] UKSC 2 (United Kingdom Supreme Court). For further examples, albeit in a somewhat different key, see also W. Sadurski, '"Solange, Chapter 3": Constitutional Courts in Central Europe – Democracy – European Union' (2008) 14:1 *European Law Journal* 1.

[52] The European Court of Human Rights explained in its judgment first that such actions in compliance with EU law would be presumed 'justified as long as the relevant organisation is considered to protect fundamental rights, as regards both the substantive guarantees offered and the mechanisms controlling their observance, in a manner which can be considered at least equivalent to that for which the Convention provides'. Unlike the German Court, the ECHR, however, announced that it would scrutinize in individual cases whether the protection of Convention rights was 'manifestly deficient' and if so consider the presumption in favour of legality rebutted; see *Bosphorus Hava Yolları Turizm Ve Ticaret Anonim Şirketi v. Ireland* [GC], 30 June 2005, No. 45036/98 (ECHR), para. 156. See more below, Fn. 70.

[53] Opinion of AG Maduro in Joined Cases C-402/05 P and C-415/05 P, *Yassin Abdullah Kadi and Others v. Council of the European Union and Others* [2008] ECR I-6351; see also the CFI in the follow-up *Kadi II* Case T-85/09, *Yassin Abdullah Kadi v. European Commission* [2010] ECR II-5177, para. 127: 'That must remain the case, at the very least, so long as the re-examination procedure operated by the Sanctions Committee clearly fails to offer guarantees of effective judicial protection, as the Court of Justice considered to be the case at paragraph 322 of *Kadi*'.

with individuals sanctioned by the UN Security Council, given that at the time, such individuals had no way of challenging their sanctions within the UN system itself.[54]

8.3.2.2 *Reverse-Solange*

More recently, the *Solange*-rationale has been revived in the academic literature in the context of the European rule of law crisis. Armin von Bogdandy and Iris Canor, writing with a number of co-authors, have argued for an expansion of the CJEU's competences in cases where we encounter serious deficits regarding the rule of law in individual Member States.[55] Labelled *Reverse-Solange*, this proposal is geared to address the problem that the European Union, strictly speaking, has very limited means to ensure adherence to core principles of democracy and the rule of law outside the scope of European law. For while there exists a Charter of Fundamental Rights that applies to actions of the European Union itself, Member States are only bound by the Charter when they implement European law, according to Art. 51 CFR.[56] Ultimately, this proposal envisages the European Court of Justice assuming the function of a constitutional court in states where serious rule of law deficits exist with respect to core rights and values as protected by Art. 2 TEU.

[54] The *Kadi* case arose from a challenge to the freezing of financial assets of Mr. Kadi on the basis of an EU Regulation, which implemented a UN Security Council resolution, requiring Member States to take action against persons and organizations suspected of being associated with Osama bin Laden. Mr. Kadi argued that he had been violated in his fundamental rights given inter alia that he himself had never been heard and never had been provided with the chance to challenge his inclusion in the Security Council sanctions list, which was correct at that time. This situation had created a gap in the protection as rights because UN members were legally obliged to implement the resolution under the UN Charter, an obligation that moreover takes precedence over conflicting international obligations – including their obligation under the European Treaties – as a matter of Art. 103 UN Charter. However, the Court did not adopt the Solange-language but a constitutionalist framing, asserting the primacy of European constitutional principles, including Mr. Kadi's fundamental rights, on the basis of the autonomy of the Community and its supremacy with respect to Member States obligations under the UN Charter. This is also true for the follow-up decision in *Kadi II*, see Joined Cases C-584/10 P, C-593/10 P and C-595/10 P, *European Commission and Others v. Yassin Abdullah Kadi* [2013].

[55] A. von Bogdandy et al., 'Protecting EU Values: Reverse Solange and the Rule of Law Framework', in A. Jakab and D. Kochenov (eds.), *The Enforcement of EU Law and Values: Ensuring Member States' Compliance* (Oxford University Press, 2017), p. 221.

[56] Ibid. Art. 51 CFR has been interpreted broadly by the CJEU in its jurisprudence, but it nevertheless restricts the Charter's applicability significantly.

8.4 Questions and Lessons

All of this raises the question what our framework and the previous insights from this book can bring to the EU case – and what in turn the EU stories might teach us going forward.

To start with, it bears emphasizing that the idea of effectiveness holds an important place as a source of political legitimacy both within and outside of nation states, its inherently administrative character and focus on risk-regulation notwithstanding.[57] Of course, this does not necessarily imply that it should operate as a yardstick for legality, as opposed to a consideration legislators or constitution drafters should take into account when designing policies and even institutions. Given the 'liquid' structures of authority we encounter in the international realm,[58] but also in the European one, this is not surprising. However, in an EU context, this deserves particular attention because the European Union is much more federalized, much closer to a state than other international organizations, and it exercises much more power. Unlike other international organizations, the European Union can meaningfully be described in constitutional terms.[59] However, in the European Union, democratic and functionalist modes of legitimacy have long been in tension with each other,[60] even if we accept that input- and output-legitimacy are not necessarily mutually exclusive but rather complementary.[61]

Some scholars have more recently suggested that the path of integration through law in the Union has come to end, and that governance in the EU is increasingly driven by more informal arrangements and measures of questionable legality, drawing on necessity and emergency rather than constitutional tropes.[62] They reference developments during the financial crisis that were based on a very insecure legal footing, if at all:

[57] Isiksel, *Europe's Functional Constitution*, pp. 7 and 72–3.

[58] N. Krisch, 'Liquid Authority in Global Governance' (2017) 9:2 *International Theory* 237; for more, see Chapter 6.

[59] E.g., Isiksel, *Europe's Functional Constitution*, as well as the nuanced argument by F. Bignami, 'Rethinking the Legal Foundations of the European Constitutional Order: The Lessons of the New Historical Research' (2013) 28:5 *American University International Law Review* 1311.

[60] Isiksel, *Europe's Functional Constitution*, p. 90.

[61] C. S. Sternberg, 'Political Legitimacy between Democracy and Effectiveness: Trade-Offs, Interdependencies, and Discursive Constructions by the EU Institutions' (2015) 7:4 *European Political Science Review* 615.

[62] White, *Politics of Last Resort*, chapter 3 in particular; C. Kreuder-Sonnen and J. White, 'Europe and the Transnational Politics of Emergency' (2022) 29:6 *Journal of European Public Policy* 953; N. Scicluna, 'Integration Through the Disintegration of Law? The ECB

the Troika, the expansion of the ECB's powers during the crisis, and the European stability mechanism, upheld by the European Court of Justice in *Pringle*.[63] Though it remains somewhat unclear how far this trend in the EU has gone – and how much it is mostly a response to the series of crises shaking the Union from the 2010s onwards – these observations tie in with what seems to be a broader global trend towards more informality in international affairs. Recent scholarship shows that decision-makers increasingly choose informal arrangements over formal ones (for different reasons).[64] From a constitutional theory perspective, such arrangements are no less troubling than the more formal structures and institutions we have gotten used to. While they may be better at preserving domestic decision-making powers (if this is what we worry about), they also typically involve fairly opaque decision-making arrangements, which often hinge on personal networks.[65]

All of this suggests two things. First, it is important to face up to functionalism as a key source of legitimacy in the European Union, one that will hold a more important place here than in domestic states. In this regard, the European Union is much like other international organizations. And because supranationalism will remain contested and problematic, a certain degree of legal flexibility will be necessary to respond to shifting political and legal landscapes. Yet, it also seems important that this openness should not get out of hand. Both in the interests of the Member States and the Union, legal guardrails are necessary, from a strategic perspective, but more importantly from a normative one. It is core to the idea of modern constitutionalism that the exercise of legal power be legally bound. This suggests that the more recent emergency-driven logic of integration as well as the unqualified *effet utile* approach the CJEU has often adopted in the past both go too far. It also illustrates why arguments from failure might have an important place in this context, by offering a principled and legal but narrow path for intervention in some cases. Given its constitutional character, the EU is in many

and EU Constitutionalism in the Crisis' (2018) 25:12 *Journal of European Public Policy* 1874.

63 Case C-370/12, *Thomas Pringle v. Government of Ireland and Others* [2012].

64 C. B. Roger, *The Origins of Informality: Why the Legal Foundations of Global Governance Are Shifting, and Why It Matters* (Oxford University Press, 2020); K. W. Abbott and T. J. Biersteker (eds.), *Informal Governance in World Politics* (Cambridge University Press, 2024), pp. 265–71.

65 J. White, 'The De-institutionalisation of Power Beyond the State' (2022) 28:1 *European Journal of International Relations* 187.

ways a more suitable legal environment for such arguments than most other international organizations. The European Treaties clearly stipulate principles of mutual solidarity and cooperation (e.g. Preamble, Art. 2, 3, 4, etc. TEU), albeit that solidarity may in practice often be lacking between Member States, as demonstrated during the financial crisis.[66]

8.4.1 Arguments from Failure

The framework developed here also provides a clearer perspective on some of the more specific examples and cases discussed in Section 8.3, to which I now return.

8.4.1.1 *Solange*-Arguments

In constitutional theory, approaches like *Solange* are typically discussed in the context of ideas of constitutional pluralism or even judicial dialogue in Europe. Multiple courts are seen as being in a conversation about rights protection in the context of determining their own jurisdiction vis-à-vis one another.[67] As such, these decisions represent not just an example of an approach that adopts a comparative institutional analysis as its key lens, but we may also label the *Solange*-arguments a form of 'legal process theory', with close parallels to comparative political process theory. The difference is that we are here concerned with deficits in rights protection rather than democratic processes, while acknowledging that both are closely related. Yet, while the *Solange*-approach may be intuitively convincing to manage jurisdictional conflicts in a multilevel system, it is also problematic. As briefly discussed in Chapter 2, Alexander Somek delivers perhaps the most stinging attack on this line of jurisprudence, describing the *Solange*-approach as a return to 'the law of the jungle', where ultimately political powers prevail.[68] Where

[66] See, e.g., A. Sangiovanni, 'Solidarity in the European Union' (2013) 33:2 *Oxford Journal of Legal Studies* 213. See also Aileen Kavanagh's work on collaborative constitutionalism, which includes some references to the ECHR and the European Union as well; A. Kavanagh, *The Collaborative Constitution* (Cambridge University Press, 2023), Conclusion.

[67] E.g., A. S. Sweet, 'A Cosmopolitan Legal Order: Constitutional Pluralism and Rights Adjudication in Europe' (2012) 1:1 *Global Constitutionalism* 53; for a comprehensive discussion, M. Avbelj and J. Komárek (eds.), *Constitutional Pluralism in the European Union and Beyond* (Bloomsbury Publishing, 2012); focusing on Kadi and more critically, G. de Búrca, 'The European Court of Justice and the International Legal Order After Kadi' (2010) 51:1 *Harvard Journal of International Law* 1.

[68] A. Somek, *The Cosmopolitan Constitution*, p. 198.

defenders of constitutional pluralism such as Mattias Kumm reframe this jurisprudence as part of a practice of mutual justification and an expression of the principle of subsidiarity, Somek considers it as an example of an administrative approach to constitutionalism whose focus is on 'interface conflicts and their management'.[69] Ultimately, he concludes, ideas of good governance triumph over democratic self-government.[70] Rather than providing 'comprehensive regulation of the exercise of public authority', the constitution becomes 'a constitution of conflict'.[71] In other words, what is legal depends on regulatory output rather than on whether the institution acting is part of a government elected directly by the people over whom it exercises authority.

Though Somek's argument is important in providing a more critical perspective on the constitutional pluralism literature, it seems to me that his critique has a lot more bite with regard to *effet utile* arguments and the principles of subsidiarity and proportionality in EU law than with regard to the target at which he directs it, the *Solange*-jurisprudence.

For the *Solange*-jurisprudence does not truly open the gates to a situation of 'bourgeois anarchy', where individuals are in a position to choose their loyalties and decide whom to trust.[72] This becomes clear when we take a look at the original cases themselves. In neither of the two German *Solange*-decisions were the plaintiffs put in a position to make a choice where to pursue their rights claims, that is in the European Union or Germany. Nor did the decisions introduce a case-by-case approach to the matter. Instead, they allowed the German Court to set out generally the responsibilities of European and German courts in dealing with rights violations, in the context of the European Union exercising public power. This distinguishes the decisions from the *Bosphorus* judgment of the ECtHR, which adopts a more flexible approach to the issue, albeit one that has given rise to some uncertainty.[73] At the same time, the ECtHR

[69] Ibid., p. 237; referring to Kumm's redescription of the Solange-jurisprudence, M. Kumm, 'The Jurisprudence of Constitutional Conflict'.

[70] A. Somek, *The Cosmopolitan Constitution*, pp. 237–8.

[71] Ibid., p. 236.

[72] Ibid., p. 200–1.

[73] See, e.g., on the development of the Court's case law S. Imamović, 'Post-EU Accession to the ECHR: The Argument for Why the ECtHR Should Abandon the Bosphorus Doctrine' (2024) 39:1 *Utrecht Journal of International and European Law* 17; V. Pergantis, 'Recalibrating the "Strict Obligations" Requirement of the Bosphorus Doctrine of Equivalent Protection: The Strasbourg Court vis-à-vis the EU Principle of Mutual Trust' (2024) 20:3 *European Constitutional Law Review* 392.

also clearly had jurisdiction in the *Bosphorus* case, which it chose not to exercise in favour of European and domestic courts. In other words, *democratic* legitimacy was not at stake here because the judgment involved (unlike *Solange I*) a withdrawal of a supranational court rather than an assertion of power.

Moreover, when the German Constitutional Court in *Solange II* relinquished its jurisdiction over European law, it did not represent a simple judicial retreat to make room for greater political powers, as Somek's metaphor of the law of the jungle suggests. Rather, it involved a recognition that, ideally, rights violations should be addressed within the legal system whose authorities exercise power in the specific case. In other words, the German Court decided not to exercise review in cases where it was never ideal for German courts to exercise jurisdiction in the first place, and where it had done so only to establish a baseline of rights protection. Thus, unless we argue against *any* kind of rights review in a supranational system, on the basis that rights presuppose a demos or a social contract or in any event a closer political community than the EU can offer,[74] I am not persuaded by this line of argument. Nor can we credibly reconcile such an approach with support for an organization like the European Union, which exercises significant public power, and which we should therefore be able to hold accountable in a court. In other words, Somek's argument is only convincing if we are – for example for democratic reasons – opposed to supranational lawmaking by the EU more broadly. This is, of course, a perfectly legitimate position, but it is not mine and would in any event take us beyond the scope of this book and into much broader debates.

As we have seen, the first *Solange*-decision represents an argument from failure, and indeed one we can normatively defend. By expanding its jurisdiction to cover European law, the German Court responded to the fact that European law was considered to prevail over domestic

[74] There is of course a debate on whether international courts too represent a political community or a demos – for an argument to that effect, see A. von Bogdandy and I. Venzke, 'In Whose Name? An Investigation of International Courts' Public Authority and Its Democratic Justification' (2012) 23:1 *European Journal of International Law* 7. For the European Court of Justice, the question who confers legitimacy and thus of the role of the demos is a more contested one; see, e.g., the famous exchange between Jürgen Habermas and Dieter Grimm on this, D. Grimm, 'Braucht Europa Eine Verfassung?' (1995) 50:12 *Juristenzeitung* 581; J. Habermas, 'Remarks on Dieter Grimm's: Does Europe Need a Constitution' (1995) 1:3 *European Law Journal* 303. The debate has not been resolved, unsurprisingly.

constitutional law (and thus rights) while no European rights review mechanism existed at the time. Together, those two developments had opened up a gap in the European legal framework, leaving individuals without access to justice when it came to rights violations. It also bears emphasizing that the 1970s were very much the time when the German Constitutional Court had firmly established its jurisprudence, closing a range of traditional domestic loopholes where rights review had previously been considered inappropriate.[75] Expanding this approach to the European Communities clearly fit with this line of jurisprudence. Nor could considerations of functionality, necessity and costs really be seen as decisive against such a move. True, claiming jurisdiction over European law in cases of rights violations did limit the supremacy of European law. It also introduced risks of fragmentation into a system that the CJEU had designed to guarantee the uniform application of European law. Those were potential costs of the Court's decision. Yet, to say that these outweighed the need to fill a gap in rights protection seems awkward, not just from a rule of law perspective but also in light of the fact that the Union owes its power to Member States who are constitutionally bound to ensure the fundamental rights of their citizens. As a result, the first *Solange* judgment in many ways appears as an exemplary and legitimate use of an argument from failure.

8.4.1.2 Systemic Deficiencies

In contrast, the concept of systemic deficiencies represents no clear-cut case of an argument from failure. The refusal to deliver a person to another Member State in line with existing regulatory arrangements due to risks of rights violations, be it as a matter of the European Arrest Warrant or the rules on migration, raises first and foremost questions of evidence. More precisely, the key question is whether there is sufficient evidence to suggest that the migrant's or arrested person's rights will be violated if they are brought into the jurisdiction of another Member State. Thus, the case involves a conflict of norms where primary law and thus fundamental rights must prevail over the regulatory framework of EU secondary law setting out Member States' respective obligations and responsibilities. Things are only complicated by the fact that it

[75] Christoph Schönberger, 'Verwaltungsrecht als konkretisiertes Verfassungsrecht', in M. Stolleis (ed.), *Das Bonner Grundgesetz: Altes Recht und neue Verfassung in den ersten Jahrzehnten der Bundesrepublik Deutschland (1949–1969)* (Berliner Wissenschafts-Verlag, 2006), p. 53.

was not actually clear in the cases at hand that individual rights would be violated: hence, the question of evidence.

And this is where the principle of mutual trust comes in, which the CJEU has elevated to a constitutional principle.[76] More precisely, the CJEU had previously argued in its case law that regulatory cooperation between Member States would no longer be feasible in practice if officials in one state would standardly scrutinize official behaviour in others because they distrusted their application of EU law. Given existing biases and prejudices towards other Member States, this concern does not seem altogether misplaced. Setting aside the default of mutual trust thus requires strong arguments, while it seems equally clear that mutual trust cannot be limitless, given a sufficiently high risk of rights violations. The question then is how high that risk has to be and whether it needs to be assessed in general or individualized terms. The concept of systemic deficiencies serves here, on the one hand, to overcome the default of mutual trust, and thus, as an argument from failure in some ways. But it also provides a more straightforward tool for assessing factual risks, which suggests that framing the issue in terms of an argument from failure is not entirely appropriate.

Nevertheless, very much in line with what we would expect if we treated this as an argument from failure, the European Court of Justice has adopted a proportionality approach in these cases. Thus, the Court emphasized that 'minor infringements of EU law'[77] would not allow for the suspension of Dublin transfers. By contrast, violations of absolute rights under the European Convention, from which no derogation is possible, are sufficient, as violations of absolute rights under the European Charter of Fundamental Rights[78] warrant the suspension of mutual trust,[79] if the deficiencies in the protection of these rights were 'systemic or generalised, or which (. . .) affect certain groups of people, or

[76] K. Lenaerts, '*La vie après l'avis*: Exploring the Principle of Mutual (Yet Not Blind) Trust' (2017) 54:3 *Common Market Law Review* 805; A. Miglionico and F. Maiani, 'One Principle to Rule Them All? Anatomy of Mutual Trust in the Law of the Area of Freedom, Security and Justice' (2020) 57:1 *Common Market Law Review* 7.

[77] Case C-411/10, *N.S. v. Secretary of State for the Home Department and Others* [2011] ECR I-13905.

[78] E.g., the prohibition of inhuman or degrading treatment or punishment, laid down in Art. 4 of the Charter, on account of its rootedness in human dignity, Joined Cases C-404/15 and C-659/15 PPU, *Pál Aranyosi* and *Robert Căldăraru v. Generalstaatsanwaltschaft Bremen* [2016], para. 85.

[79] Ibid., paras. 85–9.

(. . .) certain places of detention'.[80] In another decision, the CJEU also seemed to suggest that a violation of the essence of a fundamental right, in this case the right to fair trial, would suffice if it constituted a violation of the 'essence of the rule of law'.[81]

From a rule of law perspective, this is problematic insofar as this approach accepts that some, albeit minor, rights violations may be tolerated in the interest of enabling the functioning of the EU's regulatory framework. There has accordingly been some debate in the literature about how to define the concept of systemic deficiencies in a way that balances the need for trust, on the one hand, and the need to prevent rights violations, on the other.[82] Insofar as it is hard to provide an individual risk assessment without relying on broader background conditions, factors like quantity, time and quality may help here to assess how problematic the situation is and how real the risks for individual plaintiffs are upon their return to the country in question. It is important, however, not to establish hurdles that are too high. The focus must be on the risk for individuals in these cases rather than an abstract assessment – and this, once again, suggests that treating the concept of systemic deficiencies as an argument from failure somewhat misses the point.

Nevertheless, the idea of 'systemic deficiencies' in the court's jurisprudence is interesting because it turns the tables on the EU's prevalent efficiency discourse. If arguments from failure were underlying the trope of the *effet utile* and the expansion of EU competences at the cost of Member States, the concept of systemic deficiencies operates in the opposite way: by stopping cooperation, thus placing the achievement of the EU's regulatory goals at risk. Because of this, it is not surprising that the CJEU has been wary of defining the concept too broadly, and still treats mutual trust as the default in Europe. By invoking the idea of systemic deficiencies, the CJEU also reverts to an internationalist rather than a supranational paradigm. It sees individual states as ultimately

80 Ibid., paras. 89 and 93.

81 Case C-216/18 PPU, *Minister for Justice and Equality v. LM* [2018], paras. 48 and 51; for a detailed discussion, see A. von Bogdandy et al., 'A Potential Constitutional Moment for the European Rule of Law: The Importance of Red Lines', in A. von Bogdandy et al. (eds.), *Defending Checks and Balances in EU Member States* (Springer, 2021), p. 385.

82 A. Lübbe, '"Systemic Flaws" and Dublin Transfers: Incompatible Tests Before the CJEU and the ECtHR?' (2015) 27:1 *International Journal of Refugee Law* 135; A. von Bogdandy and M. Ioannidis, 'Systemic Deficiency in the Rule of Law: What It Is, What Has Been Done, What Can Be Done' (2014) 51:1 *Common Market Law Review* 59.

responsible for protecting the fundamental rights of individuals, rather than working towards a European solution.

8.4.1.3 Considering *Reverse-Solange*

This leaves the *Reverse-Solange* argument. This would have the European Court of Justice act as constitutional court in cases brought by Union citizens where there are serious deficits regarding the rule of law in individual Member States with respect to certain core values and rights, as protected by Art. 2 TEU. As it stands, this proposal involves a real and explicit argument from failure. One institution – the European Court of Justice – is called upon to expand its jurisdiction to cases where it usually has no jurisdiction, as a matter of Art. 51 CFR. As such, however, it would introduce a problematic differentiation between Member States, some of whose judiciaries would be considered as insufficiently trustworthy to protect their own citizens' rights. Bogdandy and Ioannidis' early 2014 article on systemic deficits explicitly refers to the concept of failed states. It argues that systemic deficiencies are an 'intermediate' concept between 'failed' and 'normal', that is well-functioning states,[83] while drawing on the World Bank indicators, etc. to make the case for a – here still somewhat undefined – special treatment of Member States like Greece. Of course, within the EU, such a move might be more defensible. But risks of paternalism nevertheless loom large, and there is at least a whiff of neo-colonial attitudes.

In terms of our framework, the main question will be whether there is indeed room for such an argument in the context of the existing legal framework. We have already seen that the competences of the EU vis-à-vis Member States have long been understood in a flexible manner. From a subsidiarity perspective, the *Reverse-Solange* proposal seems in many ways a fairly natural approach. What argues against the proposal, however, is first and foremost the wording of Art. 51 CFR, as well as its drafting history. In terms of the framework developed in Chapters 1 and 2, it is doubtful that we have a sufficient gap in the law to accommodate an argument from failure.

Art. 51 of the Charter of Fundamental Rights of the European Union reads:

1. The provisions of this Charter are addressed to the institutions, bodies, offices and agencies of the Union with due regard for the

[83] Von Bogdandy and Ioannidis, 'Systemic Deficiency', 59.

principle of subsidiarity and to the Member States only when they are implementing Union law. (. . .)

2. The Charter does not extend the field of application of Union law beyond the powers of the Union or establish any new power or task for the Union, or modify powers and tasks as defined in the Treaties.[84]

At the time the Charter was drafted, subsection 2 loomed large in the heads of several Member States. It prompted two explicit reservations by Poland and the United Kingdom essentially restating the limit in subsection 2. What the *Reverse-Solange* proposal involves is therefore very close to the thing the Member States sought to avoid, namely the prospect of a generally applicable bill of rights that would have converted the Charter into a more genuine constitutional document at a time when a constitutional vision for the European Union had just been rejected in referenda in France and the Netherlands and encountered resistance elsewhere in the Union as well. All of this suggests that there is no gap in the law here that an argument from failure in the form of the *Reverse-Solange* proposal might fill.

Of course, the counterargument to this is that when the Charter was drafted, democratic backsliding and the rule of law crisis were not yet a major problem in the European Union. Rather, it was long assumed that once states had been accepted into the Union, they could be trusted to have a functioning and effective judicial system to protect individual rights and the rule of law. Moreover, the treaties did include some mechanisms to deal with backsliding, in particular Art. 7 TEU, but those mechanisms did not prove effective, partly for design reasons but also due to a lack of political will on the part of other governments and European institutions.[85] However, even where existing mechanisms appear insufficient to deal with a problem, it may still be the case that the legal framework in place leaves no room for an expansion of competences, and this, I believe, is the case with regard to the CJEU's jurisdiction under the Charter.

84 Highlighting by this author.

85 On Art. 7 TEU see, e.g., D. Kochenov, 'Article 7: A Commentary on a Much Talked-About "Dead" Provision', in A. von Bogdandy et al. (eds), *Defending Checks and Balances in EU Member States* (Springer, 2021), p. 127; Tom Theuns, 'The Need for an EU Expulsion Mechanism: Democratic Backsliding and the Failure of Article 7' (2022) 28 *Res Publica* 693–713. In particular, the European Commission has been a disappointment to many observers here; see, e.g., R. Uitz, '*EU Rule of Law Dialogues: Risks – in Context*', *Verfassungsblog*, 23 January 2020, https://verfassungsblog.de/eu-rule-of-law-dialogues-risks-in-context/.

Add to this that it would once again involve a general assessment of the state of the rule of law in specific countries, rather than with regard to specific issues. It would, thus, involve the CJEU's judges in what will inevitably be a very broad assessment with high political stakes. Of course, the CJEU is already making some fairly broad judgments when it comes to judicial independence. But it matters whether such an assessment serves as a basis for specific findings and interventions, or whether it serves as basis for a wide expansion of the CJEU's competences.

Nor would I be optimistic about the functionality of the *Reverse-Solange* proposal. It seems by no means clear that intervention by the CJEU would improve things much in the Member States, in particular since there is already a European court competent to assess human rights violations in the respective states, namely the European Court of Human Rights. While it is true that the European Court of Justice has more powerful financial sanctions at its disposal, it runs into other difficulties. Without an expansion of the procedural avenues for individual plaintiffs to bring cases, the doctrine would likely have limited impact. For there are very limited procedural avenues for individual plaintiffs to bring violations of their rights under the Charter to the CJEU on their own, only an option for domestic courts to bring a preliminary reference to the CJEU or for the Commission to bring infringement actions. In cases where domestic judiciaries have to a significant degree been captured, and where resisting judges are frequently intimidated by disciplinary procedures or administratively sidelined, many cases will therefore simply not reach the CJEU in the first place. And while backsliding in some countries has come with significant human rights violations, in particular of minorities such as the LGBTQ community or (non-white) immigrants, the broader problem is not only and perhaps not even primarily a fundamental rights issue. It is a structural problem involving the capture of independent institutions, the intimidation and/or abolition of checks and balances and the dismantling of oppositional civil society networks and media.[86] Not all of these issues can easily be litigated in fundamental rights terms. Not least, the *Reverse-Solange* approach would come with significant costs given its differentiation between Member States and intervention in core areas of their sovereignty.

[86] L. Schneider, 'Responses by the CJEU to the European Crisis of Democracy and the Rule of Law Working Papers' (2020) *Forum Transregionale Studien 2/2020*, p. 20 f.

8.5. Conclusion

Rather than further pushing the boundaries of integration through arguments from failure like *Reverse-Solange*, we should therefore rein in this logic in the European Union. Yes, the treaties are hard to change. Yes, legal innovation can be very difficult in a supranational context where different Member States have different interests. But functionalism and flexibility cannot be boundless. They need to come with limitations for the sake of preserving and fostering democratic legitimacy in Europe. The more the Union federalizes, the less convincing its current functionalist logic will become. This is why the continued reliance on a loose purposive approach to the interpretation of the treaties has, with Maastricht and subsequent treaties, rightfully attracted more criticism. Such limits could be drawn either by a court or chamber other than the CJEU, as Joseph Weiler and others have suggested,[87] or by a thoroughly reformed Court of Justice whose procedural and organizational design ensures greater democratic responsiveness, as suggested recently in a very interesting study by Christoph Krenn.[88] But the time for ever-more federalization in the interest of achieving certain regulatory outputs in the Union should be over – and this in turn suggests why arguments from failure might come to play a more specific and limited role in this context in the future.

Perhaps surprisingly, the CJEU's broad purposive approach to interpretation in some respects parallels what we observe in some countries of the Global South where scholars often call for courts to set aside separation of powers concerns in the interest of bringing about certain outcomes. Of course, the goals and rights are very different; in the European Union, the goal is the realization of the common market; in Global South countries, addressing poverty is often a foremost concern. Nevertheless, we find in both contexts a strong functionalist current in the discussion, emphasizing the importance of realizing key legal rights or policy goals against a background of real and perceived failure. It is therefore perhaps not surprising that the concept of transformative constitutionalism has more recently been put forward as a way to describe the CJEU's impact on European countries and as an inspiration

87 J. Weiler and D. Sarmiento, 'The EU Judiciary After Weiss – Proposing A New Mixed Chamber of the Court of Justice: A Reply to Our Critics', EJILtalk, 8 July 2020.

88 C. Krenn, *The Procedural and Organisational Law of the European Court of Justice: An Incomplete Transformation* (Cambridge University Press, 2022).

for European lawyers, too.[89] As instructive as the parallels are, however, this proposal is as mistaken, for a variety of reasons. This is not so much because of the debate about whether it qualifies as a liberal[90] or post-liberal concept,[91] but because transformative constitutionalism entails an imperative to change not just state structures but society more broadly, to bring it in line with constitutional values.[92] This large-scale progressive vision distinguishes it from the largely liberal and sometimes neoliberal agenda pursued in the founding of the European Communities that sought to withdraw certain economic issues from politics in order to isolate states from political pressures for socialist changes of state and society.[93] It also does not fit a supranational setting where courts will have and should have a more restrained role. The more courts drive and enable social change towards a specific ideal of a just society, the more important it is that they are deeply connected with that society in a way that is not feasible or indeed desirable for a supranational court. Thus, EU law with its emphasis on the effective realization of certain policy goals and even individual rights can help illuminate the consequences of adopting too flexible an approach to legal interpretation and competences, where effectiveness arguments crowd out considerations of legality or the separation of powers.

[89] A. von Bogdandy, *Strukturwandel des öffentlichen Rechts: Entstehung und Demokratisierung der europäischen Gesellschaft (Suhrkamp, 2022)* and A. von Bogdandy and L. D. Spieker, 'Transformative Constitutionalism in Luxembourg: How the Court Can Support Democratic Transitions' (2023) 29:2 *Columbia Journal of European Law* 65.

[90] T. Roux, 'Transformative Constitutionalism and the Best Interpretation of the South African Constitution: Distinction Without a Difference?' (2009) 20:2 *Stellenbosch Law Review* 258; see also more poignantly T. Roux, 'The Global South and Liberal Constitutionalism: Incommensurable Opposites?', *AUSPUBLAW*, 7 July 2021, https://tinyurl.com/mskpcpsx; P. Dann, 'Liberal Constitutionalism and Postcolonialism in the South and Beyond: On Liberalism as an Open Source and the Insights of Decolonial Critiques' (2022) 20:1 *International Journal of Constitutional Law* 1.

[91] Its original author, Klare, labelled it a post-liberal concept; see K. E. Klare, 'Legal Culture and Transformative Constitutionalism' (1998) 14:1 *South African Journal on Human Rights* 146.

[92] M. Hailbronner, 'Transformative Constitutionalism: Not Only in the Global South' (2017) 65:3 *American Journal of Comparative Law* 527.

[93] Wilkinson, *Authoritarian Liberalism.*

Conclusion and Perspectives

9.1 Summary

I started out writing this book convinced of the benefits of structural reform litigation. I believed it might be an approach that courts in Europe, including the German one, should occasionally adopt to address structural problems and dysfunctions. I still believe this to be true. Yet, in the course of my research, I have also become much more critical of such arguments and the discourses of effectiveness and improvement that surround them.

The most important lesson of this book is that we need to take arguments from failure seriously as a concept of comparative public law. Arguments from failure are commonplace in public law and international law. But while arguments from failure may be related to emergency arguments or arguments about implied powers, they are not identical with either of them nor with arguments about the effective realization of certain key goals or values. Instead, they come with a distinct structure and represent a distinct idea, based on a broad understanding of the separation of powers as a tool to restrain, but also to enable effective government.

Many institutions and office-holders in very different settings invoke the real or perceived failure of other institutions to justify an expansion of their own competences. This is true in international settings and within nation states as well as in different institutional constellations. Global South scholars often draw on arguments from failure to try and convince judges to take on more robust roles in designing and monitoring specific remedies to realize socio-economic rights and ultimately a more equal and just society. In contrast, the European Court of Justice's language of efficiency, underpinned by arguments from failure, has more often than not been deployed to realize a neo-liberal economic vision of the common market in Europe. In the international realm, too, arguments from failure have contributed to legitimize structural adjustment programs and elements of the war on terror, continuing long-standing legacies of (neo-)colonialism. And yet, at the same time, they are also at the root of some of international law's proudest achievements – the creation and development of supranational human rights institutions. The riddle posed by these different ideological underpinnings cannot be satisfactorily resolved by linking all these examples to the emergence of a hegemonical Western capitalism based on an overarching logic of efficiency. The ideological differences we observe are real ones. Transformative constitutionalism is not simply the human face of legal neo-liberalism, whatever precisely it entails and whether it is ultimately postliberal or not. Rather, arguments from failure – like the broader theme of efficiency in which they are embedded – are empty vessels that may be employed for a wide variety of political projects and purposes.

This makes it hard, and to some degree impossible, to evaluate such arguments normatively without saying more about the underlying political and legal discourses. This is another lesson of this book: Whenever we confront and seek to evaluate arguments from failure, we need to know more about the political and legal context, including the broader institutional arrangements and legal rules in place. In other words, the question is not simply one of asking if the risk or problem at hand justifies institutional action without explicit textual authority. Rather, the first question will always have to be whether we are operating in a context where it makes sense to talk of ideas of mutual checks and inter-institutional cooperation, on the basis of which one institution might step in when another is failing. This will typically be the case within nation states, but in an international context it will often be a more challenging proposition, as we have seen. And even where we are operating within such a broader context, we will want to know more about what the specific competences of the institutions involved are and how their relationship is legally structured. In some cases, existing rules may open up possibilities for assistance or a temporary takeover quite naturally – and the more that is true, the less we need arguments from failure and might draw on a doctrine of implied powers instead. In other cases, such interventions may be much more of a stretch in legal terms. It will also matter whether the institutions seeking to assert new powers are situated in a broader institutional context and what the characteristics of the legal order in question are. In other words, are we dealing with a system with comprehensive regulatory arrangements seeking to provide for all circumstances or are we dealing with a set of piecemeal arrangements only, potentially designed a long time ago and hard to change? In the latter case, there is much more room for arguments from failure.

The legitimation and respective political power of the institutions involved also play a role. Thus, I have argued that we should consider if there exist other, more democratic means to address the problem at hand. This means that we need to consider the democratic legitimacy of the different institutions involved. In other words, it matters if these are (comparatively) inclusive institutions, such as the General Assembly of the United Nations, or not. Finally, we will want to know whether they are situated in a hegemonic position, where an abuse of powers is more likely and more dangerous, or not. In the former case, we will scrutinize any arguments from failure more carefully and apply stricter standards, whereas in the latter case – as with courts – we may be more generous.

If our analysis in those terms bears out that there is simply no room for any arguments from failure in a given context because the legal framework is strictly comprehensive and/or there are other more democratic means to address the problem, then this is where we have to stop. We face a case where arguments from failure should not be considered legitimate as a matter of comparative constitutional theory.

In contrast, *if* there is in principle room for arguments from failure, we must then engage with the proportionality of the expansion of powers sought in light of the failure in question. This is also where I engage the definitional question of what counts as institutional failure. As we have seen, attempts to define institutional failure in any precise manner are riddled with difficulties, given how rarely we will have an objective yardstick of what constitutes adequate performance. And while lawyers will want to rely on the violation of legal rules to determine failure, not every rights violation can qualify, as I have argued in the introduction to this book. If and when a rights violation must be considered a failure thus depends on the intended institutional responses. In other words, failure and the response to it are not just related in practice, but also conceptually. Insofar as we can approach the question on an abstract basis, it is through the lens of proportionality – and here lessons learnt from the emergency literature prove useful. Thus, we will have to assess both the functionality, necessity and overall proportionality of the alleged failure and the response to it.

This involves asking if the intended intervention is actually likely to improve matters as well as whether the failure itself warrants the takeover of the issue by another institution. It matters, therefore, if we are dealing with clear violations of human, constitutional or quasi-constitutional provisions or rights. We will further inquire how long the situation has been going on, how many people are affected and if these are particularly vulnerable people and/or particularly important and long-entrenched rights, or not.

This framework is necessarily vague, as proportionality tests generally are. Unfortunately, there is no way around that if we want to eschew the trap of universalizing where room for different institutional arrangements, politics, laws and legal and political cultures needs to be preserved. I have attempted in this book to make that room while also offering some guidance in tackling arguments from failure not just in courts and in the context of structural reform litigation but in other circumstances as well.

However, perhaps the most important point ultimately is how much the first prong of our framework, the broader institutional and legal analysis, matters in confronting arguments from failure. Proportionality tests fulfil an important function. But they also open the door to the sliding scale of necessity arguments: The greater the problem, the more will be justified to grapple with it. This problem is familiar from the emergency literature. Arguments from failure risk falling into the same trap – and perhaps especially so in circumstances where we are confronted with severe human rights abuses. Yet, we should resist the temptation to think that to alleviate grave suffering or indeed stop climate change, everything is permitted. Rules and competences continue to matter, albeit not in the way we associate – rightly or wrongly – with legal formalism, in the sense of narrow technical ('heartless') constraints that force us to remain inactive in such situations. Instead, they matter as part of a response that needs to be both workable and legitimate.

9.2 Challenges

How and why is all of this relevant? There are several reasons why public lawyers should care about the lessons from this book. First, many states are currently grappling with the challenges of effective and good governance. Second, and despite this, in many states our understanding of what constitutionalism entails has greatly expanded in the past two decades. Individually and in combination, these two factors will put further pressure on constitutional law to deliver 'results', and this has implications that public lawyers have yet to grapple with. Understanding and analyzing arguments from failure is one part of such a necessarily broader endeavour.

Start with the first point, which is often taken for granted for Global South jurisdictions. However, nearly all states currently face a range of political challenges, from ongoing wars in Ukraine and Gaza and the rise of right-wing authoritarian movements in many regions of the world to climate change. This happens at a time when many states are experiencing crises of governance, from states with persistent fragility problems to those that have been relatively stable democracies, as, for example, the United Kingdom, where a range of factors have contributed to broader dysfunctionalities of British political institutions.[1] And even where we – rightly or wrongly – have long expected things to work well, as in Europe or indeed in Germany, we find pockets of dysfunctionality, and sometimes more than that. Administration in the German state of Berlin has not for some time now conformed to the – albeit always exaggerated – ideal of German administrative capacity. Serious deficits have arisen not just in areas such as migrants' affairs but also when it comes to something as central as organizing elections.[2] Not least, some states in Southern Europe have long been considered – rightfully or not – as dysfunctional in important respects. Talk about the 'Latin-Americanization' of the European Human Rights system[3] echoes similar concerns, directed mainly towards Central and Eastern Europe. These problems are partly driven and partly exacerbated by a broader loss of trust in state institutions in nearly all regions of the world.[4] This loss of trust is often coupled with increasing political fragmentation, as the traditional post-war party system comes apart, as well as in some regions with a trend towards political polarization.

At the same time, we are experiencing a shift in our understanding of constitutionalism, one which has been ongoing for some decades at this point. The shift is away from the traditional negative-freedom-oriented model of constitutionalism towards a more comprehensive and social democratic, aspirational[5] or transformative idea of constitutionalism.[6] Traditional or standard accounts of democracy usually start from the premise that citizens are free to decide collectively what goals and projects the state should pursue, within the boundaries of existing constitutional law, including individual rights. In the classic liberal

[1] S. Freedman, *Failed State: Why Nothing Works and How We Fix It* (Pan Macmillan, 2024).

[2] VerfGH 154/21, 16 November 2022 (Constitutional Court of Berlin, Germany).

[3] See first C. M. Cerna, 'The Inter-American System for the Protection of Human Rights' (2004) 16:1 *Florida Journal of International Law* 195; subsequently, J. L. Cavallaro and S. E. Brewer, 'Reevaluating Regional Human Rights Litigation in the Twenty-First Century: The Case of the Inter-American Court' (2008) 102:4 *American Journal of International Law* 768.

[4] J. Perry, 'Trust in Public Institutions: Trends and Implications for Economic Security', *UN-DESA Policy Brief* 108, 15 June 2021, https://tinyurl.com/ctejxjkx.

[5] A. Somek, *The Cosmopolitan Constitution* (Oxford University Press, 2014); M. Loughlin, *Against Constitutionalism* (Harvard University Press, 2022).

[6] M. Hailbronner, 'Transformative Constitutionalism: Not Only in the Global South' (2017) 65:3 *American Journal of Comparative Law* 527.

understanding of rights, therefore, rights are understood as limitations of the powers that the constitution elsewhere grants to the state. In other words: Competences enable the state, rights limit its powers. This picture no longer adequately describes constitutionalism as it exists today in a wide range of states whose constitutions either include positive rights or directive principles and/or whose courts have read rights or directive principles to entail positive obligations for states to act. In other words, parliamentary majorities are not entirely free in the policies they pursue, but the constitution requires them to do certain things. This shift comes with many positive aspects; in particular, it allows us to understand and frame structural power imbalances and inequality as constitutional challenges that demand a political response. At the same time, it is part of a broader trend described by Kumm as the 'era of the total constitution', where all political questions can in principle be reframed as constitutional questions.[7]

We can observe a similar development in the context of human rights law. Its scope, too, has been considerably expanded over the past decades, treating ever more political issues as questions of human rights. Today, both left progressives and conservatives frequently rely on human rights language to put forward their own political agendas. It is the left that has had the larger impact on this development so far, though this may be changing.[8]

With this shift has come the expectation that law – in particular constitutional law and human rights – will and should be the tool to address and redress all injustice. As a result, the question will often arise if state institutions have done enough to protect a given right or constitutional value. This understanding will put pressure on states to respond – and on existing legal rules to be set aside where it appears necessary to better protect constitutional goals and rights.

As I said, there is much to like about this development. And of course there never was an age of 'neutral' or apolitical human or constitutional rights. They have always enshrined demands won in past political struggles by particular political groups. Retrenching such rights and confining them to what they used to mean fifty years ago or after the Second World War is not an attractive proposition from a politically left perspective – and it would come with some significant losses for those

[7] Loughlin, *Against Constitutionalism*, p. 131. M. Kumm, 'Who Is Afraid of the Total Constitution? Constitutional Rights as Principles and the Constitutionalization of Private Law' (2006) 7:4 *German Law Journal* 341–69; K. Möller, 'Justifying the Culture of Justification' (2019) 17:4 *International Journal of Constitutional Law* 1078, 1081.

[8] G. de Búrca/K. G. Young, 'The (Mis)Appropriation of Human Rights by the New Global Right: An Introduction to the Symposium' (2023) 21:1 *International Journal of Constitutional Law* 205.

groups most in need of protection. Nevertheless, the heightened expectations that come with the expansion of rights and law to remedy injustice represent a shift towards output rather than input legitimacy in constitutional law, with the effective protection of rights being the output in question. This is why we have seen parallels in this book between forms of legal argument in Global South contexts and in the European Union.

Of course, considerations of effectiveness have always been relevant in constitutional law, perhaps in particular in the context of proportionality analysis. This becomes particularly clear in the work of Robert Alexy. He describes constitutional rights as optimization principles that should be realized to the greatest extent possible – a task that can be realized with the help of the proportionality principle, where rights limitations are justified as long as they are proportional to the goal pursued by the government.[9] Some scholars, such as Carl Schmitt, have accordingly understood attempts to reframe constitutional law as values as part of a move from legal to essentially economic forms of arguments.[10] Others have argued that 'necessity' represents an administrative way of thinking that is ultimately not compatible with legality as a limitation on the 'overall teleological compass of administrative action'.[11] Such claims have a basis in proportionality's origins in Prussian administrative law principles and private law thinking at the end of the nineteenth century.[12] That said, functionalist arguments are not confined to proportionality. The kind of considerations raised in proportionality analysis are standard even in systems that eschew proportionality as a constitutional principle, such as the United States.[13]

[9] R. Alexy, *A Theory of Constitutional Rights* (Oxford University Press, 2002).

[10] C. Schmitt, *Die Tyrannei der Werte* (Duncker & Humblot, 1967).

[11] A. Somek, 'Administration Without Sovereignty', in P. Dobner and M. Loughlin (eds.), *The Twilight of Constitutionalism?* (Oxford University Press, 2010), p. 267; see also Cohen and Porat, who view the shift towards a proportionality approach to rights view as a shift towards an administrative model of constitutional law, M. Cohen-Eliya and I. Porat, 'Proportionality and the Culture of Justification' (2011) 59:2 *The American Journal of Comparative Law* 463.

[12] M. Cohen–Eliya and I. Porat, 'American Balancing and German Proportionality: The Historical Origins', in B. Bix and H. Spector (eds.), *Rights: Concepts and Contexts* (Routledge, 2017), p. 463.

[13] For example, US scholars noted in the late 1990s how the Supreme Court adopted a mix of 'functionalist' and 'formalist' approaches to separation of powers questions. See P. L. Strauss, 'Formal and Functional Approaches to Separation of Powers Questions: A Foolish Inconsistency' (1987) 72:3 *Cornell Law Review* 488; see also Eskridge on this, arguing that courts usually combined several approaches: W. N. Eskridge, 'Relationships Between Formalism and Functionalism in Separation of Powers Cases' (1998) 22:1 *Harvard Law Review* 21.

What then are the consequences of all this? Are we observing the triumph of a new administrative and essentially output-focused paradigm of constitutional legality (constitutionalism 3.0), as Somek argues? We might also recall Hannah Arendt's warning about a utilitarian approach to law, which is worth quoting here:

> (Hitler's motto that "Right is what is good for the German people" is only the vulgarized form of a conception of law which can be found everywhere and which in practice will remain ineffectual only so long as older traditions that are still effective in the constitutions prevent this.) A conception of law which identifies what is right with the notion of what is good for – for the individual, or the family, or the people, or the largest number – becomes inevitable once the absolute and transcendent measurements of religion or the law of nature have lost their authority. And this predicament is by no means solved if the unit to which the "good for" applies is as large as mankind itself. For it is quite conceivable, and even within the realm of practical political possibilities, that one fine day a highly organized and mechanized humanity will conclude quite democratically-namely by majority decision – that for humanity as a whole it would be better to liquidate certain parts thereof.[14]

All of this is a long way of saying that pressure to reach certain outcomes and results poses risks both to democracy and the rule of law. This is demonstrated by the example of the European Union and even more so by plenty of authoritarian and semi-authoritarian regimes. And such risks increase as the ability of governments to deliver results is stagnating or indeed decreasing in response to current challenges.

9.3 Perspectives

How can we respond to this and where do we go from here? As I have argued above, I don't believe that we should endeavour to return to a more classically liberal understanding of rights and constitutionalism that focuses on constraining political power. Such an understanding privileges the status quo and risks cementing existing social and political hierarchies. If we believe constitutionalism has something to say on these things, there is no way around the total constitution.

As public lawyers, it is our task to recognize the temptations that come with total constitutions and confront them in a clear-eyed manner. It means that we need to take effectiveness seriously as a source of constitutional legitimacy, in practice, but also in theory. Though there

[14] H. Arendt, *The Origins of Totalitarianism* (Harcourt Brace & Company, 1973), p. 299.

is more to be said here,[15] effectiveness and the doctrines and tools to realize effective government are part and parcel of both the theory and practice of government. Taking effectiveness seriously enables us to highlight trade-offs and conflicts that arise between the goals of making the government effective and the realization of collective or individual autonomy.[16] These conflicts should be teased out and openly addressed so as not to leave effectiveness arguments to the wrong people, to be deployed to whittle down constitutional constraints. Legality matters and constitutional provisions allocating functions and competences to different bodies need to be taken seriously. In many ways, therefore, this book is about when and why *not* to draw on arguments from failure, namely in most cases. The challenge will be to strike a balance: a balance between updating the law, on the one hand, in order to allow institutional adaptation to new problems and challenges as well as temporary fixes in some cases, while also preserving some limits and restraints on state power, on the other.

Add to this that the role of parliaments and administrative organs in protecting and realizing constitutional rights and/or directive principles needs to be rethought. This is all the more true as many of the newly construed positive rights or duties will involve spending new money. They thus involve questions of distribution and redistribution where a collective and democratic mode of decision-making is particularly important. In some systems, specific mechanisms to ensure a central role for parliament are already institutionally entrenched, such as in some Commonwealth countries, or exist in other, less explicit forms of weak review. In others, such as my own home jurisdiction of Germany, this is a challenge yet to be confronted. While there cannot be one model of review that will fit all systems and all contexts, Rosalind Dixon's proposal for a responsive theory of review provides an important template for thinking about these questions in different legal systems.[17]

Comparative perspectives on public law can inform such research and thinking. Public lawyers in Europe and elsewhere should therefore start looking more at countries where the challenges described here are more

15 See for a preliminary argument M. Hailbronner, 'Output-Legitimacy and Its Limitations in Constitutional Theory', in A. Klafki (ed.), *Patterns of Legitimacy* (Nomos), p. 151, with further references. For a more comprehensive discussion on thinking about 'policy goals' (Zwecke) in public law, see T. Wischmeyer, *Zwecke im Recht des Verfassungsstaates: Geschichte und Theorie einer juristischen Denkfigur* (Mohr Siebeck, 2015).

16 T. Isiksel, *Europe's Functional Constitution: A Theory of Constitutionalism Beyond the State* (Oxford University Press, 2016).

17 R. Dixon, *Responsive Judicial Review* (Oxford University Press, 2023).

commonplace and judges and lawyers have been grappling with them for some time. This means in particular looking outside of Europe and – albeit not only – to Global South jurisdictions, where they will encounter both lacking state capacities and low levels of trust in public institutions as well as a broad – often transformative – understanding of constitutional law at the same time. In doing so, we will be able to learn – sometimes by inspiration through new ideas, sometimes by learning to avoid what has gone awry elsewhere. Indian public interest litigation thus may offer both inspiration and a cautionary tale of what can go wrong. European lawyers may also begin to see the United States in a new light – no longer as a beacon of the most admirable constitutional system in the world nor for that matter simply as a corrupt oligarchy, but as a state with both long-entrenched dysfunctionalities and plenty of creative politics and lawyering seeking to fix things and confront the challenges that come with such efforts. Such comparative work is not what judges and law clerks can do in the context of deciding individual cases, but it requires time and cooperation between institutions and academics in different parts of the world.

Many open questions and challenges remain. This book grapples only with a specific aspect of a much broader set of effectiveness arguments in public law. But as we have seen, arguments from failure share many of the risks as well as the promise associated with this line of arguments, albeit that they present us with a distinct structure and logic of its own. In excavating and analyzing that structure, I hope to have cast a light on the broader themes running through this book and made some progress in grappling with such arguments as a matter of constitutional theory as and when they arise. I have no doubt that many readers will remain sceptical that there can be one framework to grapple with the very different constellations in which we encounter arguments from failure. So am I. This book contains less a set of answers than a framework for paying attention. If we simply pay closer attention to arguments from failure, instead of unreflectively adopting a necessity approach, as we so often do, this itself would be a good outcome.

BIBLIOGRAPHY

Abbott, Kenneth W. and Thomas J. Biersteker (eds.), *Informal Governance in World Politics* (Cambridge University Press, 2024).

Ackerman, Bruce, *Before the Next Attack: Preserving Civil Liberties in an Age of Terrorism* (Yale University Press, 2007).

Alexy, Robert, *A Theory of Constitutional Rights* (Oxford University Press, 2010).

Andrassy, Juraj, 'Uniting for Peace' (1956) 50:3 *The American Journal of International Law* 563–82.

Antkowiak, Thomas M., 'Remedial Approaches to Human Rights Violations: The Inter-American Court of Human Rights and Beyond' (2007) 46 *Columbia Journal of Transnational Law* 351–419.

Arendt, Hannah, *The Origins of Totalitarianism* (Harcourt Brace & Company, 1973).

Avant, Deborah D., Martha Finnemore and Susan Sell, 'Who Governs the Globe?', in id. (eds.), *Who Governs the Globe?* (Cambridge University Press, 2010), pp. 1–31.

Avbelj, Matej and Jan Komárek (eds.), *Constitutional Pluralism in the European Union and Beyond* (Bloomsbury Publishing, 2012).

Backes, Chris and Gerrit van der Veen, 'Urgenda: The Final Judgment of the Dutch Supreme Court' (2020) 17:3 *Journal for European Environmental & Planning Law* 307–21.

Administratiefrechtelijke Beslissingen 2018/417.

Bandopadhyay, Saptarishi, *All Is Well: Catastrophe and the Making of the Normal State* (Oxford University Press, 2022).

Barber, Nick W., *The Principles of Constitutionalism* (Oxford University Press, 2018).

Barber, Rebecca, 'Accountability for Crimes Against the Rohingya: Possibilities for the General Assembly Where the Security Council Fails' (2019) 17:3 *Journal of International Criminal Justice* 557–84.

Bárd, Petra and Wouter van Ballegooij, 'Judicial Independence as a Precondition for Mutual Trust? The CJEU in Minister for Justice and Equality v. LM.' (2020) 9(3) *New Journal of European Criminal Law* 353–65.

Barkow, Rachel E., 'More Supreme Than Court: The Fall of the Political Question Doctrine and the Rise of Judicial Supremacy' (2002) 102 *Columbia Law Review* 237–336.

Bar-Siman-Tov, Ittai, 'Semiprocedural Judicial Review' (2012) 6:3 *Legisprudence* 271–300.

Bass, Jack, *Unlikely Heroes* (University Alabama Press, 1990).

Bauer, Hartmut, 'Der Bundeszwang in der bundesstaatlichen Ordnung des Grundgesetzes' (2019) *Revista Catalana de Dret Públic* 1–20.

Baxi, Upendra, 'Taking Suffering Seriously: Social Action Litigation in the Supreme Court of India' (1985) 6 *Third World Legal Studies* 107–32.

Benz, Arthur, 'Demokratisches Regieren im Föderalismus: Neue Literatur zu einem alten Thema' (2019) 64 *Neue Politische Literatur* 513–35.

Bergkamp, Lucas, 'The Dutch Supreme Court's Climate Judgment: Its Consequences and Implications for Business – Revolution Through Litigation' (2020) 29:3 *European Energy and Environmental Law Review* 89–97.

Bergkamp, Lucas and Scott Stone, 'The Trojan Horse of the Paris Agreement on Climate Change: How Multi-level, Non-hierarchical Governance Poses a Threat to Constitutional Government' (2015) 4 *Environmental Liability* 119–40.

Bernstein, Anya and Cristina Rodríguez, 'The Accountable Bureaucrat' (2023) 132 *Yale Law Journal* 1600–90.

Bernstein, Anya and Glen Staszewski, 'Judicial Populism' (2021) 106 *Minnesota Law Review* 283–351.

Bhuwania, Anuj, *Courting the People: Public Interest Litigation in Post-Emergency India* (Cambridge University Press, 2017).

Bignami, Francesca, 'Rethinking the Legal Foundations of the European Constitutional Order: The Lessons of the New Historical Research' (2012) 28:5 *American University International Law Review* 1311–35.

Bilchitz, David and David Landau (eds.), *The Evolution of the Separation of Powers: Between the Global North and the Global South* (Edward Elgar Publishing, 2018).

Bilgin, Pinar and Adam David Morton, 'Historicising Representations of "Failed States": Beyond the Cold-War Annexation of the Social Sciences?' (2002) 23:1 *Third World Quarterly* 55–80.

Binder, Christina, 'Uniting for Peace Resolution (1950)' (2017), *Max Planck Encyclopedia of International Public Law* (Oxford University Press, 2013).

Blokker, Niels M., 'International Organizations or Institutions, Implied Powers', in A. Peters and R. Wolfrum (eds.), *Max Planck Encyclopedia of Public International Law* (Oxford University Press, 2008).

Bobek, Michal and David Kosař, 'Global Solutions, Local Damages: A Critical Study in Judicial Councils in Central and Eastern Europe' (2014) 15:7 *German Law Journal* 1257–92.

von Bogdandy, Armin and Luke Dimitrios Spieker, 'Transformative Constitutionalism in Luxembourg: How the Court Can Support Democratic Transitions' (2023) 29:2 *Columbia Journal of European Law* 65–91.

von Bogdandy, Armin, *Strukturwandel des öffentlichen Rechts. Entstehung und Demokratisierung der europäischen Gesellschaft* (Suhrkamp, 2022).

et al., 'A Potential Constitutional Moment for the European Rule of Law: The Importance of Red Lines', in Armin von Bogdandy et al. (eds.), *Defending Checks and Balances in EU Member States* (Springer, 2021), pp. 385–401.

'Principles of a Systemic Deficiencies Doctrine: How to Protect Checks and Balances in the Member States' (2020) 57:3 *Common Market Law Review* 705–40.

et al., 'Protecting EU Values: Reverse Solange and the Rule of Law Framework', in András Jakab and Dimitry Kochenov (eds.), *The Enforcement of EU Law and Values: Ensuring Member States' Compliance* (Oxford University Press, 2017), pp. 218–33.

von Bogdandy, Armin and Michael Ioannidis, 'Systemic Deficiency in the Rule of Law: What It Is, What Has Been Done, What Can Be Done' (2014) 51:1 *Common Market Law Review* 59–96.

von Bogdandy, Armin and Ingo Venzke, 'In Whose Name? An Investigation of International Courts' Public Authority and Its Democratic Justification' (2012) 23:1 *European Journal of International Law* 7–41.

Brenner, Samuel, '"Airbrushed Out of the Constitutional Canon": The Evolving Understanding of Giles v. Harris, 1903–1925' (2009) 107:5 *Michigan Law Review* 853–79.

Brenton, Scott, 'Does Federalism Enhance Representative Democracy? Perpetual Reform and Shifting Power in a Divided Belgium' (2022) 31:2 *Journal of Contemporary European Studies* 1–19.

Brouwer, Evelien, 'Mutual Trust and the Dublin Regulation: Protection of Fundamental Rights in the EU and the Burden of Proof' (2013) 9 *Utrecht Law Review* 135–47.

Buchanan, Allen and Robert O. Keohane, 'The Legitimacy of Global Governance Institutions', in Jovan Babic and Petar Bojanic (eds.), *World Governance: Do We Need It, Is It Possible, What Could It (All) Mean?* (Cambridge University Press, 2010), pp. 214–46.

Buchanan, James M., 'Market Failure and Political Failure' (1988) 8:1 *Cato Journal* 1–15.

Bulmer, Elliot W., 'Federalism: International IDEA Constitution-Building Primer 12' (2017), 2nd ed., *International Institute for Democracy and Electoral Assistance.*

Búrca, Gráinne de, *Reframing Human Rights in a Turbulent Era* (Oxford University Press, 2021).

'Human Rights Experimentalism' (2017) 111:2 *American Journal of International Law* 277–316.

'The European Court of Justice and the International Legal Order After Kadi' (2010) 51:1 *Harvard Journal of International Law* 1–50.

Búrca, Gráinne de and Joanne Scott, 'Introduction', in Id. (eds.), *Law and New Governance in the EU and the US* (Bloomsbury Publishing, 2006) 1–12.

Burgardt, Claus, 'Das Systemversagen in der GKV' (2014) 5 *Medizinprodukterecht* 145–9.

Çalı, Başak, '"To me, fair friend, you can never be old", William Shakespeare, "Sonnet 104": ECHR at 70 Rudolf Bernhardt Lecture, 2020' (2022) 81:4 *Zeitschrift für ausländisches öffentliches Recht und Völkerrecht/Heidelberg Journal of International Law* 895–916.

Çali, Başak and Anne Koch, 'Foxes Guarding the Foxes? The Peer Review of Human Rights Judgments by the Committee of Ministers of the Council of Europe' (2014) 14:2 *Human Rights Law Review* 301–25.

Call, Charles T., 'The Fallacy of the "Failed State"' (2008) 29:8 *Third World Quarterly* 1491–507.

Calvert, Jonathan and George Arbuthnott, *Failures of State: The Inside Story of Britain's Battle with Coronavirus* (Mudlark/Harper Collins, 2021).

Canor, Iris, 'Suspending Horizontal Solange: A Decentralized Instrument for Protecting Mutual Trust and the European Rule of Law', in Armin von Bogdandy et al. (eds.), *Defending Checks and Balances in EU Member States* (Springer, 2021), pp. 183–206.

Carey, John, 'U. N. Response to Government Oppression' (1968) 3:1 *The International Lawyer* 102–8.

Carolan, Eoin, *The New Separation of Powers: A Theory for the Modern State* (Oxford University Press, 2009).

Carroll, Maureen, 'Class Action Myopia' (2016) 65 *Duke Law Journal* 843–908.

Carswell, Andrew J., 'Unblocking the UN Security Council: The Uniting for Peace Resolution' (2013) 18:3 *Journal of Conflict and Security Law* 453–80.

Cavallaro, James L. and Stephanie Erin Brewer, 'Reevaluating Regional Human Rights Litigation in the Twenty-First Century: The Case of the Inter-American Court' (2008) 102:4 *American Journal of International Law* 768–827.

Cepeda Espinosa, Manuel José and David Landau, 'A Broad Read of Ely: Political Process Theory for Fragile Democracies' (2021) 19:2 *International Journal of Constitutional Law* 548–68.

'*Colombian Constitutional Law: Leading Cases*' (Oxford University Press, 2017).

Cepeda Espinosa, Manuel José, 'The Constitutional Protection of IDPs in Colombia', in Rodolfo Arango Rivadeneira (ed.), *Judicial Protection of Internally Displaced Persons: The Colombian Experience* (The Brookings Institution-University of Bern Project on Internal Displacement, 2009), pp. 1–48.

Cerna, Christina M., 'The Inter-American System for the Protection of Human Rights' (2004) 16:1 *Florida Journal of International Law* 195–211.

Chamon, Merijn, 'Implied Exclusive Powers in the CJEU's Post-Lisbon Jurisprudence: The Continued Development of the ERTA Doctrine' (2018) 55:4 *Common Market Law Review* 1101–42.

Chayes, Abram, 'The Role of the Judge in Public Law Litigation' (1976) 89 *Harvard Law Review* 1281–316.

Chenwi, Lillian, 'Unpacking "Progressive Realisation", Its Relation to Resources, Minimum Core and Reasonableness, and Some Methodological Considerations for Assessing Compliance' (2013) 46:3 *De Jure* 742--69.

Chilton, Adam and Mila Versteeg, 'Small-c Constitutional Rights' (2022) 20:1 *International Journal of Constitutional Law* 141–76.

Chitalkar, Poorvi and Varun Gauri, 'India: Compliance with Orders on the Right to Food', in Malcolm Langford, César Rodríguez-Garavito and Julieta Rossi (eds.), *Social Rights Judgments and the Politics of Compliance: Making It Stick* (Cambridge University Press, 2017), pp. 288–314.

Choudhry, Sujit, Madhav Khosla and Pratap Bhanu Mehta (eds.), *The Oxford Handbook of the Indian Constitution* (Oxford University Press, 2016).

Coffee Jr., John C., *Entrepreneurial Litigation: Its Rise, Fall, and Future* (Harvard University Press, 2015).

'Rescuing the Private Attorney General: Why the Model of the Lawyer as Bounty Hunter Is Not Working' (1983) 42:2 *Maryland Law Review* 215–88.

Cohen, Benjamin V., *The United Nations, Constitutional Developments, Growths, and Possibilities* (Harvard University Press, 1961), pp. 18–9.

Cohen, Joshua and Charles F. Sabel, 'Directly-Deliberative Polyarchy' (1997) 3:4 *European Law Journal* 313–42.

Cohen-Eliya, Moshe and Iddo Porat, 'American Balancing and German Proportionality: The Historical Origins', in Brian Bix and Horacio Spector (eds.), *Rights: Concepts and Contexts* (Routledge, 2017), pp. 463–86.

'Proportionality and the Culture of Justification' (2011) 59:2 *The American Journal of Comparative Law* 463–90.

Conable, Barber B., 'Foreword', in *Sub-Saharan Africa: From Crisis to Sustainable Growth* (The World Bank, Washington D.C., 1989), pp. xi–15.

Costello, Cathryn and Itamar Mann, 'Border Justice: Migration and Accountability for Human Rights Violations' (2020) 21:3 *German Law Journal* 311–34.

Couzigou, Irène, 'The Right to Self-Defence against Non-State Actors: Criteria of the "Unwilling or Unable" Test' (2017) 77 *Heidelberg Journal of International Law* 53–55.

Croissant, Aurel, 'Thailand: The Vicious Cycle of Civilian Government and Military Rule', in id. (ed.), *Comparative Politics of Southeast Asia* (Springer, 2nd ed., 2022), pp. 315–59.

Cunningham, Frank, *Theories of Democracy* (Routledge, 2002).

Czepek, Jakub, 'The Application of the Pilot Judgment Procedure and Other Forms of Handling Large-Scale Dysfunctions in the Case Law of the European Court of Human Rights' (2018) 20 *International Community Law Review* 347–73.

Daly, Tom, *The Alchemists: Questioning Our Faith in Courts as Democracy-Builders* (Cambridge University Press, 2017).

Damrosch, Lori F., 'Gross and Systematic Human Rights Violations', in Anne Peters and Rüdiger Wolfrum (eds.), *4 Max Planck Encyclopedia of Public International Law* (Oxford University Press, 2012), pp. 597–603.

Dann, Philipp, 'Liberal Constitutionalism and Postcolonialism in the South and Beyond: On Liberalism as an Open Source and the Insights of Decolonial Critiques' (2022) 20:1 *International Journal of Constitutional Law* 1–12.

The Law of Development Cooperation: A Comparative Analysis of the World Bank, the EU and Germany (Cambridge University Press, 2013).

'Verfassungsgerichtliche Kontrolle gesetzgeberischer Rationalität' (2010) 49:4 *Der Staat* 630–46.

von Danwitz, Luc, 'Der Grundsatz des gegenseitigen Vertrauens zwischen den Mitgliedstaaten der EU. Eine wertebasierte Garantie der Einheit und Wirksamkeit des Unionsrechts' (2020) 61:1 *Europarecht* 61-88.

Davis, Dennis M., 'Separation of Powers: Juristocracy or Democracy' (2016) 133 *South African Law Journal* 258–70.

De Oliveira, Emerson A. B., 'The Unconstitutional State of Affairs in Brazil's Prisons', in Rubens Becak and Jairo Lima (eds.), *The Unwritten Brazilian Constitution: Human Rights in the* Supremo Tribunal Federal (Lexington Book, 2021), pp. 233–46.

Derwort, Pim, Nicolas Jager and Jens Newig, 'Towards Productive Functions? A Systematic Review of Institutional Failure, Its Causes and Consequences' (2019) 52:2 *Policy Sciences* 281–98.

Deutsch, Ulrike and Rüdiger Wolfrum, *The European Court of Human Rights Overwhelmed by Applications: Problems and Possible Solutions* (Springer, 2009).

Dixon, Rosalind, *Responsive Judicial Review* (Oxford University Press, 2023).

Dixon, Rosalind and David Landau, *Abusive Constitutional Borrowing: Legal Globalization and the Subversion of Liberal Democracy* (Oxford University Press, 2021).

Dixon, Rosalind and Michaela Hailbronner, 'Ely in the World: The Global Legacy of *Democracy and Distrust* Forty Years On' (2021) 19:2 *International Journal of Constitutional Law* 427–38.

'The Forms, Functions, and Varieties of Weak(ened) Judicial Review' (2019) 17:3 *International Journal of Constitutional Law* 904–930.

Dixon, Rosalind and David Landau, 'Competitive Democracy and the Constitutional Minimum Core', in Tom Ginsburg and Aziz Huq (eds.), *Assessing Constitutional Performance* (Cambridge University Press, 2016), pp. 268–92.

'The Core Case for Weak-Form Judicial Review' (2016) 38:6 *Cardozo Law Review* 2193–232.

'Creating Dialogue about Socioeconomic Rights: Strong-form versus Weak-form Judicial Review Revisited' (2007) 5:3 *International Journal of Constitutional Law* 391–418.

Dorf, Michael C. and Charles F. Sabel, 'A Constitution of Democratic Experimentalism' (1998) 98:2 *Columbia Law Review* 267–473.

Dupuy, Pierre-Marie, 'The Constitutional Dimension of the Charter of the United Nations Revisited' (1997) 1:1 *Max Planck Yearbook of United Nations Law Online* xix–33.

Duranti, Marco, *The Conservative Human Rights Revolution: European Identity, Transnational Politics, and the Origins of the European Convention* (Oxford University Press, 2016).

Dyzenhaus, David, 'Legal Theory in the Collapse of Weimar: Contemporary Lessons?' (1997) 91 *American Political Science Review* 121–34.

Dzehtsiarou, Kanstantsin, *Can the European Court of Human Rights Shape European Public Order?* (Cambridge University Press, 2021).

Eggleston, Neil W. and Amanda Elbogen, 'The Trump Administration and the Breakdown of Intra-Executive Legal Process' (2018) 127 *The Yale Law Journal* 825–47.

Eisenberg, Theodore and Stephen C. Yeazell, 'The Ordinary and the Extraordinary in Institutional Litigation' (1980) 93:3 *Harvard Law Review* 465–517.

Ely, John Hart, *Democracy and Distrust: A Theory of Judicial Review* (Harvard University Press, 1980).

von Engelhardt, Marie, *Dealing with Fragile States: The Law and Practice of International Development Organizations*, PhD diss., Humboldt University, 2015, available at https://edoc.hu-berlin.de/bitstream/handle/18452/18078/engelhardt.pdf?sequence=1&isAllowed=y.

Epp, Charles R., *Making Rights Real: Activists, Bureaucrats, and the Creation of the Legalistic State* (University of Chicago Press, 2009).

The Rights Revolution: Lawyers, Activists, and Supreme Courts in Comparative Perspective (University of Chicago Press, 1998).

Ermacora, Felix, 'Procedures to Deal with Human Rights Violations: A Hopeful Start in the United Nations?' (1974) 7 *Human Rights Journal* 670–89.

Eskridge, William N. Jr., 'Relationships Between Formalism and Functionalism in Separation of Powers Cases' (1998) 22:1 *Harvard Law Review* 21–9.

Fahner, Johannes Hendrik, *Judicial Deference in International Adjudication: A Comparative Analysis* (Bloomsbury Publishing, 2020).

Fassbender, Bardo, 'The United Nations Charter as Constitution of the International Community' (1998) 36 *Columbia Journal of Transnational Law* 529–620.

Ferejohn, John and Pasquale Pasquino, 'The Law of the Exception: A Typology of Emergency Powers' (2004) 2:2 *International Journal of Constitutional Law* 210–39.

Ferraz, Octavio Luiz Motta, *Health as a Human Right: The Politics and Judicialisation of Health in Brazil* (Cambridge University Press, 2020).

Figueroa Garcia-Herreros, Nicolas, *A Critique of Populist Jurisprudence: Courts, Democracy, and Constitutional Change in Colombia and Venezuela*, PhD diss., The New School, 2016.

Fischer Kuh, Katharina, 'The Legitimacy of Judicial Climate Engagement' (2019) 46:3 *Ecology Law Quarterly* 731–64.

Fish, Stanley, *Is There a Text in This Class? The Authority of Interpretive Communities* (Harvard University Press, 1980).

Fish Hodgson, Timothy, 'The Mysteriously Appearing and Disappearing Doctrine of Separation of Powers: Toward a Distinctly South Africa Doctrine for a More Radically Transformative Constitution' (2018) 34:1 *South African Journal on Human Rights* 57–90.

Fiss, Owen M., 'Foreword: The Forms of Justice' (1979) 93:1 *Harvard Law Review* 1–58.

Fletcher, William A., 'The Discretionary Constitution: Institutional Remedies and Judicial Legitimacy' (1982) 91:4 *The Yale Law Journal* 635–97.

Fombad, Charles Manga (ed.), *The Separation of Powers in African Constitutionalism* (Oxford University Press, 2016).

Fowkes, James, 'Normal Rights, Just New: Understanding the Judicial Enforcement of Socioeconomic Rights' (2020) 68:4 *The American Journal of Comparative Law* 722–59.

'Transformative Constitutionalism and the Global South: The View from South Africa', in Armin von Bogdandy et al. (eds.), *Transformative Constitutionalism in Latin America: A New Latin American Ius Commune* (Oxford University Press, 2017), pp. 97–122.

Building the Constitution: The Practice of Constitutional Interpretation in Post-Apartheid South Africa (Cambridge University Press, 2016).

'Civil Procedure in Public Interest Litigation: Tradition, Collaboration and the Managerial Judge' (2012) 1:3 *Cambridge Journal of International and Comparative Law* 235–53.

Franck, Thomas M., *Recourse to Force: State Action Against Threats and Armed Attacks* (Cambridge University Press, 2002).

'U.S. Foreign Policy and the U.N.' (1986) 14 *Denver Journal of International Law & Policy* 159–70.

Frankenberg, Günter, 'Constitutional Transfer: The IKEA Theory Revisited' (2010) 8:3 *International Journal of Constitutional Law* 563–79.

Freedman, Sam, *Failed State: Why Nothing Works and How We Fix It* (Pan Macmillan, 2024).

Fuller, Lon L. and Kenneth I. Winston, 'The Forms and Limits of Adjudication' (1978) 92:2 *Harvard Law Review* 353–409.

García Morales, María Jesús, 'Bundeszwang und Sezession in Spanien: Der Fall Katalonien' (2019) *Die öffentliche Verwaltung* 1–13.

Gardbaum, Stephen, 'Comparative Political Process Theory' (2020) 18:4 *International Journal of Constitutional Law* 1429–57.

The New Commonwealth Model of Constitutionalism: Theory and Practice (Cambridge University Press, 2013).

Gargarella, Roberto, *The Law as a Conversation Among Equals* (Cambridge University Press, 2022).

Latin American Constitutionalism, 1810–2010: The Engine Room of the Constitution (Oxford University Press, 2013).

'Dialogic Justice in the Enforcement of Social Rights: Some Initial Arguments', in Alicia Ely Yamin and Siri Gloppen (eds.), *Litigating Health Rights: Can Courts Bring More Justice to Health?* (Harvard University Press, 2011), pp. 232–43.

Gauri, Varun, 'Public Interest Litigation in India: Overreaching or Underachieving?' (2009) *The World Bank*, Policy Research Working Paper 5109.

Gauri, Varun and Daniel M. Brinks, *Courting Social Justice: Judicial Enforcement of Social and Economic Rights in the Developing World* (Cambridge University Press, 2008).

Geiss, Robin, *"Failed States": Die normative Erfassung gescheiterter Staaten* (Duncker & Humblot, 2005).

Ginsburg, Tom, Aziz Huq and David Landau, 'The Comparative Constitutional Law of Presidential Impeachment' (2021) 88 *The University of Chicago Law Review* 81–164.

Ginsburg, Tom and Aziz Huq, *How to Save a Constitutional Democracy* (University of Chicago Press, 2018).

Griffin, Stephen M., *Broken Trust: Dysfunctional Government and Constitutional Reform* (University Press of Kansas, 2015).

Grimm, Dieter, 'Braucht Europa eine Verfassung?' (1995) 50:12 *JuristenZeitung* 581–91.

Gross, Oren, 'The Prohibition on Torture and the Limits of the Law', in Sanford Levinson (ed.), *Torture: A Collection* (Oxford University Press, 2004), pp. 229–56.

Gruffydd Jones, Branwen, 'The Global Political Economy of Social Crisis: Towards a Critique of the "Failed State" Ideology' (2008) 15:2 *Review of International Political Economy* 180–205.

Habermas, Jürgen, *Between Facts and Norms: Contributions to a Discourse Theory on Law and Democracy* (MIT Press, 1996).

'Remarks on Dieter Grimm's: Does Europe Need a Constitution' (1995) 1 *European Law Journal* 303–7.

Hailbronner, Michaela, 'Output-Legitimacy and Its Limitations in Constitutional Theory', in Anika Klafki (ed.), *Patterns of Legitimacy* (Nomos 2024), pp. 151–66.

'Combatting Malfunction or Optimizing Democracy? Lessons from Germany for a Comparative Political Process Theory' (2021) 19:2 *International Journal of Constitutional Law* 492–514.

'Political Process Review: Beyond Distrust' (2020) 18:4 *International Journal of Constitutional Law* 1458–65.

'Beyond Legitimacy: Europe's Crisis of Constitutional Democracy', in Mark Graber, Sandy Levinson and Mark Tushnet (eds.), *Constitutional Democracy in Crisis?* (Oxford University Press, 2018), pp. 277–95.

'Transformative Constitutionalism: Not Only in the Global South' (2017) 65:3 *American Journal of Comparative Law* 527–65.

'Constitutional Legitimacy and the Separation of Powers in Africa: Looking forward', in Charles Manga Fombad (ed.), *The Separation of Powers in African Constitutionalism* (Oxford University Press, 2016), pp. 385–9.

Traditions and Transformations: The Rise of German Constitutionalism (Oxford University Press, 2015).

Hamilton, Alexander, Madison, James and Jay, John, *The Federalist Papers*, Clinton Rossiter (ed.) (Dutton/Signet, 2012).

Hammarskjöld, Dag, 'Do We Need the United Nations?' Address before the Students Association. Copenhagen, 2 May 1959, in Andrew Wellington Cordier, Wilder Foote and Max Harrelson (eds.) (1974) 4 *Public Papers of the Secretaries-General of The United Nations 1958-1960.*

Harms, Katharina, 'Kompetenzen des Bundes aus der "Natur der Sache"?' (1994) 33:3 *Der Staat* 409–28.

Heckman, Charles A., 'Keeping Legal History Legal and Judicial Activism in Perspective: A Reply to Richard Pildes' (2002) 19 *Constitutional Commentary* 625–44.

Hellwig, Timothy and David Samuels, 'Electoral Accountability and the Variety of Democratic Regimes' (2008) 38:1 *British Journal of Political Science* 65–90.

Helman, Gerald B. and Steven R. Ratner, 'Saving Failed States' (1992–1993) 89 *Foreign Policy* 3–20.

Heri, Corina, *Responsive Human Rights: Vulnerability, Ill-Treatment and the ECtHR* (Hart Publishing, 2021).

Herzog, Roman and Gerken, Lüder, 'Stoppt den Europäischen Gerichtshof', Frankfurter Allgemeine Zeitung, 8 September 2008, p. 8.

Hirschl, Ran, *Comparative Matters: The Renaissance of Comparative Constitutional Law* (Oxford University Press, 2014).

Towards Juristocracy: The Origins and Consequences of the New Constitutionalism (Harvard University Press, 2009).

Hobbes, Thomas, 'Leviathan', John Charles Addison Gaskin (ed.) (Oxford University Press, 2008).

Huneeus, Alexandra, 'Reforming the State from Afar: Structural Reform Litigation at the Human Rights Courts' (2015) 40:1 *Yale Journal of International Law* 1–40.

Imamović, Šejla, 'Post-EU Accession to the ECHR: The Argument for Why the ECtHR Should Abandon the Bosphorus Doctrine' (2024) 39:1 *Utrecht Journal of International and European Law* 17–29.

Inman, Robert and Daniel L. Rubinfeld, *Democratic Federalism: The Economics, Politics, and Law of Federal Governance* (Princeton University Press, 2020).

Isiksel, Turkuler, *Europe's Functional Constitution: A Theory of Constitutionalism Beyond the State* (Oxford University Press, 2016).

Issacharoff, Samuel, *Fragile Democracies: Contested Power in the Era of Constitutional Courts* (Cambridge University Press, 2015).

Issacharoff, Samuel and Richard H. Pildes, 'Politics as Markets: Partisan Lockups of the Democratic Process' (1998) 50:3 *Stanford Law Review* 643–717.

Jacobsohn, Gary and Miguel Schor (eds.), *Comparative Constitutional Theory* (Edward Elgar Publishing, 2018).

Jaffrelot, Christophe and Pratinav Anil, *India's First Dictatorship: The Emergency, 1975–1977* (Oxford University Press, 2021).

Jensen, Steven L. B., *The Making of International Human Rights: The 1960s, Decolonization, and the Reconstruction of Global Values* (Cambridge University Press, 2016).

Kaiser, Anna-Bettina, *Ausnahmeverfassungsrecht* (Mohr Siebeck, 2020).

Karlan, Pamela S., 'Politics by Other Means' (1999) 85:8 *Virginia Law Review* 1697–724.

Kavanagh, Aileen, *The Collaborative Constitution* (Cambridge University Press, 2023)

'The Constitutional Separation of Powers', in David Dyzenhaus and Malcolm Thorburn (eds.), *Philosophical Foundations of Constitutional Law* (Oxford University Press, 2016), pp. 221–39.

Kelley, Mark, 'Saving 60(b)(5): The Future of Institutional Reform Litigation' (2015) 125 *The Yale Law Journal* 272–312.

Kersbergen, Kees van and Bertjan Verbeek, 'The Politics of Subsidiarity in the European Union' (1994) 32 *Journal of Common Market Studies* 215–36.

Khaitan, Tarunabh, 'Guarantor (or "Fourth Branch") Institutions', in Jeff King and Richard Bellamy (eds.), *Cambridge Handbook of Constitutional Theory* (Cambridge University Press, forthcoming).

Khosla, Madhav and Mark Tushnet, 'Courts, Constitutionalism, and State Capacity: A Preliminary Inquiry' (2022) 70:1 *The American Journal of Comparative Law* 95–138.

King, Jeff, *Judging Social Rights* (Cambridge University Press, 2012).

Kingsbury, Benedict and Megan Donaldson, 'Global Administrative Law', in Anne Peters and Rüdiger Wolfrum (eds.), *4 Max Planck Encyclopedia of Public International Law* (Oxford University Press, 2012), pp. 468 ff.

Klabbers, Jan, 'The EJIL Foreword: The Transformation of International Organizations Law' (2015) 26:1 *European Journal of International Law* 9–82.

Klare, Karl E., 'Legal Culture and Transformative Constitutionalism' (1998) 14:1 *South African Journal on Human Rights* 146–88.

Klarman, Michael J., *From Jim Crow to Civil Rights: The Supreme Court and the Struggle for Racial Equality* (Oxford University Press, 2006).

Brown v. Board of Education and the Civil Rights Movement (*Oxford University Press,* 2007).

Klatt, Matthias, 'Positive Obligations Under the European Convention on Human Rights' (2011) 71 *Zeitschrift für ausländisches öffentliches Recht und Völkerrecht* 691–718.

Kleinlein, Thomas, 'The Procedural Approach of the European Court of Human Rights: Between Subsidiarity and Dynamic Evolution' (2019) 68:1 *International & Comparative Law Quarterly* 91–110.

'Consensus and Contestability: The ECtHR and the Combined Potential of European Consensus and Procedural Rationality Control' (2017) 28:3 *European Journal of International Law* 871–93.

Klonoff, Robert H., 'The Decline of Class Actions' (2017) 90 *Washington University Law Review* 729–838.

Kochenov, Dimitry, 'Article 7: A Commentary on a Much Talked-About "Dead" Provision', in Armin von Bogdandy, et al. (eds.), *Defending Checks and Balances in EU Member States* (Springer, 2021), pp. 127–54.

Komesar, Neil K., *Law's Limits: Rule of Law and the Supply and Demand of Rights* (Cambridge University Press, 2001).

Imperfect Alternatives: Choosing Institutions in Law, Economics, and Public Policy (University of Chicago Press, 1994).

Krenn, Christoph, *The Procedural and Organisational Law of the European Court of Justice: An Incomplete Transformation* (Cambridge University Press, 2022).

Kreuder-Sonnen, Christian and Jonathan White 'Europe and the Transnational Politics of Emergency' (2022) 29:6 *Journal of European Public Policy* 953–965.

Emergency Powers of International Organizations: Between Normalization and Containment (Oxford University Press, 2019).

Krisch, Nico, 'Liquid Authority in Global Governance' (2017) 9:2 *International Theory* 237–60.

Kumm, Mattias, 'Constitutionalism and Experimentalist Governance' (2012) 6:3 *Regulation & Governance* 401–9.

'Institutionalising Socratic Contestation: The Rationalist Human Rights Paradigm, Legitimate Authority and the Point of Judicial Review' (2008) 1:2 *European Journal of Legal Studies* 153–83.

'Who Is Afraid of the Total Constitution? Constitutional Rights as Principles and the Constitutionalization of Private Law,' (2006) 7:4 *German Law Journal* pp. 341–69.

'The Jurisprudence of Constitutional Conflict: Constitutional Supremacy in Europe Before and After the Constitutional Treaty' (2005) 11 *European Law Journal* 262–307.

Kurban, Dilek, 'Forsaking Individual Justice: The Implications of the European Court of Human Rights' Pilot Judgment Procedure for Victims of Gross and Systematic Violations' (2016), 16:4 *Human Rights Law Review* pp. 731–69.

Kuwali, Dan, 'The End of Humanitarian Intervention: Evaluation of the African Union's Right of Intervention' (2009) 9 *African Journal on Conflict Resolution* 41–61.

Kyritsis, Dimitrios, *Where Our Protection Lies: Separation of Powers and Constitutional Review* (Oxford University Press, 2017).

Laclau, Ernesto, *On Populist Reason* (Verso, 2005).

Landau, Joseph, 'Process Scrutiny: Motivational Inquiry and Constitutional Rights' (2019) 119:8 *Columbia Law Review* 2147–204.

Landau, David, 'Institutional Failure and Intertemporal Theories of Judicial Role in the Global South', in David Bilchitz and David Landau (eds.), *The Evolution of the Separation of Powers: Between the Global North and the Global South* (Edward Elgar Publishing, 2018), pp. 31–56.

'A Dynamic Theory of Judicial Role' (2014) 55:5 *Boston College Law Review* 1501–62.

'The Reality of Social Rights Enforcement' (2012) 53:1 *Harvard International Law* 190–247.

'Political Institutions and Judicial Role in Comparative Constitutional Law' (2010) 51:2 *Harvard International Law Journal* 319–78.

Landemore, Helen, *Open Democracy* (University of Princeton Press, 2020).

Lang, Heinrich, '§ 27 Krankenbehandlung', in Ulrich Becker and Thorsten Kingreen (eds.), *SGB V – Gesetzliche Krankenversicherung* (8th edn., C.H. Beck, 2022).

Lazar, Nomi Claire, *States of Emergency in Liberal Democracies* (Cambridge University Press, 2009).

Lecourt, Robert, 'Le rôle du droit dans l'unification européenne' (1964) 17–18 *Bulletin de l'Association des juristes européens* 5–23.

Legrand, Pierre, 'The Impossibility of "Legal Transplants"' (1997) 4 *Maastricht Journal of European & Comparative Law* 111–24.

Leijten, Ingrid, 'Human rights v. Insufficient climate action: The Urgenda case' (2019) 37:2 *Netherlands Quarterly of Human Rights* 112–8.

Lenaerts, Koen, 'La vie après l'avis: Exploring the Principle of Mutual (Yet Not Blind) Trust' (2017) 54:3 *Common Market Law Review* 805–40.

Lepsius, Oliver, 'Die maßstabsetzende Gewalt', in Matthias Jestaedt et al. (eds.), *Das entgrenzte Gericht* (3rd edn., Suhrkamp, 2019), pp. 159–281.

Levi-Faur, David, 'From "Big Government" to "Big Governance"?', in id. (ed.), *The Oxford Handbook of Governance* (Oxford University Press, 2012), pp. 3–18.

Levinson, Sanford and Jack M. Balkin, *Democracy and Dysfunction* (University of Chicago Press, 2019).

Lewis, David E., *The Politics of Presidential Appointments: Political Control and Bureaucratic Performance* (Princeton University Press, 2008).

'Revisiting the Administrative Presidency: Policy, Patronage, and Agency Competence' (2009) 39:1 *Presidential Studies Quarterly* 60–73.

Liebenberg, Sandra 'Engaging the Paradoxes of the Universal and Particular in Human Rights Adjudication: The Possibilities and Pitfalls of "Meaningful Engagement"' (2012) 12 *African Human Rights Law Journal* 1–29.

'The Art of the (Im)Possible? Justice Froneman's Contribution to Designing Remedies for Structural Human Rights Violations' (2022) 12:1 *Constitutional Court Review* 137–70.

Liebenberg, Sandra and Katherine G. Young, 'Adjudicating Social Rights: Can Democratic Experimentalism Help?', in Helena Alviar García, Karl Klare and Lucy A. Williams (eds.), *Socio-Economic Rights in Theory and Practice: Critical Inquiries* (Routledge, 2015), pp. 237–57.

Locke, John, *Two Treatises of Government* (Cambridge University Press, 2013, Peter Laslett edition).

Second Treatise on Government (1689).

Loevy, Karin, *Emergencies in Public Law: The Legal Politics of Containment* (Cambridge University Press, 2016).

Loughlin, Martin, *Against Constitutionalism* (Harvard University Press, 2022).

Lübbe, Anna, '"Systemic Flaws" and Dublin Transfers: Incompatible Tests Before the CJEU and the ECtHR?' (2015) 27:1 *International Journal of Refugee Law* 135–40.

Luhmann, Niklas, *Rechtssoziologie* (Springer, 2008).

Lustig, Doreen and Joseph H. H. Weiler, 'Judicial Review in the Contemporary World: Retrospective and Prospective' (2018) 16:2 *International Journal of Constitutional Law* 315–72.

Madlingozi, Tshepo, 'Social Justice in a Time of Neo-Apartheid Constitutionalism: Critiquing the Anti-Black Economy of Recognition, Incorporation and Distribution' (2017) 28:1 *Stellenbosch Law Review* 123–47.

Mahomed, Faraaz, 'The Fourth Branch: Challenges and Opportunities for a Robust and Meaningful Role for South Africa's State Institutions Supporting Democracy', in David Bilchitz and David Landau (eds.), *The Evolution of the Separation of Powers: Between the Global North and the Global South* (Edward Elgar Publishing, 2018), pp. 177–205.

Marciano, Alain and Stephen G. Medema, 'Market Failure in Context: Introduction' (2015) 47 *History of Political Economy* 1–19.

Mason, Stephen, 'The Post Office Horizon Scandal: A Brief Chronology' (2021) 18 *Digital Evidence and Electronic Signature Law Review* 1–9.

Mate, Manoj, 'The Rise of Judicial Governance in the Supreme Court of India' (2015) 33 *Boston University International Law Journal* 169–224.

Maxwell, Lucy, Sarah Mead and Dennis van Berkel, 'Standards for Adjudicating the Next Generation of Urgenda-Style Climate Cases' (2022) 13:1 *Journal of Human Rights and the Environment* 35–63.

Mayer, Benoit, 'The Contribution of Urgenda to the Mitigation of Climate Change' (2022) XX *Journal of Environmental Law* 1–18.

McCarthy-Cotter, Leanne-Marie and Matthew V. Flinders, 'Accountability in Liberal Democratic, Parliamentary Systems', in Edoardo Ongaro and Sandra Van Thiel (eds.), *The Palgrave Handbook of Public Administration and Management in Europe* (Palgrave Macmillan, 2017).

Medina-Quiroga, Cecilia, *The Battle of Human Rights: Gross, Systematic Violations and the Inter-American System* (Springer Netherlands, 1988).

Meinel, Florian, 'Confidence and Control in Parliamentary Government: Parliamentary Questioning, Executive Knowledge, and the Transformation of Democratic Accountability' (2018) 66:2 *The American Journal of Comparative Law* 317–67.

Melling, Graham and Anne Dennett, 'The Security Council Veto and Syria: Responding to Mass Atrocities through the "Uniting for Peace" Resolution' (2017) 57 *Indian Journal of International Law* 285–307.

Gergen, Mark P., John M. Golden and Henry E. Smith, 'The Supreme Court's Accidental Revolution? The Test for Permanent Injunctions' (2012) 112 *Columbia Law Review* 203–249.

Merrill, Thomas W., 'Capture Theory and the Courts: 1967–1983' (1997) 72:4 *Chicago-Kent Law Review* 1039–117.

Mhango, Mtendeweka, 'Is It Time for a Coherent Political Question Doctrine in South Africa? Lessons from the United States' (2014) 7:4 *South African Journal of Legal Studies* 457–93.

Miglionico, Andrea and Francesco Maiani, '"One Principle to Rule Them All? Anatomy of Mutual Trust in the Law of the Area of Freedom, Security and Justice"' (2020) 57: 1 *Common Market Law Review*, 7–44.

Mishkin, Paul J., 'Federal Courts as State Reformers' (1978) 35:3 *Washington and Lee Law Review* 949–76.

Mjöll Arnardóttir, Oddný, '*Res Interpretata, Erga Omnes* Effect and the Role of the Margin of Appreciation in Giving Domestic Effect to the Judgments of the European Court of Human Rights' (2017) 28:3 *European Journal of International Law* 819–43.

Modiri, Joel M., 'Conquest and Constitutionalism: First Thoughts on an Alternative Jurisprudence' (2018) 34:3 *South African Journal on Human Rights* 300–25.

Moffitt, Benjamin, 'How to Perform Crisis: A Model for Understanding the Key Role of Crisis in Contemporary Populism' (2015) 50:2 *Government and Opposition* 189–217.

Möller, Kai, 'Justifying the Culture of Justification' (2019) 17:4 *International Journal of Constitutional Law* 1078–97.

Möllers, Christoph, 'Legalität, Legitimität und Legitimation', in Matthias Jestaedt et al. (eds.), *Das entgrenzte Gericht* (3rd edn., Suhrkamp, 2019), pp. 281–423.

The Three Branches: A Comparative Model of Separation of Powers (Oxford University Press, 2013).

Monnet, Jean, *Memoirs*, Richard Mayne (trans.) (Third Millenium Publishing, 2015).

Monnet, John C., 'The Latest Phase of Negro Disfranchisement' (2009) 62 *Oklahoma Law Review* 407.

Morsink, Johannes, *The Universal Declaration of Human Rights: Origins, Drafting, and Intent, Pennsylvania Studies in Human Rights* (University of Pennsylvania Press, 1999).

Mukherjee, Gaurav and Juha Tuovinen, 'Designing Remedies for a Recalcitrant Administration' (2020) 36:4 *South African Journal on Human Rights* 386–409.

Müller, Jan-Werner, *What Is Populism?* (University of Pennsylvania Press, 2016).

Muralidhar, S., 'Public Interest Litigation' (1997–1998) 33–34 *Annual Survey of Indian Law*.

Murphy, Peri U. and Pasquale Pasquino, 'Long Lasting State of Emergency in Turkey and the Recent Constitutional Amendments Under Its Shade' (2023) 10:2 *International Journal of Human Rights and Constitutional Studies* 99–113.

Murray, Donnette, 'Flawed and Unnecessary: the "Unwilling or Unable" Doctrine Pertaining to States' Use of Force in Self-Defence against Non-State Actors' (2017) 30 *Hague Yearbook of International Law* 59–118.

Nahlawi, Yasmine, 'Overcoming Russian and Chinese Vetoes on Syria Through Uniting for Peace' (2019) 24:1 *Journal of Conflict and Security Law* 111–43.

North, Douglass, *Institutions, Institutional Change and Economic Performance* (Cambridge University Press, 1990).

Ockham, William of, *Dialogus*, available at http://publications.thebritishacademy.ac.uk/pubs/dialogus/t31d1new.html#zp16.

Odermatt, Jed, 'Patterns of Avoidance: Political Questions Before International Courts' (2018) 14:2 *International Journal of Law in Context* 221–36.

Orford, Anne, *International Authority and the Responsibility to Protect* (Cambridge University Press, 2011).

Pagden, Anthony, 'The Genesis of "Governance" and Enlightenment Conceptions of the Cosmopolitan World Order' (1998) 50:155 *International Social Science Journal* 7–15.

Page, Edward C., *Policy Without Politicians: Bureaucratic Influence in Comparative Perspective* (Oxford University Press, 2012).

Payandeh, Mehrdad, 'Das Gebot der Folgerichtigkeit: Rationalitätsgewinn oder Irrweg der Grundrechtsdogmatik?' (2011) 136:4 *Archiv des öffentlichen Rechts* 578–615.

Pergantis, Vassilis, 'Recalibrating the "Strict Obligations" Requirement of the Bosphorus Doctrine of Equivalent Protection: The Strasbourg Court Vis-à-Vis the EU Principle of Mutual Trust' (2024) 20:3 *European Constitutional Law Review* 392–423.

Petersen, Niels, *Proportionality and Judicial Activism: Fundamental Rights Adjudication in Canada, Germany and South Africa* (Cambridge University Press, 2017).

'Legislative Inconsistency and the "Smoking Out" of Illicit Motives' (2016) 64:1 *The American Journal of Comparative Law* 121–45.

Pildes, Richard H., 'Keeping Legal History Meaningful' (2002) 19 *Constitutional Commentary* 645–61.

Pildes, Richard H., 'Democracy, Anti-Democracy, and the Canon' (2000) 17 *Constitutional Commentary* 295–319.

Popper, Karl, *The Open Society and Its Enemies. Volume I: The Spell of Plato* (Routledge 2010).

Pozen, David E., 'Self-Help and the Separation of Powers' (2014) 124:1 *The Yale Law Journal* 2–90.

Prado, Mariana Mota and Michael J. Trebilcock, *Institutional Bypasses: A Strategy to Promote Reforms for Development* (Cambridge University Press, 2019).

Prakash, Aseem and Matthew Potoski, 'Dysfunctional Institutions? Toward a New Agenda in Governance Studies' (2016) 10:2 *Regulation & Governance* 115–25.

Quinot, Geo and Sandra Liebenberg, 'Narrowing the Band: Reasonableness Review in Administrative Justice and Socio-Economic Rights Jurisprudence in South Africa' (2011) 22 *Stellenbosch Law Review* 639–63.

Ramsden, Michael, 'Uniting for Peace and Humanitarian Intervention: The Authorising Function of the U.N. General Assembly' (2016) 25:2 *Washington International Law Journal* 267–306.

Rasmussen, Morten, 'Establishing a Constitutional Practice of European Law: The History of the Legal Service of the European Executive' (2012) 21:3 *Contemporary European History* 375–397.

Ray, Brian, *Engaging with Social Rights: Procedure, Participation and Democracy in South Africa's Second Wave* (Cambridge University Press, 2016).

Reicher, Harry, 'The Uniting for Peace Resolution on the Thirtieth Anniversary of its Passage' (1981) 20:1 *Columbia Journal of Transnational Law* 1–49.

Resnik, Judith, 'Managerial Judges' (1982) 96:2 *Harvard Law Review* 374–448.

Roach, Kent, *Remedies for Human Rights Violations: A Two-Track Approach to Supra-national and National Law, Cambridge Studies on Constitutional Law*, Vol. 27 (Cambridge University Press, 2021).

'Polycentricity and Queue Jumping in Public Law Remedies: A Two-Track Response' (2016) 66:1 *University of Toronto Law Journal* 3–52.

Roach, Kent and Geoff Budlender, 'Mandatory Relief and Supervisory Jurisdiction: When Is It Appropriate, Just and Equitable?' (2005) 122:2 *South African Law Journal* 325–51.

Robinson, Nick, 'Expanding Judiciaries: India and the Rise of the Good Governance Court' (2009) 8 *Washington University Global Studies Law Review* 1–70.

Rodríguez-Garavito, César and Diana Rodríguez-Franco, *Radical Deprivation on Trial* (Cambridge University Press, 2015).

Rodríguez-Garavito, César, 'Beyond the Courtroom: The Impact of Judicial Activism on Socioeconomic Rights in Latin America' (2011) 89 *Texas Law Review* 1669-98.

Roger, Charles B., *The Origins of Informality: Why the Legal Foundations of Global Governance Are Shifting, and Why It Matters* (Oxford University Press, 2020).

Rombouts, Heidy, Pietro Sardaro and Stef Vandeginste, 'The Right to Reparation for Victims of Gross and Systematic Violations of Human Rights', in Koen de Feyter et al. (eds.), *Out of the Ashes: Reparation for Victims of Gross and Systematic Human Rights Violations* (Intersentia, 2005), pp. 345–503.

Romero Páez, Nicolás Augusto, 'La doctrina del estado de cosas inconstitucional en Colombia: – Novedades del neonstitucionalismo y la "inconstitucionalidad de la Realidad"' (2012) 1 *Derecho Público Iberoamericano* 243–63.

Rosanvallon, Pierre, *Counter-Democracy: Politics in an Age of Distrust* (Cambridge University Press, 2008).

Rosenberg, Gerald N., *The Hollow Hope* (University of Chicago Press, 2008).

Roux, Theunis, 'Grand Narratives of Transition and the Quest for Democratic Constitutionalism in India and South Africa' (2024) 57 *Verfassung in Recht und Übersee/World Comparative Law* 5–71.

'The Global South and Liberal Constitutionalism: Incommensurable Opposites?' on *AUSPUBLAW*, 7 July 2021.

'*In Defence of Empirical Entanglement*: The Methodological Flaw in Waldron's Case Against Judicial Review' (2015) 73 *UNSW Law Research Paper*, available at https://papers.ssrn.com/sol3/papers.cfm?abstract_id=2712058.

The Politics of Principle: The First South African Constitutional Court, 1995–2005 (Cambridge University Press, 2013).

'Transformative Constitutionalism and the Best Interpretation of the South African Constitution: Distinction Without a Difference?' (2009) 20:2 *Stellenbosch Law Review* 258–85.

Rubin, Edward L., *Beyond Camelot* (Princeton University Press, 2007).

Russell, Meg, 'Brexit and Parliament: The Anatomy of a Perfect Storm' (2021) 74:2 *Parliamentary Affairs* 443–463.

Sabel, Charles F. and Jonathan Zeitlin, 'Learning from Difference: The New Architecture of Experimentalist Governance in the European Union' (2008) 14:3 *European Law Journal* 271–327.

Sabel, Charles F. and William H. Simon, 'Destabilization Rights: How Public Law Litigation Succeeds' (2004) 117 *Harvard Law Review* 1016–101.

Sadl, Urska, 'The Role of *Effet Utile* in Preserving the Continuity and Authority of European Union Law: Evidence from the Citation Web of the Pre-accession Case Law of the Court of Justice of the EU' (2015) 8:1 *European Journal of Legal Studies* 18–45.

Sadurski, Wojciech, '"Solange, Chapter 3": Constitutional Courts in Central Europe – Democracy – European Union' (2008) 14:1 *European Law Journal* 1–35.

Sagar, Rahul, 'Chapter 13: Emergency Powers', in Sujit Choudhry, Madhav Khosla and Pratap Bhanu Mehta (eds.), *The Oxford Handbook of the Indian Constitution* (Oxford University Press, 2016), pp. 213–31.

Sandler, Ross and David Schoenbrod, *Democracy by Decree: What Happens When Courts Run Government* (Yale University Press, 2003).

Sangiovanni, Andrea, 'Solidarity in the European Union' (2013) 33:2 *Oxford Journal of Legal Studies* 213–41.

Sathe, Satyaranjan Purushottam, *Judicial Activism in India: Transgressing Borders and Enforcing Limits* (2nd edn., Oxford University Press, 2003).

Scharpf, Fritz W., *Governing in Europe: Effective and Democratic?* (Oxford University Press, 1999).

Scheppele, Kim Lane, 'Small Emergencies' (2005) 40 *Georgia Law Review* 835–62.

Scheuerman, William E., 'Survey Article: Emergency Powers and the Rule of Law After 9/11' (2006) 14:1 *Journal of Political Philosophy* 61–84.

Schmitt, Carl, *Die Tyrannei der Werte* (Duncker & Humblot, 1967).

Politische Theologie: Vier Kapitel zur Lehre von der Souveränität (Duncker & Humblot, 1922).

Schneider, Linda, *Responses by the CJEU to the European Crisis of Democracy and the Rule of Law* (Forum Transregionale Studien, 2020).

Scicluna, Nicole, 'Integration through the Disintegration of Law? The ECB and EU Constitutionalism in the Crisis' (2018) 25:12 *Journal of European Public Policy* 1874–91.

Schumpeter, Joseph A., Capitalism, Socialism and Democracy (Harper, 1950).

Setzer, Joana and Lisa C. Vanhala, 'Climate Change Litigation: A Review of Research on Courts and Litigants in Climate Governance' (2019) 10:3 *Wiley Interdisciplinary Reviews: Climate Change* 580.

Shapiro, Scott J., 'Law, Plans, and Practical Reason' (2002) 8:4 *Legal Theory* 387–441.

Sharman, Campbell, 'Parliamentary Federations and Limited Government: Constitutional Design and Redesign in Australia and Canada' (1990) 2:2 *Journal of Theoretical Politics* 205–30.

Shirvani, Foroud, 'Die Bundes – und Reichsexekution in der neueren Deutschen Verfassungsgeschichte' (2011) 50:1 *Der Staat* 102–21.

Sibanda, Sanele, 'When Do You Call Time on Compromise? South Africa's Discourse on Transformation and the Future of Transformative Constitutionalism' (2020) 24 *Law Democracy and Development* 384–412.

'Not Purpose-Made! Transformative Constitutionalism, Post-Independence Constitutionalism and the Struggle to Eradicate Poverty' (2011) 22:3 *Stellenbosch Law Review* 482–500.

Simon, William H., 'Toyota Jurisprudence: Legal Theory and Rolling Rule Regimes', in Gráinne de Búrca and Joane Scott (eds.), *Law and New Governance in the EU and the US* (Bloomsbury Publishing, 2006), pp. 37–64.

Sinclair, Guy Fiti, *To Reform the World* (Oxford University Press, 2017).

Skubiszewski, Krzysztof, 'Implied Powers of International Organizations', in Yoram Dinstein and Mala Tabory (eds.), *International Law at a Time of Perplexity: Essays in Honour of Shabtai Rosenne* (Martinus Nijhoff Publishers, 1989), pp. 855–69.

Smith, Adam, *The Wealth of Nations* (1776).

Somek, Alexander, *The Cosmopolitan Constitution* (Oxford University Press, 2014).

'Administration Without Sovereignty', in Petra Dobner and Martin Loughlin (eds.), *The Twilight of Constitutionalism?* (Oxford University Press, 2010), pp. 267–88.

Starski, Paulina, *The 'Unwilling or Unable' State as a Challenge to International Law*, Habilitation thesis, Bucerius Law School (2020).

Sternberg, Claudia S., 'Political Legitimacy Between Democracy and Effectiveness: Trade-offs, Interdependencies, and Discursive Constructions by the EU Institutions' (2015) 7:4 *European Political Science Review* 615–38.

Strauss, Peter L., 'Formal and Functional Approaches to Separation of Powers Questions: A Foolish Inconsistency' (1987) 72:3 *Cornell Law Review* 488–526.

Sundstøl Eriksen, Stein, '"State Failure" in Theory and Practice: The Idea of the State and the Contradictions of State Formation' (2011) 37:1 *Review of International Studies* 229–47.

Sunstein, Cass R., 'Nonsectarian Welfare Statements' (2016) 10:2 *Regulation & Governance*, 126–33.

'What's Standing After Lujan? Of Citizen Suits, "Injuries," and Article III' (1992) 91:2 *Michigan Law Review* 163–236.

Susi, Mart, 'The Definition of a Structural Problem in the Case-Law of the European Court of Human Rights Since 2010' (2012) 55 *German Yearbook of International Law* 385–419.

Sweet, Alec Stone, 'A Cosmopolitian Legal Order: Constitutional Pluralism and Rights Adjudication in Europe' (2012) 1:1 *Global Constitutionalism* 53–90.

Szele, Bálint, '"Crises are Opportunities" Jean Monnet and the First Steps Towards Europe' (2003) 2:2 *European Integration Studies* 5–15.

Tardu, Maxime E., 'United Nations Response to Gross Violations of Human Rights: The 1503 Procedure' (1980) 20:3 *Santa Clara Law Review* 559.

Taylor, Helen, 'Forcing the Court's Remedial Hand: Non-compliance as a Catalyst for Remedial Innovation' (2019) 9:1 *Constitutional Court Review* 247–81.

Teubner, Günther, *Constitutional Fragments: Societal Constitutionalism and Globalization* (Oxford University Press, 2012).

'Constitutionalising Polycontexturality' (2011) 20 *Social and Legal Studies* 210–29.

Theuns, Tom, 'The Need for an EU Expulsion Mechanism: Democratic Backsliding and the Failure of Article 7' (2022) 28 *Res Publica* 693–713.

Thiruvengadam, Arun K., 'Swallowing a Bitter PIL? Reflections on Progressive Strategies for Public Interest Litigation in India', in Oscar Vilhena et al. (eds.), *Transformative Constitutionalism: Comparing the Apex Courts in Brazil, India and South Africa* (Pretoria University Press, 2013), pp. 519–31.

Thornhill, Chris and Carina Rodriguez de Araújo Calabria, 'Global Constitutionalism and Democracy: The Case of Colombia' (2020) 2 *Jus Cogens* 155–83.

Thürer, Daniel, 'The "Failed State" and International Law' (1999) 81:836 *International Review of the Red Cross* 731–761.

Timmer, Alexandra, 'A Quiet Revolution: Vulnerability in the European Court of Human Rights', in Martha Albertson Fineman and Anna Grear (eds.), *Vulnerability* (Routledge, 2016), pp. 147–70.

Tokatlı, Mahir, 'Impeachment as Last Resort to Safeguard Democracy? Removing the Head of Government in Different Institutional Settings' (2024) 65:2 *Politische Vierteljahresschrift* 395–415.

Tolley, Howard Jr., *The U.N. Commission on Human Rights* (Westview Press, 1987).

'The Concealed Crack in the Citadel: The United Nations Commission on Human Rights Response to Confidential Communications' (1984) 6:4 *Human Rights Quarterly* 420–62.

Tomuschat, Christian, '"Uniting for Peace": ein Rückblick nach 50 Jahren' (2001) 76:2/3 *Die Friedens-Warte* 289–303.

Tsebelis, George, 'Decision Making in Political Systems: Veto Players in Presidentialism, Parliamentarism, Multicameralism and Multipartyism' (1995) 25:3 *British Journal of Political Science* 289–325.

Tushnet, Mark, *The New Fourth Branch: Institutions for Protecting Constitutional Democracy* (Cambridge University Press, 2021).

Weak Courts, Strong Rights: Judicial Review and Social Welfare Rights in Comparative Constitutional Law (Princeton University Press, 2009).

'Law and Prudence in the Law of Justiciability: The Transformation and Disappearance of the Political Question Doctrine' (2002) 80 *North Carolina Law Review* 1203–35.

'Policy Distortion and Democratic Debilitation: Comparative Illumination of the Countermajoritarian Difficulty' (1995) 94:2 *Michigan Law Review* 247-301.

Tzouvala, Ntina, *Capitalism as Civilisation: A History of International Law, Cambridge Studies in International and Comparative Law*, Vol. 142 (Cambridge University Press, 2020).

'TWAIL and the "Unwilling or Unable" Doctrine: Continuities and Ruptures' (2015) 109 *American Journal of International Law* 266–70.

Uitz, Renáta, 'EU Rule of Law Dialogues: Risks – in Context', *Verfassungsblog*, 23 January 2020, https://verfassungsblog.de/eu-rule-of-law-dialogues-risks-in-context/.

Unger, Roberto Mangabeira, *False Necessity: Anti-necessitarian Social Theory in the Service of Radical Democracy* (Cambridge University Press, 1987).

Urquhart, Brian, *Hammarskjold* (Knopf, 1972).

Van der Schyff, Gerhard, 'The Prohibition on Constitutional Review by the Judiciary in the Netherlands in Critical Perspective: The Case and Roadmap for Reform' (2020) 21:5 *German Law Journal* 884–903.

Vauchez, Antoine, 'Integration Through Law: Contribution to a Socio-History of EU Political Commonsense' (2008) 10 *EUI Working Papers* (European University Institute).

Venzke, Ingo and Joana Mendes, 'The Idea of Relative Authority in European and International Law' (2018) 16:1 *International Journal of Constitutional Law* 75–100.

Vilbert, Frank, *The Rise of the Unelected: Democracy and the New Separation of Powers* (Cambridge University Press, 2009).

Waldron, Jeremy, *Political Theory* (Harvard University Press, 2016).

'The Core of the Case Against Judicial Review', (2006) 115:6 *The Yale Law Journal* 1346–405.

Wegener, Bernhard, 'Urgenda – Weltrettung per Gerichtsbeschluss' (2019) *Zeitschrift für Umweltrecht* 3–13.

Weiler, Joseph H. H., 'In the Face of Crisis: Input Legitimacy, Output Legitimacy and the Political Messianism of European Integration' (2012) 34:7 *Journal of European Integration* 825–41.

'The Transformation of Europe' (1991) 100:8 *The Yale Law Journal* 2403–83.

Wewerinke-Singh, Margaretha and Ashleigh McCoach, 'The State of the Netherlands v Urgenda Foundation: Distilling Best Practice and Lessons Learnt for Future Rights-Based Climate Litigation' (2021) 30:2 *Review of European, Comparative & International Environmental Law* 275–83.

White, Jonathan, 'The De-institutionalisation of Power Beyond the State' (2022) 28:1 *European Journal of International Relations* 187–208.

Politics of Last Resort: Governing by Emergency in the European Union (Oxford University Press, 2019).

White, Michael D. et al., 'Federal Civil Litigation as an Instrument of Police Reform: A Natural Experiment Exploring the Effects of the Floyd Ruling on Stop-and-Frisk Activities in New York City' (2016) 14 *Ohio State Journal of Criminal Law* 9–66.

White, Nigel David, 'The United Nations System: Conference, Contract or Constitutional Order' (2000) 4 *Singapore Journal of International & Comparative Law* 281–99.

Whittington, Keith E., 'Impeachment in a System of Checks and Balances' (2022) 87:3 Missouri Law Review 835–61.

Political Foundations of Judicial Supremacy: The Presidency, the Supreme Court, and Constitutional Leadership in U.S. History (Princeton University Press, 2007).

Wildhaber, Luzius, 'Pilot Judgments in Cases of Structural or Systemic Problems on the National Level', in Ulrike Deutsch and Rüdiger Wolfrum (eds.), *The European Court of Human Rights Overwhelmed by Applications: Problems and Possible Solutions* (Springer, 2009), pp. 69–75.

Wilkinson, Michael A., *Authoritarian Liberalism and the Transformation of Modern Europe* (Oxford University Press, 2021).

Wischmeyer, Thomas, *Zwecke im Recht des Verfassungsstaates: Geschichte und Theorie einer juristischen Denkfigur* (Mohr Siebeck, 2015).

'Generating Trust Through Law? Judicial Cooperation in the European Union and the "Principle of Mutual Trust"' 17:3 (2016) *German Law Journal* 339–82.

Yamin, Alicia Ely, Oscar Parra-Vera and Camila Gianella, 'Colombia: Judicial Protection of the Right to Health: An Elusive Promise?', in Alicia Ely Yamin and Siri Gloppen (eds.), *Litigating Health Rights: Can Courts Bring More Justice to Health?* (Harvard University Press, 2011), pp. 103–31.

Yap, Po Jen, 'Remedial Discretion and Dilemmas in Asia' (2019) 69:1 *University of Toronto Law Journal* 84–104.

Constitutional Remedies in Asia (Routledge, 2019).

'New Democracies and Novel Remedies' (2017) 1 *Public Law* 30–45.

Young, Katharine, 'The Canons of Social and Economic Rights' (2021) 553:1 *Boston College Law School Legal Studies Research Paper* 1–18.

Zittoun, Philippe, 'Analysing Policy Failure as an Argumentative Strategy in the Policymaking Process: A Pragmatist Perspective' (2015) 30:3 *Public Policy and Administration* 243–60.

INDEX

Printed by Integrated Books International,
United States of America